W9-AXH-117

THE ENFORCERS

THE HISTORY OF COMMUNICATION

Robert W. McChesney and John C. Nerone, editors

A list of books in the series appears at the end of this book.

THE
ENFORCERS

HOW LITTLE-KNOWN TRADE REPORTERS EXPOSED

THE KEATING FIVE

AND ADVANCED BUSINESS JOURNALISM

ROB WELLS

with a foreword by David Cay Johnston

**UNIVERSITY OF
ILLINOIS PRESS**
Urbana, Chicago, and Springfield

© 2019 by the Board of Trustees
of the University of Illinois
All rights reserved
Manufactured in the United States of America
1 2 3 4 5 C P 5 4 3 2 1
∞ This book is printed on acid-free paper.

All charts were developed by the author from his
research and content analysis.

Library of Congress Cataloging-in-Publication Data
Names: Wells, Rob, author. | Johnston, David Cay, 1948–
    author of introduction.
Title: The enforcers : how little-known trade reporters
    exposed the Keating five and advanced business
    journalism / Rob Wells ; with a foreword by David
    Cay Johnston.
Description: Urbana : University of Illinois Press, 2019.
    | Series: The history of communication | Includes
    bibliographical references and index. | Identifiers:
    LCCN 2019018155 (print) | LCCN 2019019558 (ebook)
    | ISBN 9780252051807 (ebook) | ISBN 9780252042942
    (hardcover : alk. paper) | ISBN 9780252084768 (pbk.
    : alk. paper)
Subjects: LCSH: Lincoln Savings & Loan Association—
    Corrupt practices. | Savings and loan association
    failures—California. | Keating, Charles H. |
    Securities fraud—United States. | Saving and loan
    association failures—California—Press coverage. |
    Journalism, Commercial—United States.
Classification: LCC HG2626.178 (ebook) | LCC HG2626.178
    W35 2019 (print) | DDC 364.1/323092273—dc23
LC record available at https://lccn.loc.gov/2019018155

CONTENTS

Foreword   vii

Acknowledgments   xi

Introduction   1

1   The Reporter and His Industry   21

2   The Enforcers   45

3   The Developer   60

4   Advertising and Controversy   85

5   Keating's War with the Press   107

6   Media and the Keating Five   135

7   "The Charles Keating of Florida"   160

8   The Future of Business Journalism   172

Appendix: Methodology   191

Notes   199

Index   243

Photographs follow page 128

FOREWORD

DAVID CAY JOHNSTON

Most Americans have never heard of *National Thrift News*, but they owe it a debt of gratitude.

More than three decades ago, its fearless publisher and its diligent reporters were the first to report on the vast criminal enterprise run by Charles Keating through Lincoln Savings and Loan. Yet nearly two years had passed between 1987, when this trade paper, its circulation only about 12,000, broke the news and the time major newspapers began reporting on Keating's crimes.

This lightly capitalized and very specialized publication revealed investigations of federal banking regulators into Keating's complex crooked dealings—a tale few know even if they learned a great deal much later about Keating himself. Keating used piles of cash, easy credit, and jobs to corrupt higher-level federal regulators to keep his swindle going. He employed big law firms to threaten ruinous litigation to anyone who dared even look for the truth. He even lured into his cause a bipartisan collection of US senators, who became known as the Keating Five and whose reputations were deservedly tarnished for their months-long involvement in the Lincoln S&L scam, during which many more people lost their life savings.

Rob Wells, a longtime financial journalist and now a professor teaching reporting to young people, takes a critical look at the role of the press in what became known as the Savings and Loan Scandals of the late 1980s and early

1990s. He is far from the first to examine Keating or other corrupt bankers of that era.

But this book is the first to focus on the role of the trade press, the specialized industry publications that are often far ahead of general-interest newspapers and magazines in the role of watchdogs warning us about wrongdoing in industry and among those whose duty it to regulate in the public interest.

While the story of *National Thrift News* (now *National Mortgage News*) and Keating's costly crimes form the core of this book about accountability journalism, Wells goes far beyond his central case study. The role of the trade press in covering David Paul of Centrust Bank, whose gleaming Miami tower formed the backdrop for the opening credits of the stylish television series *Miami Vice*, gets examined. So, too, does coverage of Ghaith Pharaon, the Saudi investor best known as a front for the notorious Bank of Credit and Commerce International or BCCI, which specialized in laundering money for drug lords and gun runners. Wells shows us that Pharaon also bailed out Bert Lance, Jimmy Carter's federal budget director, by buying Lance's National Bank of Georgia for twice what it was worth and other troubling conduct.

Wells shows how the trade press is crucial to uncovering financial and other misdeeds, which by their very nature damage our economy, make us less safe, and reduce wealth. *Aviation Week and Space Technology*, *Aquatics International*, and *Engineering News-Record* are among the little-known trade papers that Wells shows to have at times been in the forefront of uncovering corruption and also watchdogging the government agencies that are supposed to regulate industry for the benefit of the public.

Many of these trade publications have reputations as the bibles of their industry. To survive, they must provide highly credible news, since their audience consists for the most part of inside players, meeting in some ways a higher standard than general-interest newspapers, magazines, and broadcast news outlets.

The vital role of trade versus the best mainstream press came home to me one day two decades ago as I settled into a first-class seat on a jetliner flying between two US banking centers, New York City and Charlotte, North Carolina. In the window seat next to me was a thirty-something man in a tailored white shirt with fancy cufflinks and a very expensive suit. He devoted much of the two-hour flight to reading—nay, to scrutinizing—*American Banker*. He was not alone. The man across the aisle and the woman one row in front of him up also buried themselves in this daily trade paper. Only one of them ever opened up the *New York Times*, the newspaper I worked for at the time.

During thirteen years at the *Times* exposing how US tax systems actually work, I similarly scrutinized a little-known weekly publication called *Tax Notes*. For decades, it waged costly battles in court to obtain Internal Revenue Service documents showing how the tax system was administered, documents often available to high-priced tax accountants and lawyers but not John Q. and Joan R. Taxpayer.

Each week, the federal, state, and global editions of *Tax Notes* published more than two hundred pages of tax news. And none of that space was taken up by ads, either. Tax deserves such scrutiny because it is by far the largest single economic activity in America and around the world, though you would hardly know that from the amount and quality of tax coverage in the mainstream press. When I left the *Times*, I made the unusual move of becoming a columnist for *Tax Notes*. It was unusual because mainstream newsrooms look down on trade papers as little more than training grounds for young reporters hoping to reach the big leagues. What I saw, however, was an opportunity to reach a sophisticated and influential audience.

While mainstream magazines like the *New Yorker* hawk subscriptions at as little as $5 per year, many trade publications cost $2,500 a year. They can charge such high prices because theirs is truly news their readers not only can use but need if their careers are to flourish.

By delving into the role of trade press in the Keating and some other scandals, Wells throws a spotlight on the strengths, shortcomings, and blind spots of US journalism. He is rigorous in his reporting and unsparing in both his criticisms and his praise.

Of particular significance to Wells is the diminishing number of journalists in America and the dramatic increase in the number of people paid to influence what you see in the news trade or general interest media. When I was a nineteen-year-old staff writer for the *San Jose Mercury* in 1968, the number of flacks, as reporters call corporate publicists, was not much greater than the number of reporters. And back then, reporters could often get direct access to corporate executives, as an enterprising *Des Moines Register* reporter showed in 1973 by dialing the presidents of the Fortune 500 companies. Nearly half took the call, but today few if any would, instead having an aide divert such blind calls to their staff of flacks.

Since 2000, the number of reporters and correspondents in the United States has fallen by almost half, from close to 43,000 to little more than 22,000, federal Bureau of Labor Statistics data show. Meanwhile, public relations jobs grow like dandelions in spring. In 2016, there were five publicists for every reporter, a ratio that just two years later, in 2018, had grown to six to one. On average, the flacks' paychecks were 30 percent larger, Bureau of Labor Statistics data shows.

The extensive use of not just publicity-avoiding agents, but expensive major law firms to stifle inquiries, accuse reporters of imaginary improprieties, and threaten ruinous litigation are all much worse now than in the final third of the last century. And the Freedom of Information Act, which Wells used to uncover previously unknown documents, is under steady assault as governments try to hide their actions from the American people, who own our government. Wells offers smart insights into these and other threats to accountability journalism.

After you read these pages, take some time to ponder what Wells reveals and what you can do to improve accountability through journalism as a journalist or a consumer of news. And remember that those little trade papers are in many ways bright gems of US journalism.

ACKNOWLEDGMENTS

First, my deep thanks to my wife, Deborah St. Coeur, for her unconditional support, love, and positive attitude throughout this research and book project. Deborah has been enduring serious health battles through the course of this project, but she always devoted her full attention and interest to my seemingly endless discussion of Stan Strachan, Charles Keating, or business journalism. I also wish to thank my family—sisters Sue Carson, Nancy Kniesche and brother Jim Wells and their wonderful spouses and children—for their interest and support.

The idea for this book began during my doctoral studies at the University of Maryland's Philip Merrill College of Journalism as a class paper for Mark Feldstein's journalism history course. I was very lucky to be in the company of outstanding journalists and educators during my time there, all of whom helped build a solid foundation for this research. Thank you to Dean Lucy Dalglish, my all-star dissertation committee of Sarah Oates, Kalyani Chadha, Mark Feldstein, Ira Chinoy, and David Sicilia and my fantastic doctoral cohort members, Pallavi Guha and James Gachau. McKeldin librarian Maggie Saponaro helped hunt down obscure documents and data throughout the early research.

I am indebted to my mentor and friend, Kathy Roberts Forde of the University of Massachusetts at Amherst, who helped shape the book proposal and provided encouragement along the way. A special thank-you to my friends Janie Harris, Pallavi Guha of Towson University, and Tracy Lucht of Iowa State

University, who read draft chapters and provided excellent insights. Also a thank-you to Jared Favole and Cassie Cope for their feedback. And a special thank-you to Danny Nasset of the University of Illinois Press, who believed in this project and provided patient encouragement along the way, and to Geof Garvey, for his sharp and patient editing.

I am deeply grateful for the University of Arkansas for its strong support for my research, particularly Larry Foley, chair of the School of Journalism and Strategic Media, as well as Robert C. and Sandra Connor. Brandon Gorman, a graduate student in journalism, provided valuable research assistance during the spring 2018 semester. Brooke Borgognoni, a graduate student, helped get the word out on social and digital media. Joel Thornton and Molly Boyd of the Mullins Library at the University of Arkansas were very helpful with research assistance.

This book would not have been written if it were not for support from Stan Strachan's daughter, Hillary Wilson, who opened her family's scrapbooks and her father's files to me. The former staff of the *National Thrift News* patiently answered questions and dug through old files and memories to help me along the way. Thanks to Paul Muolo, Stephen Kleege, Mark Fogarty, Debra Cope, and Stephen Pizzo. Mary Fricker helped me piece together the characters and back story early in the research. I am grateful to Rich Melville and Austin Kilgore of SourceMedia, the current owner of *National Mortgage News*, for allowing me to review the early issues of the *National Thrift News* and for their insights. Thanks to Renee James, curator of the Greater Arizona Collection at Arizona State University, for her assistance in examining the voluminous Keating files.

Last, my deep gratitude to David Cay Johnston, a former *New York Times* reporter who won the Pulitzer Prize for his investigation of the tax system and was among the first to peel away the deceit at the heart of Donald Trump's business empire. David has been a mentor and ally who knows the power of the trade press, as his foreword to this book clearly shows.

THE ENFORCERS

INTRODUCTION

Stan Strachan, Stephen Kleege, and Paul Muolo huddled around a speaker-phone, talking to Charles H. Keating Jr., one of the most powerful and promi-nent men in U.S. finance. These three journalists in September 1987 were asking questions about Keating's political influence, his ability to compel five U.S. senators to run interference and pressure federal regulators to back off on en-forcement actions against his failing Lincoln Savings and Loan. Neither party knew it at the time, but this interview and the resulting article would set in mo-tion events that led to a major political scandal and Keating's eventual downfall and imprisonment on fraud charges.

National Thrift News was the first to expose the Keating Five group of sena-tors and their efforts in doing the bidding of a wealthy campaign contributor. Keating gave campaign contributions estimated at $1.3 million to the five sena-tors: Democrats Don Riegle of Michigan, Alan Cranston of California, John Glenn of Ohio, Dennis DeConcini of Arizona, and Republican John McCain of Arizona, the Vietnam War hero and later Republican Party nominee for presi-dent. Keating had been waging an intensifying legal and regulatory war with the Federal Home Loan Bank Board, which was seeking to curtail speculative lending and investment activities at Keating's Lincoln Savings and Loan. His plan to persuade five U.S. senators to grill and intimidate bank regulators was designed to let Keating run Lincoln as he pleased. "Every state in the union gets only two U.S. senators," Judy Grande, a former president of the National Press Club, said. "But Charles Keating had five working for him."[1]

The Keating Five affair emerged as one of the seminal influence-peddling scandals of the 1980s and stored the savings-and-loan crisis in cultural memory. The savings-and-loan scandal and the exposure of these veteran senators' association with Keating tarnished their reputations and undermined their careers.[2] Keating was once asked whether his campaign contributions were aimed at getting politicians to act on his behalf. His reply: "I want to say in the most forceful way I can: I certainly hope so."[3] Keating and his American Continental Corporation team engaged in "a looting" of Lincoln Savings, U.S. District Judge Stanley Sporkin wrote. "This was not done crudely," Sporkin noted. "Indeed, it was done with a great deal of sophistication. The transactions were all made to have an aura of legality about them."[4] Regulators sued Keating, and he was convicted of seventeen counts of securities fraud and sentenced to ten years in prison. Lincoln's failure cost taxpayers an estimated $3.4 billion. "We're looking at the biggest bank heist in history,"[5] then-U.S. Rep. Jim Leach, an Iowa Republican, said at the time.

By fall 1989, unrelenting press coverage made Keating into a household name, synonymous with the savings-and-loan debacle, one of the worst banking crises of the twentieth century, which cost taxpayers an estimated $125 billion to clean up. Grande, a former *Cleveland Plain Dealer* Washington bureau chief, put it simply: "If there is a single man in America who has come to personify the savings and loan disaster, it is Charles H. Keating Jr."

On the phone call with the *National Thrift News* reporters, the mismatch in power was palpable: Keating had a net worth of more than $40 million and controlled a real-estate and banking empire once valued at $5.5 billion.[6] Keating had lawyers on the call, who did most of the talking. The two reporters, Kleege and Muolo, were nervous as they asked detailed questions of a major financier and his legal team. "The *Thrift News*—the environment we were sitting in was second-hand furniture and grimy garment district windows and exposed pipes on the ceiling," Kleege recalled. "And we sort of pictured Keating sitting in a board room somewhere with a nice conference table and his lawyers around him."

Keating, a Phoenix developer, knew how to wield political power, having been involved in national politics at some level since the 1960s. Strachan, by contrast, ran a small trade newspaper, barely ten years old, with a staff of about nineteen and a weekly circulation of 12,334. Although the journalists had significant skill and experience, the *National Thrift News* had a low public profile; the general public could not buy this specialized newspaper on the newsstands in lower Manhattan, or anywhere else, for that matter. The *National Thrift News* was mailed to banking executives, regulators, and reporters at larger newspapers, who mined it for tips and story ideas. (The term *thrift* is synonymous with a savings and loan, a type of bank focused on making home mortgage loans.) Yet this small newspaper was doing a job that its larger counterparts were not doing by holding the powerful to account. The *National Thrift News* staff followed the best practices of professional investigative journalism, obtaining key documents and getting insiders to divulge details. "We had a long phone conversation with Keating," Kleege recalled of that interview. Keating "would take the question and put us on hold and ask the lawyers what he should say and answer it."

The *National Thrift News* first reported in September 1987 about Keating's bold attempt to have five U.S. senators bully regulators and described some of the regulators' serious concerns about the condition of Lincoln Savings. This was a major work of investigative journalism involving a high-profile and politically connected financier. The reaction from competing news organizations? "Nothing happened," Strachan wrote about the immediate aftermath of their story. Other news outlets largely ignored the *National Thrift News* report for nearly one-and-a-half years. Not until Lincoln collapsed in April 1989 did the major papers and television stations take a closer look at Keating and begin reporting on his dealings. A flood of newspaper and television coverage ensued when Congress opened an investigation, leading to investigative hearings in the House Banking Committee and the Senate Ethics Committee that portrayed Keating as a prime villain of the savings-and-loan crisis.

The mainstream media's failure to pursue the Keating Five story in 1987 was symptomatic of a broader negligence in the coverage of the savings-and-loan crisis. Journalists at top-tier news organizations admitted they were late in realizing how the savings-and-loan industry's problems were a national story. "We nibbled at it," Albert Hunt, former *Wall Street Journal* Washington bureau chief, told Howard Kurtz. "We should have been covering it more in '86 and '87. It was elusive. It was a Texas story. It was a Michigan story. It was a Maryland story. It was a California story. But no one put it together."[7] Journalist Ellen Hume offered similar sentiments about why the mainstream media came late to the savings-and-loan story: "It was all too complicated and boring to interest many mainstream journalists."[8] Michael Gartner, the former president of NBC News, said television news was slow to report the story because the savings-and-loan crisis was difficult to visualize. Without images, Gartner said, "television can't do facts."[9] Meanwhile, regulators minimized the extent of the thrift crisis, describing the Texas and Arizona thrift problems as regional issues and not part of a national trend. Allen Pusey of the *Dallas Morning News* recalled that "The national press took its cue from the regulators, who were downplaying the whole thing."[10]

Although the *National Thrift News* reporting was ignored initially, the newspaper eventually won the recognition it deserved, not only within the genre of trade journalism, but also within the broader field of journalism. For example, it won a George Polk Award for financial reporting in 1988 for its coverage of the savings-and-loan crisis, a rare honor for a trade newspaper. The New York Financial Writers Association gave Strachan a lifetime achievement award in 1990. Myron Kandel, a pioneer in broadcast financial journalism, said he nominated Strachan for a Pulitzer Prize.[11]

THE TRADE PRESS

This exclusive report by the *National Thrift News* and the mainstream media's attempt to ignore it form the centerpiece of this book. I use the *National Thrift News* reporting on the Keating story as a case study for discussing larger problems with business journalism, and, at the same time, for describing how business reporting can modernize and improve. In doing so, the book examines the overlooked genre of trade journalism, those specialty publications that serve specific industries such as *American Lawyer* or *National Jeweler*, and its role in providing accountability and investigative reporting. Trade journals, with their detailed coverage of industries and access to decision makers, play an influential role in shaping coverage of mainstream media[12] and, in many cases, can raise important societal issues. This genre is an economically prosperous corner of the journalism universe. The trade press earned nearly $12 billion in print and digital advertising revenue in 2016, according to Connectiv, a trade association for the business-to-business and media information industry.[13] By this measure, the trade press is larger than cable and network television news programming, which generated $7.3 billion on advertising revenue in 2016, according to the Pew Center's annual State of the Media Report.[14] Despite the economic might of the trade press, scholarship on this sector is sparse, as noted by journalism historian Kathleen Endres: "It is unclear why the business press has not been studied as extensively as newspapers, broadcasting, advertising, public relations, or consumer magazines. It is older than many of these areas. It remains a lucrative branch of American journalism. It performs a service to the industries it covers."[15]

What makes the *National Thrift News* so fascinating was its willingness to confront powerful industry figures such as Keating with bold reporting that in many ways defied conventional wisdom about the trade press, often dismissed

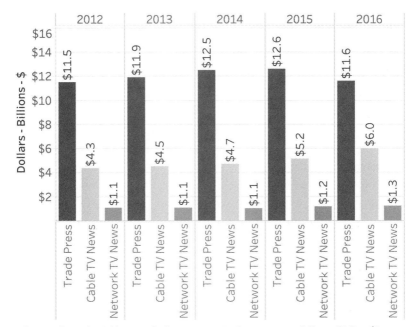

Trade press is bigger than cable, network television news. Total 2016 revenues in billions of dollars. (Sources: Pew Research Center, State of the Media, 2017; Connectiv, 2018, Trade Print and Digital Advertising.)

as a public-relations arm of industry. I examine this question by considering the *National Thrift News* through the political economy theory of media studies. The political economy theory, grounded in the research of Karl Marx and advanced by Noam Chomsky and others, describes how the economic power of corporations, through their advertising dollars and political connections, helps mute critical press coverage. For political economy theorists, Keating should be Exhibit A: a wealthy developer who used his economic power to file lawsuits to silence critics and his money to influence state, local, and national politicians. Yet the *National Thrift News* pursued Keating anyway, ahead of the press pack. I explain how the *National Thrift News* was able to do this extraordinary reporting and draw broader lessons for all types of journalists covering businesses. The *National Thrift News* excelled because its journalists knew the subject matter, were part of the community, and used their close engagement with the industry to their competitive advantage in conducting investigative reporting on the savings-and-loan crisis.

The detailed case studies of the Keating media coverage and reporting on the failure of Centrust Savings and Loan in Miami are supplemented with interviews with more than a dozen extraordinary trade press journalists, all of whom are recognized for investigative reporting that has benefited the broader society. Trade publications have long been criticized for being captive to the industries they cover. Yet this book challenges that narrative by providing new evidence of accountability and investigative journalism in this little-studied genre of journalism. The book contains interviews with a dozen winners of the Timothy White Award, which recognizes courageous reporting by trade journalists. The awards are "given to an editor whose work displays extraordinary courage, integrity, and passion" and for standing up "to outside pressures—whether from advertisers, industry executives or upper management," according to the Software and Information Industry Association, a top association for the trade press. The interviews help situate the *National Thrift News* in a tradition of in-depth reporting in the trade press. "What passes for investigative journalism in the mainstream press is sort of almost every day reporting in the trade press," said Mike Fabey, U.S. editor for the defense industry publication, *Jane's Fighting Ships*.[16] Fabey, then reporter for *Aviation Week and Space Technology*, won a Timothy White Award for his articles questioning the seaworthiness of the *U.S.S. Freedom* and severe construction problems with the U.S. Navy's multibillion-dollar Littoral Ship program. According to Fabey, the U.S. Navy and defense contractor Lockheed Martin sought to block the reporting.[17] Revelations about the ship's problems led Congress to investigate, forcing the Navy to address the problems and spend millions in repairs. Fabey said this type of in-depth journalism occurs often in trade publications: "In the trade press, we dig through records, records that other folks look at when they are doing investigations. That's our daily bread."[18]

The Timothy White Awards provide numerous examples of watchdog reporting that can benefit the broader society, not just the narrow audience of business executives. Rob Blackwell, editor of the *American Banker* newspaper, won this award for his coverage of Wells Fargo and Company and its use of fake consumer accounts. Gary Thill directed investigations at *Aquatics International*, such as a pattern of sexual abuse by swimming coaches. Julie Friedman of *American Lawyer* documented the financial unraveling of a major law firm, Dewey and LeBoeuf. Richard Korman exposed bullying in the construction industry and a fraud in the surety bond business for *Engineering News-Record*.[19] Maryfran Johnson, former editor in chief of *Computerworld*, was recognized for standing up to Oracle Corporation chief executive Lawrence Ellison. "I think that truly great reporting and good journalism, I think it shines a light out of anywhere it is. It doesn't matter if it is a magazine for people who work in the shoe industry," Johnson said. "It's all about telling real stories and representing your readers as honestly and (with) as much integrity as you can. To me that is what journalism is all about."[20]

These cases, of course, represent a small sample of the trade press genre. Yet these interviews and findings are significant in that they describe for an academic audience, perhaps for the first time, evidence of accountability and watchdog reporting in a genre bypassed by journalism studies scholars. The *National Thrift News* encourages us to think of the trade press more broadly. Paul Starr has written about the "diffusion of knowledge" as a normative characteristic of the press in the early U.S. republic.[21] Perhaps trade publications can extend a form of "industrial education" to the broader public and warn today's consumers about threats and opportunities in their financial lives? Why shouldn't the trade press, with this potent analytic content, be part of a broader diffusion of knowledge for the rest of society?

IMPROVING BUSINESS REPORTING

In the savings-and-loan crisis, the critique of national news media coverage was stark. A 1993 federal commission named to study the crisis, the National Commission on Financial Institution Reform, Recovery and Enforcement, wrote, "The news media were largely silent during the period when most of the damage was being done. The news media missed one of the most costly public debacles in U.S. history. Ordinarily, issues often do not become pressing in Washington until made so by the news media. Failure of the news media to point out mounting problems in the S&L industry helped the process run unchecked."[22]

Coverage of the savings-and-loan crisis was not the first failure by business journalists, by any means. There is a substantial body of criticism, dating back to the 1920s, about missed opportunities for business reporters to sound the alarm about impending financial crises or hold businesses to account. In the wake of the 1929 stock market Great Crash, Harold Carswell faulted reporters for relying too much on the boosterism of the New York Stock Exchange and failing to write about the rising speculative risks.[23] Such a media critique was revisited after the bursting of the dot-com investment bubble in 2000, which led to a loss of $5 trillion in paper wealth; the 2001 collapse of Enron Corporation, the largest corporate bankruptcy at the time, which put four thousand people out of work and ruined the pensions of some fifteen thousand others; the 2008 downfall of Bernard Madoff's investment scheme, which led to a $65 billion loss in investment gains for some twenty-one thousand people; and the 2008 global financial crisis, the most severe economic downturn since the Great Depression, where some 8.3 million people lost their jobs in 2008–9 and retirement savings accounts lost one-third or more of their value.[24]

The criticism that business journalism is too cozy with the markets comes up time and time again in the academic literature: Carswell on the 1929 stock market crash, Gillian Doyle and Robert McChesney on the Enron Corporation collapse and Dean Starkman on the 2008 financial crisis.[25] A common thread in this criticism is business journalists' lack of independence from the business and markets they cover. For example, Justin Lewis found "substantive empirical evidence" that public-relations professionals help shape content in news stories. "Nearly one in five newspaper stories and 17 per cent of broadcast stories were verifiably derived mainly or wholly from PR material or activity. . . . The main source of PR activity overall is the business/corporate world, which originated 38 per cent of the PR material that found its way into press articles and 32 per cent of broadcast news items."[26] Lewis and Andrew Williams concluded, "Taken together, these data present a picture of the journalistic processes of news gathering and news reporting in which any meaningful independent journalistic activity by the media is the exception rather than the rule."[27] Keith Butterick also found that business journalism plays an important role in supporting corporate ideology:

> Financial and business journalism has an ideological function because it accepts and helps to sustain a neoliberal view of business. At the heart of this is the almost universal acceptance that the sole function of a company is to enhance the value of its shareholders. This is neoliberalism in business. The ideological component in financial and business news discourse has two effects. Firstly, it helps to establish the ideological hegemony of free market capitalism; and secondly, and related to the first point, it underscores the argument that the Anglo-Saxon model of capitalism has no alternative.[28]

Why have so many business journalists missed reporting on the early signs of a financial crisis? To answer this, I examine the early history of business journalism. Business journalism initially was compromised and co-opted, acting as a member of the business estate. It has not formed a strong watchdog culture as a result of its intimate relationship with the markets and businesses it covers.[29] These connections are numerous and roots are deep. From the beginning, brokers and merchants relied on the business press to help establish prices and make the early capitalist markets function efficiently.[30] Paul Julius Reuter, founder of the eponymous news service, took this idea one step further: "News moves markets . . . news is a market."[31] Historian Wayne Parsons viewed business journalism and capitalism as evolving together: "The historical importance of the financial press does not lie so much in its contribution to the development of a literary form as in its role in defining a capitalist language and culture: free markets, individualism, profit and speculation."[32]

Changing and improving business journalism and bringing it out of the backwater and into the mainstream of American watchdog journalism is an urgent matter. The power and influence of large businesses and financial markets over American life has expanded dramatically in recent years as deregulation has reduced the government's oversight role.[33] We live in an era of financial turbulence that is due to the disruptions of technology and globalized financial markets,[34] and these forces show few signs of abating.

WATCHDOG JOURNALISM

This book focuses on the *National Thrift News* as a case study of how watchdog reporting can operate in business journalism. To understand the mechanism, I examine the origins of watchdog reporting, how it stems from the normative ideal of journalism performing a surveillance function over the government and powerful institutions. The concepts date back to Enlightenment philosophers Jeremy Bentham and Immanuel Kant and the writings of James Madison, the fourth U.S. president. Edmund Burke envisioned journalism as a Fourth Estate, a separate entity coequal with the three branches of government. This examination of the roots of watchdog reporting addresses how we understand the news media's power, how journalists use it, and how the business community and the government seek to curtail it.

Watchdog journalism can take two forms. First, it can involve originally produced journalism that sheds light on an abuse. Second, it can involve rebroadcasting information generated by analysts, legal cases, regulators, or other entities that also perform an oversight function.[35] Veteran business journalist Diana Henriques asserted that the press is one of the remaining institutions left standing to counter the power of the complex markets and companies: "Today, the voice of labor has been reduced to a whisper, the consumer advocates and other nonprofit guardians are scattered and poorly funded, government regulation has become a dirty word, and Big Business stands alone on the stage, free at last from any meaningful countervailing social or civic power—except the power of the press. Business now dominates every corner of the world we cover to a degree that would have been unthinkable two generations ago."[36] Against this backdrop, I argue that we need to adopt a broader view of business journalism, one in which the primary audience is consumers. "'Business' journalism isn't some subspecialty," Matt Murray, editor of the *Wall Street Journal*, argued in a Twitter posting.

"Business, markets and economics are the forces that animate our world, the jobs we have, the products we buy. For all the attention it gets, politics is often a reaction to these forces."[37] Such a focus on consumers and their needs points forward for the news industry as it struggles with the decline in newsroom revenues and radical downsizing. The answer is to provide compelling, original content that exposes corruption and serves the broader society. The *National Thrift News* was founded as a business to provide hard news about its industry and it made money with this business model of accountability journalism. Kleege recalled that Strachan "recognized that the industry was in trouble and he didn't shy away from the story because that was the most important thing to the industry at the time. He antagonized advertisers but still didn't shy away of it."[38] A former federal housing regulator—Eugene Carlson, former communications director for the Office of Federal Housing Enterprise Oversight—described the *National Thrift News* reputation: "It is one thing for a well-heeled television network, general circulation magazine, or big city newspaper to broadcast or publish a story that might offend an advertiser. . . . It is quite another matter for a relatively small trade newspaper to relentlessly and aggressively cover the industry whose advertising dollars comprise its very lifeblood. But that's exactly the no-holds barred approach that Stan and his crew of reporters brought to their coverage of the mortgage industry."[39]

The story of the *National Thrift News* shows how even small newsrooms can innovate in the face of strong advertiser influence. I argue that this type of aggressive, independent business journalism is needed now more than ever. We live in an age defined by a neoliberal order, celebrated by Friedrich Hayek and Milton Friedman, where individual consumers and investors need quality information to function in a free market and make crucial decisions in modern life, especially in retirement planning and navigating health insurance. To put it plainly, consumers are "on their own." Randy Martin wrote of this sociological shift in *Financialization of Daily Life*, how this current era of finance merges the business and life cycles, the professional and the personal. Financialization "asks people from all walks of life to accept risks into their homes that were hitherto the province of professionals. Without significant capital, people are being asked to think like capitalists," he wrote.[40] Consumers and investors are looking for strong business journalism to survive in this free market, whether in making correct investment decisions or in identifying the bad actors. In this vision of capitalism, market players demand quality information so that participants can decide how to assess and price risk. Business journalism can fill a vital societal need to assist consumers as they make what are essentially life-or-death decisions in the markets. This examination of a new type of independent business journalism is particularly timely as the Trump administration is pursuing a deregulatory agenda and investigators are examining conflicts of interest in his business holdings.

BUSINESS RELATIONSHIP WITH THE PRESS

This book explores the complex relationships and interactions between business people and the press, how their fortunes can rise and fall as a result of similar economic forces and how their roles in the capitalist system create tension and put them at odds with one another. Consider the relationship between Strachan and David L. Paul, owner of Centrust Savings and Loan in Miami, a thrift that followed Keating's playbook of risky bets on junk bonds and political influence peddling. Paul was even described as the Charles Keating of Florida. The downfall of Centrust cost taxpayers $1.7 billion, the fourth-largest savings-and-loan failure. Paul was sentenced to eleven years in prison on bank fraud charges; he was also one of Strachan's sources and a family friend. The Strachan and Paul relationship, while unusual, typifies the complex business and interpersonal dealings in trade journalism, where reporters and industry figures interact closely.

As regulators began to close in on Paul and Centrust, *National Thrift News* reporters started to pursue stories about their boss's friend. Strachan allowed his young reporters to pursue negative stories about Paul, and their stories were printed in *National Thrift News*. Stephen Pizzo, an investigative journalist for *National Thrift News*, recalled his conversations with Strachan about Paul. "We started writing some very tough stuff on David Paul," Pizzo recalled. "He said boy you guys ought to be right. . . . It wasn't the David Paul that he thought he knew." Despite this, Strachan allowed the critical stories to be published in the newspaper. "He never spiked a single story," Pizzo said.[41]

This book seeks to examine the foundational tensions between reporters and business people by highlighting normative divides between journalism and business. Trade journals are shaped by their industries and the broader economic forces, and the *National Thrift News* was no exception. Strachan and the *National Thrift News* emerged in the mid-1970s, a period when demand for business journalism surged amid a turbulent business and political climate. "As runaway inflation, deregulation, and recession clouded the economic environment, the corporate leaders turned increasingly to new business publications for their informational needs,"[42] Endres wrote. Continued growth in the financial markets, coupled with the growing consumer demand for business news and information, created what Damian Tambini called "a golden age of financial journalism."[43] Business people and general readers demanded business reporting to help them understand trends such as rampant inflation or the decline in U.S. manufacturing dominance.[44] Business newspaper advertising soared as a result, rising 40 percent to $1 billion between 1970 and 1976.[45] "The 1970s appeared to be a pivotal decade in the expansion of the specialized business press field," Endres wrote. In such an environment—a growing housing sector, innovations in the fixed-income markets, and rapid change due to government deregulation—the *National Thrift News* found a ready audience for its harder-edged brand of journalism.

The tensions and allegiances between business reporters and industry are evident in the lives of Strachan and Keating. Although they came from different backgrounds and operated in different spheres, they had quite a bit in common. Both were leaders in the savings-and-loan industry, albeit in significantly different roles, and both depended on the industry for their livelihoods. They found business opportunities in the growing markets—Keating through banking, Strachan by providing a news service for the industry. Both were operating in an environment shaped by the broader forces of deregulation and market upheaval that began in the inflation spiral of the 1970s and continued into the following decade. Keating saw himself as a visionary developer of the Arizona desert, using his Lincoln Savings and Loan to help finance the elaborate, five-star Phoenician resort at the base of Camelback Mountain. He fought tirelessly against regulatory and political oversight, which he viewed as barriers to his goal. Strachan, by contrast, became the industry's moral compass as it was undergoing rapid transformation in wake of deregulation and modernization of the financial markets.

One stark way to illustrate the normative divide between the businesses and the press involves examining their discourse. For example, consider how property developers talk; it is a discourse of promotion, a type of language not always wedded to the facts. This rhetorical tradition of property developers dates back to Colonial-era U.S. businessmen who engaged in what Daniel Boorstin called the "Booster Talk," a mixture of the present and future tense, blending "fact and hope ... asserting what could not yet be disproved."[46] Keating's proclamations about his new desert city Estrella west of Phoenix or creation of the Phoenician resort hotel reflected a vision of the future not yet realized. As regulators sought to determine the present value of these ambitious property developments, Keating urged the long view, saying the value would be realized with more time and a better market. Donald Trump described a similar outlook in his 1987 *Art of the Deal*. Trump spoke of promotion through "bravado

... truthful hyperbole. It's an innocent form of exaggeration."[47] For journalists, it was maddening to unwrap the layers of spin and promotion from Keating or Trump and determine the current truth of the project's financial condition and the financial stability of a company or savings and loan. This expansive, optimistic language of promoters and entrepreneurs stands in tension with the core mission of journalism to "seek truth and report it."[48] Rhetoric and truth are not necessarily aligned. Aristotle noted the importance of performance in rhetoric or, as he put it succinctly, "the whole business of rhetoric being concerned with appearances"[49] that involve skillful manipulation of an audience's emotions.

The analysis of businesses' influence on journalists, particularly on what stories are considered newsworthy, is guided by Lance Bennett's indexing hypothesis. This theory shows how journalists' story selection tracks the priorities of the political and business elite and how issues are bypassed if they are not on the elites' agenda. "Despite the seemingly obvious role of the press to sort out facts and evidence, journalists have a surprisingly difficult time when politicians serve up distortions and outright lies," Bennett wrote.[50] The indexing hypothesis shows "opinions voiced in news stories came overwhelmingly from government officials."[51] Bennett cited research showing a high rate of misinformed viewers at major news outlets such as Fox News, CBS, and ABC. One reason: the unwillingness to speak truth to power. "Even the best news organizations left large numbers of people misinformed simply because they did not check or challenge what those politicians who spoke out were saying," Bennett wrote. "It also appears that the more mainstream or popular news organizations were least likely to challenge government propaganda."[52] The *National Thrift News* sought to combat this mindset by challenging the official narrative and by empowering its reporters—the newspaper was called a "reporter's paper," after all. These steps toward greater press independence helps minimize a dysfunctional dependence on government and powerful officials "as its reference on reality."[53]

CONTENT ANALYSIS

To examine the dysfunctional media coverage of the savings-and-loan crisis, I provide results of a content analysis of national media coverage of Keating by the *Wall Street Journal*, the *New York Times*, the *American Banker*, the *Associated Press*, and the *National Thrift News*. This analysis of 460 articles from 1986 to 1990 measured how *National Thrift News'* reporting differed from that of mainstream business publications. It also examined how the *National Thrift*

News trade publication status helped or hurt its reporting. The study was divided into two time periods: before and after the April 13, 1989, bankruptcy of Lincoln's parent company and subsequent seizure by regulators. The review shows how early mainstream press coverage of Keating missed warning signs about his political manipulation of the regulatory process and how the *National Thrift News* caught these problems. It shows how the *National Thrift News* engaged in detailed beat reporting where the *New York Times*, the *Associated Press*, *American Banker*, and the *Wall Street Journal* did not. It then describes how the media coverage shifted once Keating moved into the sphere of legitimate controversy, or after the Lincoln Savings failure in April 1989. This coverage pattern is consistent with Bennett's indexing hypothesis.

The analysis leads to a discussion of the fundamental differences between trade publications and mainstream newspapers. Briefly put, this book defines mainstream business journalism broadly as reporting on business, finance and economic news, generally for a mass audience; the *Wall Street Journal*, the *Associated Press*, and the *New York Times* are among mainstream business journalism providers. The trade press is a specialized subcategory of business journalism and refers to the news organizations that cover business topics for very specific audiences; for example, *Aviation Week* covers defense news for companies such as Lockheed, the leaders at the Pentagon, and oversight committees in the U.S. Congress. The analysis shows that only after the Lincoln Savings collapse did revelations of Keating's political manipulation and the Keating Five meeting emerge as a narrative in press coverage. The Keating Five developed into a major national news story in the fall of 1989 as congressional hearings described political favors and fraud. Keating and Lincoln Savings transformed from a business news story into front-page news and Keating became a villain in popular political culture. House Banking Chairman Henry Gonzalez, a Texas Democrat, said his committee chose to investigate Keating and Lincoln Savings for a simple reason: It was the prototype "of everything that went wrong."[54]

A second case study focuses on media coverage of David Paul and his Centrust Savings Bank in Miami. It includes a content analysis of the 516 articles between 1984 and 1993 of *National Thrift News*, the *New York Times*, the *Wall Street Journal*, *American Banker*, and the *St. Petersburg (FL) Times*. This case study examines the relationship between Strachan and Paul as well as the articles about Centrust printed in the *National Thrift News*, and so it tests the narrative of Strachan's reputation for journalistic independence. The research finds that *National Thrift News* carried adequate coverage of the Centrust case in that the newspaper discovered and reported on unflattering behavior by Paul. But the paper was not the first with key developments. This research was supplemented by a review of archival material in the Greater Arizona Collection at the Arizona State University Library, which holds the records of American Continental Corporation from 1971 through 1993, additional legal research, and interviews with the Timothy White Award winners.

KEATING AND LIBEL

One measure of Keating's economic power and his ability to influence media coverage was his reputation for litigation and his tendency to threaten media outlets with libel lawsuits. This material documented how a wealthy and politically powerful businessman sought to use his economic might to intimidate the press and regulators. The scale of Keating's use and abuse of the legal system is difficult to comprehend. The U.S. House Banking Committee in 1989 published an eleven-page list of the outside law firms hired by American Continental or Lincoln Savings: it lists eighty-two law firms and fifty-one individual attorneys.[55] One regulator asserted Keating's litigation strategy was an attempt to gain control of all three branches of government "if one defines his frequent use of lawsuits as an attempt to control the judicial branch."[56]

This archival research uncovered significant new material about Keating and his relationship with the press. The research included internal legal memos about American Continental, the legal strategy of Lincoln Savings with the news media, and a confidential libel suit settlement with *Arizona Trend* magazine. It also documents the reach of Keating's legal and political power: Keating's legal team was able to convince the Justice Department to investigate media leaks at the Federal Home Loan Bank Board. Through a Freedom of Information Act request, I traced the Federal Bureau of Investigation's inquiry through the bank board, which did not result in any charges, but certainly sent a message to regulators. I also discovered Keating frequently hired private investigators and had used one firm to intimidate a lower-level Federal Home Loan Bank Board examiner who ruled against Lincoln Savings. The archives show how Keating played hardball with minor controversies, such as sending threatening legal letters to a state worker and a community activist criticizing one of his Phoenix developments. The archives also showed that Keating's aggressive campaign against the regulators began to backfire in 1988. I discovered internal company memos that showed one major bond dealer backed away from purchasing American Continental bonds and another major regional bank stopped doing business with Keating's company in early 1988 amid questions about the company's operations.[57]

Keating began his legal battle with the media as an antipornography crusader in Cincinnati in the 1960s. Through that experience, Keating sued magazine and book publishers, filmmakers, and theater owners and gained a national political profile. President Richard Nixon named Keating to an antipornography commission in 1969. His campaign against adult theaters and magazines led to a confrontation with and the eventual prosecution of *Hustler* publisher Larry Flynt. With these battles, Keating used the courts as a weapon against his enemies, a template for the fights with the media and regulators during the savings-and-loan crisis. U.S. District Judge Stanley Sporkin, writing in a decision involving the Lincoln seizure, described Keating's pattern of intimidation:

> All too often Keating and those individuals working with him adopted strategies to thwart and frustrate the regulatory process. Such tactics included making it difficult for the board's (Federal Home Loan Bank Board's) examiners to obtain records and threats to institute lawsuits. These tactics were somewhat successful in that through their intimidating effect they delayed the board from taking prompt action.[58]

In Phoenix in the early 1980s, Keating road-tested the pattern he used in the Keating Five scandal of buying political access and threatening the press. Keating pushed through major housing developments that sought to transform the desert landscape, projects such as Estrella Ranch outside Phoenix that featured artificial lakes filled with precious desert groundwater. Environmentalists and community leaders took to the press to protest, and the ensuring coverage led Keating to engage in numerous fights with the Phoenix news media. *Arizona Republic* columnist Gail Tabor summarized the criticism, describing Keating as "too busy destroying our groundwater supply and turning the desert into one big artificial lake."[59] American Continental in November 1986 threatened a weekly community newspaper, the *West Valley View*, with a libel lawsuit over a story about artificial lakes on the Estrella Ranch development. Addressing complaints about unfair news coverage, editor Vin Suprynowicz said his reporter visited the development and attempted to talk to people but was threatened with arrest.

Keating's legal threats against the news media provide yet another example of the clash in cultures between journalism and corporations. Journalists regard threats of lawsuits as a direct assault on their autonomy and therefore an existential danger. The threat of a libel lawsuit creates a dynamic within the culture of journalism that tends to deepen the conflict. "It's never been an effective tactic to bully us. It generally makes us dig in our heels," said Blackwell, editor in chief of *American Banker*. Blackwell said it's unusual for banks to make such explicit threats because they result in a shutdown in negotiations. Most banks will instead argue about the relative fairness of coverage rather than threatening a lawsuit, he said. In other words, Keating's use of lawsuits and legal threats suggests just how far out of sync he was with the industry norms. At the same time, Keating and his legal team seemed well aware of how their legal threats would be received by the media. A 1980 internal company memo described the coverage and tone of the *Arizona Republic* and *Phoenix Gazette*, the morning and evening newspapers in Phoenix, then both owned by Eugene C. Pulliam: "They are rarely, if ever, sued and if sued, and they are somehow in the wrong, very little if anything is said about it. . . . My recommendation would be to proceed cautiously and calculate each step extending its recourse to the farthest possible conclusion before engaging this media in war."[60]

PARALLELS TO TRUMP

Keating's use of the courts to intimidate and stifle press coverage is a long-held strategy by business executives to silence critics, one practiced by Donald Trump in his business career. By one estimate, Trump has made forty-three public threats of lawsuits and filed five lawsuits against the press.[61] As of this writing, Trump's attorneys threatened author Michael Wolff and his publisher with a libel lawsuit over publication of *Fire and Fury*, an account of the inner dealings of the White House that raised questions about Trump's mental capacity and stability.[62] Keating and Trump shared many other characteristics, ranging from their public rhetoric, autocratic managerial style, and appetite for risk. Both faced accusations of nepotism from their extensive employment of their children and other family members. Nearly all of Keating's six children and many of their spouses worked for either American Continental or Lincoln Savings. Keating held strong political views related to his Catholic faith, such as opposition to abortion, but he was willing to support politicians with opposing views in order to pursue business objectives. For example, Keating contributed heavily to abortion-rights supporter Senator Alan Cranston, a Democrat from California. This is another similarity to Trump, who supported Hillary Clinton in the 2008 election. "In 2008, I supported Hillary Clinton," Trump said. "It was for business."[63]

Keating saw he was under attack by the news media and regulators, a pattern of narcissism and paranoia like that displayed by Trump in the investigation by special counsel Robert Mueller over Russian interference with the 2016 elections. Like Trump, Keating framed the regulatory action and media criticism in highly personal terms:

> I think I am prepared emotionally as I can be for the assault that is coming on the name and integrity of Charlie Keating. By toying with the files, by trumped up charges, leaks, distortions and outright lies, by sheer political and regulatory power and misconduct, they will try to force us to capitulate to avoid being painted as a scoundrel, or worse. But I will not, I cannot, play the game. It is an obscene thing, I believe, to see a vigorous American enterprise destroyed and a caring family shattered.[64]

RECOMMENDATIONS

Although this case study focuses on the late 1980s, the themes in this book remain timely and urgent because of the restructuring of the journalism business. Maha Rafi Atal, in a study of digital advertising at six leading news organizations, described the current dilemma well: "At both legacy and online news organizations, advertiser pressures combine with other newsroom practices to diminish the scope for critical and investigative business journalism."[65] This has led to a growing void in investigative journalism at the local level. For example, the Freedom of Information Act requests by local newspapers declined by almost a half between 2005 and 2010.[66] "There's broad consensus that the crisis in local journalism is a crisis for democracy and the health of communities," Steven Waldman and Charles Sennott wrote.[67] A more independent business journalism needs to challenge the "reactiveness" of daily journalism, in which news organizations' coverage decisions are set by announcements from the White House or Twitter postings by the president. "Most journalists lack the time or commitment to investigate the richest dimensions of breaking news events,"[68] David Protess wrote.

The interviews, historical analysis, and content analysis in this project distilled broad lessons for other news organizations, and I summarize them with a list of recommendations for journalists, educators, and news executives to help business journalism evolve and better serve society. There are three central factors that supported accountability journalism at the *National Thrift News* and at other trade publications: ownership of the media organization, a strong grounding in traditional journalistic values, and the willingness to assert journalistic autonomy from commercial influences. These three are closely linked and flow from the news organization ownership. As part owner, Strachan had the autonomy to set the newsroom culture and the tone of the reporting. Strachan could lead by example and set a tone by which innovation could flourish in the newsroom and where he could take risks. He did so through a simple yet powerful mission. The *National Thrift News* was "a reporter's paper," one at which journalists could set the news agenda and not be led by the industry. This tone allowed top *National Thrift News* reporters to use their daily beat reporting to write an important book on the savings-and-loan crisis, *Inside Job*, one of the definitive works about the role of organized crime in the savings-and-loan crisis. To his young reporters, Strachan demonstrated autonomy in this complex web of relationships between businesses and journalists and showed them how to operate as industry insider and outside watchdog and to pursue a news agenda of smart beat reporting of companies and industries. This allowed the paper to pursue investigative reporting.

My recommendations call for reporters to pursue what journalist Michael Hudson calls a type of "early warning journalism" that seeks to highlight financial abuses before they become systemic crises.[69] I ask journalists to set the agenda whenever possible in the news coverage and exert skepticism about how elites narrowly define what is and what is not news. Doing so involves more aggressive outreach for news sources, such as neighborhood and community groups. Journalists should work with greater collaboration on complex topics, with the recent Panama Papers investigation of international tax shelters involving some three hundred reporters on six continents serving as a valuable template for the industry, an effort that won the 2017 Pulitzer Prize.

In addition, new startup digital newsrooms should consider the business model of the *National Thrift News*: a focus on a specific topic or industry that will pay for in-depth news and write the stories to serve these specific readers, and when the occasion merits, to a broader audience. General readers and mainstream media would benefit by paying attention to the large amount of material in the trade press that performs an effective oversight of business. "In some ways," Fabey said, "the trade press is one of the last bastions of really good day in and day out journalism."[70]

1

THE REPORTER AND HIS INDUSTRY

Stan Strachan was eight years old when he emigrated to the United States from England, an experience that profoundly shaped his worldview, providing a sense of idealism about the United States and greatly influencing his journalism. "He believed in the American dream and the standards that America was supposed to be built on, and he didn't want to compromise those," Strachan's daughter, Hillary Wilson, said. "When he saw those being compromised, it was outrageous to him." Her father's sense of outrage at cheating and wrongdoing "came from moving here and being an immigrant," she said.[1] Strachan's reporters and business associates all saw that mix of idealism and outrage at injustice, traits that guided his journalism and informed the coverage of *National Thrift News*.

Stanley Kenneth Strachan was born in Finsbury in central London on August 22, 1938, to working-class parents, George and Rebecca Strachan.[2] George Strachan was a tailor's presser, or an assistant to a tailor. In 1947, Strachan, his parents, and younger brother Ronald boarded the passenger liner S.S. *Washington* in Southampton, England, and sailed to New York. After an eight-day voyage, the family arrived in good health at Ellis Island on January 22, 1947. They were to stay in Brooklyn with George Strachan's mother, Esther. George Strachan also had a sister, Mary Rimert, living in Brooklyn. The Strachan family was coming to stay permanently and desired to become U.S. citizens.

From the beginning, Strachan was willing to take a stand on principle, according to family legend. Wilson recalled a family story that her father confronted a neighborhood Mafia boss and complained that the mob associates were selling drugs in a playground frequented by his little brother and other neighborhood children. The Mafia leader agreed with Strachan about the problem and the playground drug dealing stopped, according to family lore.[3]

Family photo albums show a few early photos of a young Stan Strachan and his brother. One showed the two at the beach, perhaps Coney Island, both looking a bit pasty white and without much muscle tone. Stan Strachan was a teenager, slightly hunched, wearing black-rimmed glasses. He leaned somewhat impatiently toward the camera on a crowded summer's day at the boardwalk. Dressed in swim trunks, Stan Strachan looked like he spent more time in the library than in the gym. The photo of Strachan reveals an intensity that he carried into his adult life. The family photos show Strachan gaining weight as he aged and growing a thick, almost rabbinical beard. C-SPAN captured Strachan's personality during a May 1, 1989, National Press Club event on the savings-and-loan crisis. In the footage, Strachan appears as the quintessential old-school journalist—a balding, portly man in a somewhat rumpled suit, with a full beard and large glasses. Strachan's presentation, however, is anything but rumpled. Without notes, he spoke fluently, with precise recall of dates and facts about complex regulatory issues and the history of the savings-and-loan crisis, all with a distinct New York accent.[4] Strachan's daughter said the videotaped event captured her father's prodigious memory and his capacity to amass and articulate complex subjects without notes: "All of it was in his head," she said.[5]

Friends credited Strachan for being a devoted to his family, to his wife Tobyann, and to their only child, Hillary. Mark Fogarty, a *National Thrift News* editor who succeeded Strachan, described the depths of Strachan's feelings toward his family. Fogarty recalled attending the funeral of Strachan's brother, Ron Strachan, in 1989. Stan Strachan gave an emotional eulogy. "Tears were rolling down his cheeks and he didn't bother to brush them away," Fogarty said. "He didn't think it was inappropriate to cry over your brother dying early."[6] That moment, witnessing his hard-charging boss crying in public, made an impression: "Men are taught not to show their feelings, but Stan taught me that day it was all right for a man not to be ashamed of any true feeling," Fogarty said.

During the civil-rights era, Strachan signed up to join the Freedom Marches in the South. He underwent training in nonviolent civil disobedience in New York, a screening process used to determine whether a person could withstand the personal and physical abuse that activists suffered while standing with African Americans and confronting racists. At a meeting in Brooklyn, the trainers would yell and scream and even punch the prospective volunteers to prepare them for the hostility and violence in Alabama, Arkansas, and beyond.

"When they punched him, he punched them back," Wilson recalled. "And so he wasn't accepted to go down and march."

Paul Muolo, a former *National Thrift News* reporter who covered significant investigative projects at the paper, recalled Strachan expressing a significant moral and ethical viewpoint during their newsroom conversations. "Stan was very much sympathetic to the Civil Rights movement.... As a person, you'll talk to Stan in the office about non-financial issues like civil rights and jazz music and Vietnam War. He was definitely someone who felt strongly people of color in the early 80s weren't getting a fair shake." Muolo said.[7]

Strachan attended public schools in Brooklyn but did not attend college. He had to drop out of high school to work to help support his family, eventually completing his high school studies at night school, according to Wilson. Strachan began his journalism career as a copy boy for the *New York Journal-American*, an afternoon daily newspaper. Strachan then worked as a sportswriter and police reporter for a weekly newspaper in Toms River, New Jersey. He strengthened his proficiency with numbers and statistics through sports reporting.[8] Strachan began his financial journalism career in 1961 when he joined the *American Banker* newspaper as a junior reporter. Former *American Banker* editor Brad Henderson recalled that Strachan was "one of the most prolific reporters the paper ever employed."[9] Strachan rose to become assistant managing editor, and his outsize personality made a lasting impression. "Not only was he one of the most insightful and prolific people ever to work here, but he endeared himself to scores of colleagues through such antics as setting his typewriter ablaze—with a cigarette ash—and banning whistling in the newsroom (on grounds that it was bad luck)," wrote Phil Roosevelt, a former *American Banker* editor.[10] Many former colleagues wrote about Strachan's intensity in the newsroom. "His standards were high, and he did not suffer fools gladly," recalled Al Daly, a former *American Banker* reporter. "Once, when he was acting managing editor and I was covering a convention, I phoned in a story. When I was finished, I heard his voice booming across the newsroom: 'This lead is terrible! Tell him to send a new one!'"[11]

Strachan left the *American Banker* around 1971 and was an independent journalist and freelance writer, reporting for the *New York Times* and other publications.[12] In 1974, he married Tobyann Nemetz, a speech pathologist who had attended the University of Washington and earned a master's degree in education from New York University. By all accounts, the couple had a strong and affectionate relationship; Strachan gave typewritten poems to his wife for Valentine's Day.[13] In 1980, the couple had their only child, Hillary. During the mid-1970s, Strachan bounced around in the industry and even worked for several months in public relations for Bank of America in San Francisco in late 1975. He and Tobyann quickly became homesick. They moved back to New York and he began as *National Thrift News* editor in August 1976.

Strachan's career in financial news came as the industry faced a significant turning point in the post–World War II growth that was fueled by the Baby Boom generation. The rapidly expanding housing market presented many opportunities for builders, developers, bankers—and the news media. As eager families sought loans to buy homes, the savings-and-loan industry saw explosive growth in the home mortgage business. In 1970, the savings-and-loan industry reported assets of $176.2 billion, a figure that grew 229 percent to $579.3 billion by 1979. Two veteran business executives, Wesley Lindow and John Glynn, saw an opportunity to start a newspaper for this growing industry. The savings-and-loan industry was poorly served at the time by the existing financial media. The industry was covered only by a monthly magazine published by an industry association that offered no hard news. Their business proposal envisioned "a first-rate newspaper containing original reporting" featuring in-depth coverage and "analytical and interpretive treatment of events" aimed at savings-and-loan and mortgage executives.[14] As this industry grew, savings-and-loan executives needed hard news and they needed it delivered quickly. Lindow and Glynn's pitch to advertisers: "As the population continues to grow, so will the S&L market."[15] Certainly, the market to be served was significant; a record $2.7 billion in deposits flowed into the nation's savings and loans in April 1975.

Lindow and Glynn had the skills and contacts to launch a newspaper such as *National Thrift News*. Lindow was a former president of Irving Trust, a major New York bank founded in 1851, and Glynn was a former top executive of the Sperry Corporation, an equipment and electronics manufacturer. Lindow knew the banking industry well, having served as head economic analyst for the U.S. Treasury Department in World War II during the Truman administration and then as a consultant to the treasury secretary. He also consulted for the Federal Home Loan Bank Board and for the superintendent of banks in New York and held other prominent positions in the industry.[16] Lindow and Glynn recruited Strachan as the editor, a journalist with an ideal profile to lead a trade newspaper. Like Lindow, Strachan had extensive experience, contacts, visibility, and a personal belief in the industry's importance.

National Thrift News began as a barebones operation in fall 1976. Its first office was in an apartment on New York's West Side. Back issues of the newspaper were filed in the bathtub.[17] The October 14, 1976, edition listed six employees: Thomas Rollo, publisher; Strachan, editor; managers for production, classified advertising, circulation; and an auditor.[18] Strachan was given a 10 percent

Table 1.1. Stan Strachan Timeline

Year	Event
1938	Strachan is born in England, August 22, 1938.
1947	Strachan and family move to New York, settle in Brooklyn with relatives.
1950s	Attends high school in Brooklyn.
Late 1950s	Works at various newspapers in New York and New Jersey as copy boy, police reporter, sports reporter.
1961	Joins *American Banker*, rises to become assistant managing editor.
1971–76	Freelance writing, independent journalist; reports for *New York Times*, other newspapers.
1974	Marries Tobyann Nemetz.
1976	Hired as editor of *National Thrift News*; first issue September 30, 1976; given ownership stake in company.
1980	Tobyann and Stan Strachan have a daughter, Hillary.
1988	*National Thrift News* wins George Polk Award for Keating Five, S&L coverage.
1989–90	Industry crisis leads to eventual renaming of paper as *National Mortgage News*.
Late 1980s	Regular economic, business commentator on CNN.
1990	Awarded New York Financial Writers Association Elliott V. Bell lifetime achievement award for a distinguished career as a reporter and editor in financial journalism.
1995	Faulkner and Gray acquires *National Mortgage News*.
1996	Strachan no longer editor, remains as publisher.
1997	Strachan dies, age fifty-eight, January 7, 1997.

ownership in the newspaper. Rollo, who served as publisher the first two years, later claimed he originated the idea of *National Thrift News* but never received his promised 30 percent stake. Rollo waged an eight-year legal battle with Lindow, Glynn, and Strachan over ownership of the paper but lost the case in U.S. District Court in 1982 and lost a related case in New York State Supreme Court in June 1990.[19] Amid this legal fight, the paper grew in circulation and staffing. By 1979, *National Thrift News* reported a total circulation of 10,754, of which 4,360 was paid circulation. *National Thrift News* subscriptions in 1979 were $35 a year. In the early years, if readers failed to renew their subscriptions, the paper continued to mail out the papers "since *National Thrift News* must guarantee advertisers a minimum of 10,000 circulation," according to the paper's auditor, Robert Gehlmeyer.[20]

Advertising records were not available, but interviews and a review of other metrics provided a general picture of the *National Thrift News* financial health. Muolo estimated that by the early 1990s, *National Thrift News* and its affiliated publications generated about $4 million in annual revenues from a combination of subscriptions, advertising, and conference fees. In its heyday, "*National Thrift News* was loaded with all of these tombstone ads from Wall Street," Muolo recalled, referring to advertisements from brokerage firms about pending deals.

"He rode quite a wave for probably ten very good years," he said. Strachan was right in the middle of a revolution of modern finance: "Stan had luckily timed it perfectly."[21]

National Thrift News and its parent, Dorset Group, were sold to publisher Faulkner and Gray in March 1995, a sale prompted by Lindow's death. Andrew L. Goodenough, then a senior vice president at Faulkner and Gray who was closely involved in the sale, estimated that *National Thrift News* and its affiliated businesses generated about $3.2 million to $3.3 million in revenues at the time of the sale. The expansion was significant from the paper's first year of operation in 1976, when, according to company records, *National Thrift News* lost $46,639. The paper was profitable by 1979, earning $134,749.[22] "*National Thrift News*, financially, was making money almost from the get-go. It was quite successful," Muolo said.

THE S&L INDUSTRY AND ITS COLLAPSE

Strachan's conception of the United States led him to identify and sympathize with the fundamental mission of the savings-and-loan industry. Founded in the United States in 1831, the savings-and-loan industry helped blue-collar families finance their home purchases. The industry was idealized in Frank Capra's 1946 classic *It's a Wonderful Life*, in which James Stewart worked with the local building and loan to finance small houses so residents could move out of overpriced slums. Lewis Ranieri, a veteran Salomon Brothers banker and one of Strachan's closest friends, said he and Strachan initially "viewed the thrift [savings-and-loan] industry like the movie. . . . The thrift industry did good by doing well, providing affordable housing for people."[23] Stephen Kleege and others said Strachan believed in the fundamental mission of savings and loans. "He saw the savings-and-loan industry as basically a good thing. It was set up to allow people to save money and make loans to buy houses," Kleege said.[24]

In the nineteenth century, thrifts—then known as "building and loans"—were primarily cooperative institutions, where working-class people would pool their money until they amassed sufficient funds to obtain a mortgage for a house. This concept was borrowed from the British building society movement in the late eighteenth century. Building-and-loan associations were small and community centered and located in a few midwestern and eastern states. In the 1890s, some 5,600 building-and-loan associations existed in the United States, and these businesses "began a long history of political involvement" in national housing policy. David Mason writes that thrift leaders believed "they were part of a broader social reform effort and not a financial industry. . . . This attitude of social uplift was so pervasive that the official motto of the national thrift trade association was 'The American Home. Safeguard of American Liberties' and its leaders consistently referred to their businesses as being part of a 'movement' as late as the 1930s."[25] The cooperative structure began to evolve into a for-profit structure in the 1920s. After the Great Depression, Congress "transformed S&Ls into agents of national housing policy" by providing them with federal deposit insurance, a type of subsidy that allowed them to attract funds at below-market rates.[26] The subsidy afforded by federal deposit insurance and government regulation sheltered S&Ls from competition and positioned the industry to grow significantly in the two decades after World War II. The industry was instrumental in financing the suburban housing and growth for Baby Boom families. The National Commission on Financial Institution Reform, Recovery and Enforcement, which examined the S&L industry collapse, said the notion of savings and loans as a pathway to homeownership, combined with the thousands of savings and loans located across the country (one in every congressional district), formed the core of the industry's remarkable political power:

> Unlike bankers who were seen as driven by profits and self-interest, S&Ls were viewed as partners in pursuing the American dream. The S&L industry, through state organizations and the national U.S. League, did a masterful job of wrapping itself in the mantle of housing and in endearing itself to those holding political power. What was good for S&Ls was good for housing. This explains in good part the tremendous political influence the industry had. The special treatment accorded S&Ls had bipartisan support, and the industry was used intensively to allocate credit to housing by both Republican and Democratic administrations and Congresses.[27]

This politically powerful industry began to bleed significantly in the mid-1970s. At that time, interest rates were soaring because of inflation. This trend put many thrifts in a regulatory and market bind: they could not pay the high interest rates on deposits because of federal regulatory limits. Because they could not offer a decent rate on savings accounts, thrifts found themselves at a competitive disadvantage relative to traditional banks and other investment options. Depositors withdrew their funds and pursued more attractive alternatives, such as investing in Treasury bonds.[28] The rising inflation was driven by a complex mix of global economic and political developments. The economy was in turmoil in the early 1970s as U.S. industries' global dominance was shaken by new competition from Europe and Japan, which were exporting inexpensive, quality consumer goods to U.S. shores. At the time, manufacturers such as Volkswagen and Sony began to get a foothold in the U.S. markets. Simultaneously, the U.S. economy was strained by both an expensive war in Vietnam and government measures to expand the Great Society social safety net. The U.S. economy, thus under considerable pressure, was destabilized by the 1973 Arab oil embargo, which helped trigger a condition known as "stagflation," or high inflation and stagnant economic growth. This turmoil set the path for the United States to lose its status as a creditor nation and instead became a debtor nation, or one that had to borrow from the rest of the world.[29]

Inflation hurt the core business of savings and loans, which primarily issued long-term mortgages at fixed rates. As interest rates rose, mortgages lost significant value, which in turn decreased the thrifts' net worth.[30] Simply put, savings and loans suffered a slow death from the mismatch of interest rates and maturities.[31] David Stockman, a top Reagan administration aide and then director of the White House Office of Management and Budget, warned in 1981 that "any honest evaluation" of the industry "would show that its equity has been wiped out."[32] William Black, the Federal Home Loan Bank regulator central in the fight with Keating, observed that by 1982, the industry was insolvent by roughly $150 billion.[33] This figure was particularly unnerving when compared to the mere $6 billion left in the savings-and-loan deposit insurance fund, known as the Federal Savings and Loan Insurance Fund (FSLIC), created to repay insured depositors of insolvent thrifts.

Congress and the White House devised a rescue plan that focused primarily on deregulation and privatization. Their intent was to reduce red tape on investments and activities in hopes of attracting new outside investment, thus allowing the thrifts to grow out of their problems. Congress and the White House also chose deregulation because the traditional Keynesian economic solutions were ineffective in curtailing the inflationary shock and resulting economic problems in the mid-1970s. The deregulation aligned with a growing neoliberal movement sought private-market solutions for economic and social ills. Conservative economist Milton Friedman was ascendant in this era as a key adviser to President Reagan and British prime minister Margaret Thatcher. This combination of deregulation, advances in computer technology, and rapid evolution of international markets set off a cycle of financial turbulence that continues to exist as of this writing.[34] Deregulation contributed to poor supervision of the mortgage markets and was a factor in the savings-and-loan collapse, as was the 2008 financial crisis.[35]

Desperate to get the economy running, President Jimmy Carter had signed the first laws initiating this deregulatory movement, the tax reductions in the 1978 Revenue Act, and red-tape cutting in the 1980 Monetary Control Act. President Reagan accelerated that trend by deregulating a wide range of industries including airlines, trucking, and banking. In 1982, Reagan signed the Garn–St. Germain Depository Institutions Act of 1982, which allowed savings and loans to offer higher interest rates and expand their lending into riskier areas. In this bill, the thrifts won both expanded powers and another significant victory: an increase in deposit insurance up to $100,000 per account. This change effectively exposed taxpayers to greater losses in the event of major thrift failures. That's because the U.S. government became the lender of last resort if the FSLIC fund was exhausted. The boost in deposit insurance coverage was just the latest evidence of the industry's political muscle. Tim McNamar, a former deputy treasury secretary, said it was lucky the thrifts didn't seek to boost deposit insurance to $1 million per account: "The thrifts were so powerful in Congress they could get anything they wanted."[36] Deregulation proceeded at the state

Table 1.2. Major Events in Savings-and-Loan Crisis

Year	Event
1980	Federal Reserve chairman Paul Volcker drives interest rates up to battle inflation; higher rates, regulations eventually leave many S&Ls insolvent.
1981	Federal Home Loan Bank Board regulatory accounting change on capital, papers over losses, postpones thrift insolvency.
1982	Garn-St. Germain Act deregulates thrifts; several state regulators totally deregulate the industry.
1985	Energy bust hits Texas thrifts, exposing bad investments; major failures surface from reckless lending; thrift deposit insurance fund, FSLIC, dwindles.
1987	Texas recession; major S&Ls failures.
	GAO: FSLIC fund insolvent by at least $3.8 billion; Congress fails to recapitalize fund.
	Keating Five meeting in Capitol.
	Gray leaves Federal Home Loan Bank, replaced by M. Danny Wall.
	Competitive Equality Banking Act of 1987: $10.8 billion recapitalization of FSLIC; postpones or prevent S&L closures.
1988	Real-estate market begins decline in northeastern United States.
	Bank Board's "Southwest Plan" to sell insolvent Texas S&Ls to the highest bidder.
	George H. W. Bush elected president; S&L crisis not part of election debate.
1989	Keating's American Continental Bankruptcy–Lincoln Failure.
	Regulators impose growth limits and other restrictions.
	Financial Institutions Reform Recovery and Enforcement Act (FIRREA) signed into law; abolishes the FHLBB and FSLIC, creates OTS, RTC.
	House Banking Committee Hearings on Keating Five.
	Wall Resigns after House hearings.
1990	Regulators seize Centrust.
	Drexel Burnham Lambert files for bankruptcy.
1993	Keating convicted of seventy-three counts of racketeering, fraud and conspiracy.
	Jury convicts Paul on sixty-eight counts of fraud.

Sources: Michael Binstein and Charles Bowden, *Trust Me: Charles Keating and the Missing Billions* New York: Random House, 1993; Federal Deposit Insurance Corporation, *The S&L Crisis: A Chrono-Bibliography,* last updated December 20, 2002, https://www.fdic.gov/bank/historical/sandl/; *Wall Street Journal,* November 20, 1990.

level as well. The state of California, home to Lincoln Savings and Loan and many others, approved the Nolan Act in 1982, which broadened savings and loans' ability to make direct investments in real-estate deals.

These deregulatory measures were applauded on Wall Street. Foreign investment returned to the United States. The financial markets also began to see a period of innovation, brought on by necessity: a desire to guard against the inflationary shock and hedge against the currency risks in newly globalized financial markets. A bond market rally began in 1982, followed by a stock market rally, aided by the success of Federal Reserve chairman Paul Volcker's efforts to reduce inflation, expand the money supply, and eventually, reduce interest rates. Between 1970 and 1998, the U.S. bond market grew at an annual rate of 19.5 percent to $13 trillion.[37] "One of the most profound transformations in postwar finance was the explosion of domestic non-financial debt," economist Henry Kaufman wrote.[38] The years between 1982 and 1990 "were one of the longest periods in post–World War II history without a downturn in the economy."[39] Stock averages tripled between 1980 and 1989, creating $2 trillion in paper wealth.[40]

MEDIA OPPORTUNITY

Strachan's newspaper possessed great expertise on finance and the mortgage business, making it well suited to benefit from growth in the bond and credit markets. One trend in this era was the rapid rise of mortgage securitization, or the process of bundling mortgage contracts together into a type of bond. The homeowners' monthly payments represent the bond's revenues. Such a transaction was a revolution for local banks and thrifts because they could sell mortgage loans to firms such as Salomon Brothers, which repackaged the loans into the bonds.[41] By selling the mortgages, a local bank was able to unload the risk of repayment onto other investors, thereby freeing up millions of dollars for new investments. Mortgage securitization also helped make the mortgage market national in scope. These innovations in the mortgage market generated considerable advertising revenue for *National Thrift News*.

As the bond market rebounded and deregulation took hold in the industry, *National Thrift News* saw advertising double. Before President Reagan signed the 1982 Garn–St. Germain deregulation bill, the size of *National Thrift News* ranged from twenty to thirty-four pages. After the 1982 bill, page counts increased from thirty-seven to sixty-six pages through 1987, a period when the stock market was booming. During these years, the newspaper was filled with numerous full-page ads from the largest institutions on Wall Street, such as

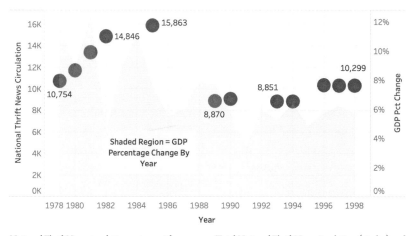

National Thrift News circulation swings with economy. Total *National Thrift News* circulation (circles) and GDP (shaded) percentage change 1979–98. Some years missing for circulation data. (Source: Standard Rate and Data Service, Bureau of National Affairs.)

Merrill Lynch, Fannie Mae, and Shearson Lehman Brothers. Some issues of *National Thrift News* in the mid-1980s reached as many as ninety-two pages. Staffing at the newspaper increased as well. Editors and reporters listed in the masthead rose from two in 1976 to a peak of eighteen in 1986.

Other news organizations capitalized on the market turbulence and resulting innovations. Reuters created a news service to report on the global foreign currency markets, which grew dramatically after the United States abandoned the gold standard in 1971. Reuters evolved by integrating its news coverage with tools for following real-time trading of currencies, futures contracts, and a myriad of derivatives. Michael Nelson, a senior Reuters executive, said growth of the international currency trading "was going to revolutionize the markets and we'd better see how we could exploit it."[42] Reuters developed new hardware and software in the 1970s "to suit the logic of a new, expansive global market economy."[43] Business for Reuters's new foreign exchange quotation system soared in the mid-1970s. "Reuters had stumbled upon a way of making money . . . and in so doing had created the first global electronic marketplace."[44]

Mortgage bonds and the Reuters foreign currency news and data service were examples of innovations that helped expand the global financial markets. Parsons wrote that "during the 1970s, there occurred not only the break-up of the old economic consensus but also the build-up of the new information systems which increased the flow of information and the capacity of markets to function internationally."[45] It was precisely the deregulatory actions and market and demographic trends of the time that attracted Keating to the savings-and-loan industry. He saw the deregulated thrift industry as a means of helping finance his ambitious commercial and residential development ideas. "You could not make money by just involving yourselves in mortgages. You had to diversify," Keating said.

The effects of deregulation were evident in other areas. Regulators and lawmakers eased capital standards, or the required reserve funds that banks and thrifts hold to pay off loan losses and address other problems. As troubles mounted in the thrift industry in the mid-1980s, regulators delayed the reckoning and permitted insolvent thrifts to remain open. Institutions on the brink of failure became known as "zombies."[46]And as the industry grew, regulators discovered they lacked the resources to oversee the industry properly. The Federal Home Loan Bank Board in Washington and its twelve district banks lacked the manpower to keep track of all the new thrift owners and the time to develop any expertise in assessing the new loans and investments being made by the industry.[47] But an even more significant problem loomed. Some regulators lacked the ability or apparently even the will to do their jobs. For example, a simple background check of Keating's regulatory history apparently was not conducted before regulators approved his application to buy Lincoln Savings and Loan. The Federal Home Loan Bank Board did not review the public record on Keating's earlier consent decree on fraud charges, which he had settled with the Securities and Exchange Commission in 1979.[48]

In a deregulated environment, some thrifts speculated in commercial real estate, and others were taken over by criminals who used the institutions to launder illegal proceeds.[49] This free-for-all environment emerged from heavy industry lobbying. The political might of the savings-and-loan industry and its influence over the regulatory system were major factors fueling the crisis; there were more than four thousand savings institutions by 1980, which gave the industry a physical presence in all 535 congressional districts.[50] It was impossible for someone to be nominated chairman of the Federal Home Loan Bank Board without the support of the U.S. League of Savings Institutions, the main trade association for thrifts.[51] "Effective lobbying of Congress by the industry exploited powerful political advantages to downplay potential losses while continuing to shield the industry from corrective but painful market forces. The Administration gave the S&L problem low priority," according to the National Commission on Financial Institution Reform.[52] The House hearings on Keating in 1989 illustrated how the deregulatory environment, combined with the economic problems and a culture of greed, led to a disaster: "What it produced was reckless lending, poor judgment and outright fraud, much of it linked to the real-estate boom and bust across the Sunbelt."[53] These were among the key political, economic, and market trends of the savings-and-loan disaster in the 1980s, at the time the worst financial crisis in the nation's history after the banking collapse in the 1930s. All told, about one-third of the 3,200 institutions failed or were merged by the early 1990s, leaving taxpayers with a bill of at least $124 billion for the cleanup.[54]

TRADE PRESS ORIGINS

Business journalism in the United States has evolved over the past 240 years from narrow commodity "price current" newspapers in South Carolina and New York to multidimensional news outlets serving a general public, such as the *Wall Street Journal, Bloomberg News,* and *Reuters.* The growth of *National Thrift News* tracked with the basic normative origins in business journalism as servants to business, one that had a symbiotic relationship with the markets. Business publications are essential to capitalism in providing news for the market, an important legacy that defined the genre's priorities and worldview. "Capitalist tool" was more than a catchy marketing phrase for *Forbes* magazine; it also captured the normative foundation of business journalism. John McCusker traced the origins of the business press to 1540 in Antwerp and the price current publications of the time, barebones sheets that described commodity prices and trade information.[55] These papers, organized by brokers and market owners, helped businesses function and markets evolve by providing data for price discovery of products and commodities, as well as advertising to match suppliers, manufacturers, merchants, and financiers.[56] The *South Carolina Price Current*—with its lists of prices for rice, Jamaican rum, cocoa, beeswax, and other goods—was one of the first business publications in the continental United States. The early U.S. newspapers carried considerable commercial information, with reports on shipping, harvests, and European market developments aimed at merchants who were eager to advertise their own products.[57] As McCusker wrote, such "business newspapers helped to perfect the market." Reporting on prices helped "cut a firm's transaction costs and (allowed) merchants to engage customers more closely, to challenge competitors more successfully" and to "generate more business for the city."[58] At a later point in history, Paul Julius Reuter, founder of the eponymous news service, took this idea a step further: "News moves markets . . . news is a market."[59] Wayne Parsons viewed business journalism and capitalism as evolving together: "The growth of economic communications was and is a precondition of capitalist development and the spread of capitalism as a concept or ideology. . . . The historical importance of the financial press does not lie so much in its contribution to the development of a literary form as in its role in defining a capitalist language and culture: free markets, individualism, profit and speculation."[60] This primitive business reporting was in sync with a normative feature of early U.S. journalism, which Daniel Boorstin described as "the Booster Press." Boorstin argued that early U.S. newspapers played a vital role in developing new frontier cities and promoting their existence. "They started by advertising the nonexistent town where they hoped to make a vigorous life. Seeking settlers from all over the country, they were probably our earliest media of national advertising. In the Old World, the papers satisfied a need; here, they excited a hope," Boorstin wrote.[61] This tight relationship of the trade press and its industry holds throughout the major phases of U.S. capitalism. Financial capitalism, represented by banker J. P. Morgan, ran generally from late 1800s to about 1912; managerial capitalism from the 1920s to the 1980s; and shareholder capitalism from the 1980s forward.[62] Both the trade press and general business journalism grew from the 1830s onward, tracking the production and reporting innovations in the field of journalism generally and benefiting from the boom in a new industrial society.

That symbiotic relationship between industry and the trade press was clear in the founding of the *National Thrift News*. As he investigated support for the proposed newspaper, Lindow traveled to Chicago to meet with Norman Strunk, then head of the U.S. League of Savings Institutions, the powerful trade association for the savings-and-loan industry. Lindow told Strunk the *National Thrift News* "would help build up the industry." Industry support was critical in Lindow's mind: "When I left I felt I had informally received his blessing for the kind of paper I had in mind."[63] He also sounded out officials with the Federal Home Loan Bank and won their support. Strachan also had a positive orientation toward the industry.

Strachan developed many close associations and friendships with industry executives. For example, Strachan "was friendly" with businessmen such as the U.S. League of Savings Institutions president William O'Connell and its lawyer William McKenna.[64] Ranieri, the Wall Street bond legend, was a close personal friend of Strachan and his family.[65] Later in his career, Strachan would be applauded when he arrived at a savings-and-loan industry event and given a reserved seat in the front of the room.[66] Strachan's knowledge and wide circle of contacts made him a popular figure in the industry. Several Wall Street executives sent lengthy and heartfelt condolence letters after Strachan's death in 1997. The close industry ties meant Strachan sometimes would check with industry officials about prospective reporting talent. Former reporter Lew Sichelman recalled he was hired after Strachan called the National Association of Homebuilders, asking whether they knew of any decent reporters.[67] The paper had a solid reputation and its reporters were knowledgeable about the complex market, factors that allowed its journalists to gain the trust of industry insiders. Being a reporter for *National Thrift News*, Sichelman recalled, allowed him to get "in the door wherever I wanted to go and talk to people I wanted to."

National Thrift News was a classic trade journal that contained routine news about mortgage bond offerings and industry executives. Only a small portion of the newspaper each week would carry probing journalism. Other articles celebrated the industry at times. Take, for example, Strachan's January 3, 1980, editorial, "Hip Hip Hoorah," that praised developments in the industry.[68] An April 10, 1980, editorial was somewhat positive about a major deregulation law, the Financial Deregulation and Monetary Control Act of 1980, which President Carter signed and which was an important step in the beginning of the deregulatory trend that accelerated in the Reagan administration. These industry-friendly editorials stand in contrast to the sterner tone in Strachan's writing later in the decade as S&L executives were jailed for fraud. Kleege said although Strachan fundamentally supported the main housing mission of the savings-and-loan industry, he was upset by the excesses he witnesses in the 1980s.

In one of the early histories of business journalism, May Belle Flynn described how the business press and industry were intertwined: "All through industrial history, there is a close relationship between basic inventions, the subsequent development of industries founded upon such inventions and finally, the emergence of publications to represent that industry."[69] The growth of both industry and the journalism was evident in the transportation field, with early trade magazines such as the *American Railroad Journal*. Founded in 1832, the journal is known among academics as the granddaddy of them all in the early business press. Henry Varnum Poor's reporting in the *American Railroad Journal* marks an important development for U.S. business journalism, for he was one of the first business reporters to demand correct financial information from the companies he covered.[70] The rise of railroads in the early nineteenth century marked a major turning point in U.S. industrial development and the evolution of modern U.S. business and regulatory regimes.[71] Others in this era were *Hunt's Merchant Magazine and Commercial Review* and the *Dry Goods Reporter and Commercial Glance*.[72] Specialized commercial publications expanded significantly after the Civil War.

From the 1830s onward, the trade press began to develop a separate identity and diverge from general business journalism. The trade press is generally defined as the publications with an explicit mission to provide information to help businesses and markets grow.[73] It is distinguished from general business journalism publications such as the *Wall Street Journal, Reuters,* and *Fortune,* which represent a broader category of reporting on business and the economy performed by general-interest and specialized publications.[74] One essential function of the trade press is that it provides technical knowledge and a type of industrial education, particularly at a time when the United States lacked a system of trade or technical schools.[75] "The need and the opportunity for a business press grew out of the introduction of the factory system, and the dawning of the realization that the making and distribution of goods depended upon economic principles," wrote Jesse H. Neal, a leader of the trade group Association of Business Papers in New York. By 1893, the trade press had grown to such a size that the *American Economist* carried an article that sought to distinguish trade press from mainstream media.

The early trade press did not make compelling reading for a general audience. Neal wrote that readers of these early journals "found little real news material, and still less reader interest."[76] Even as journalism grew in the nineteenth century, business publications printed news as information rather than news as story.[77] In other words, this early business journalism lacked a narrative structure or cultural context. Early business journalism in the price currents, with their focus on prices and transactions, was devoid of context, narrative flair, and analysis and thus did not enhance the genre's stature. As Parsons wrote, "the profession did not acquire a reputation for literary merit or high journalistic standards. Indeed, for this reason, in most accounts of the history of journalism, financial reporting is mentioned either not at all or merely en passant."[78] Peter Kjaer wrote that the technical nature of some business reporting, especially its coverage of abstract financial issues, "led many critics to conclude that business journalism today is remote from the traditional ideas of journalism, since business journalism is no longer concerned with the description and interpretation of current events on behalf of the public."[79] Yet these publications can contain significant news for the public interest. Consider that a trade publication, *Gleanings in Bee Culture,* was first to report on the Wright Brothers' flight in 1904.[80]

The demand for business journalism continued to build in the early twentieth century, especially after World War I as more individuals began investing in the stock markets. At the same time, corporations were changing. Companies were being run by a new managerial class, which needed more interpretive and analytical reporting on business issues. As the consumer society exploded after World War II, many readers began demanding news to help them navigate investment decisions. As business journalism spread to general interest media platforms such as mass distribution newspapers and television, the conflicts inherent in the trade press—its reliance on official business sources and its relationship to the industry it covers—became more apparent. Business journalism faced new demands from its readers, but critics found it failed to serve as a watchdog over businesses and markets.

BACKWATER

National Thrift News and similar publications had to navigate a history of a stigma on business journalism. These reputation problems ranged from advertiser influence over editorial content, cozy relationships with companies and government, lack of a watchdog culture, and a narrow focus on elite audiences. These factors contributed to a negative reputation for business journalism that continued through the 1980s.[81] "The standard media—mainstream newspapers, magazines, and broadcasters—had always been reliable promoters of the corporate ethic," Bagdikian wrote. "Whole sections of newspapers were always devoted to unrelieved glorification of business people, not just in advertisements where corporations pay for self-praise but in 'news' that is assumed to be dispassionate."[82]

The early, checkered history of business journalism helped establish another normative feature: business journalism became known as a backwater in the newsroom, where reporters wrote in a foreign jargon, were too close to business people, and often explicitly advocated for their interests. As Quirt has noted, the business desk developed a reputation as "a dumping ground for burned out city-side reporters and others looking for a place to camp until retirement."[83] Within newsrooms, business reporters lacked the stature of prominent beats such as politics or foreign affairs. Consider the story of Sylvia Porter, the pioneer in personal finance journalism. Fighting the widespread sexism in journalism, Porter decided to pursue business journalism as a first step for her reporting career. Lucht, for example, characterized Porter's entry into business journalism as accepting "a job in a non-prestigious field of journalism."[84]

In the early years of business journalism, its journalists were not watchdogs over the industries they covered. This genre focused on the protection of capitalism but not necessarily the protection of consumers. One vivid example involved Bertie Forbes, a columnist for Hearst newspapers, who started *Forbes* magazine in 1917. *Forbes* was among the first business magazines aimed at general readers.[85] *Forbes*'s inaugural issue contained a classic case of business journalism pandering to the powerful. An exclusive interview with John D. Rockefeller was titled "How Forbes Gets Big Men to Talk" and compared Rockefeller to Napoleon, one of many examples of business journalists pandering to companies and top executives.

For most of the twentieth century, the business pages of daily papers and the financial programs on television treated business leaders as heroic captains of industry. Business reporters of the past, for example, dealt either with press releases from the publicity departments of corporations, or, if the news medium was important enough, its reporter was periodically permitted to enter the inner sanctum of "the man himself," the head of the company, about whom the reporter would write a story. This tended to produce either sycophants or the illusion of having been admitted to the most accurate possible news that existed.[86]

Another example came from *Hunt's Merchant Magazine and Commercial Review*, which reviewed the causes of the 1857 financial panic—perhaps the first global financial crisis. The nineteen-page article dwelled on a technical discussion of whether paper money or hard currency caused the crisis but offered no details about unemployment or firms shuttered by the calamity.[87] Professional standards were late to this field. Clarence Barron, owner of the *Wall Street Journal*, engaged in such unethical practices in the early twentieth century as ordering stories promoting companies in which he owned stock.[88] Such behavior is now forbidden at the modern *Wall Street Journal* and every other mainstream business publication.[89] This is an example of business journalists acting as if they were part of the club they are covering. Quirt explained the behavior: "One reason so much of the reporting during that period lacked a measure of doubt was the curious view that business journalism had of itself. It saw itself not so much as a tough-minded chronicler of events as it did as an extension of the community it wrote about."[90]

Catering to advertisers and writing industry-favorable stories were two concerns, but business reporters also had an extensive history of engaging in outright corruption. Many accounts portrayed business journalists on the take. Journalists "demanded cold cash for news favorable to the market,"[91] Galbraith wrote of journalists in the 1920s. One of the most dramatic journalist corruption cases involved the markets columnist for the *New York Daily News*, Raleigh T. Curtis. He received $19,000 from 1929 to 1930 (worth $280,000 in 2018 dollars) from a stock promoter who was also his next-door neighbor in White Plains, New York. Curtis's bribes were detailed in 1932 U.S. Senate Banking Committee hearings.[92] One investigation found that financial writers at eight papers touted stocks in exchange for cash or other favors, including *Wall Street Journal* columnists William Gomber, who wrote the Broad Street Gossip column, and Richard Edmonson, who wrote the Abreast of the Market column.[93] Galbraith described the standards of business journalism in the 1920s in blunt terms: "Many of those who were writing about Wall Street and business in those days were drunks and incompetents."[94] Hubbard found that business editors complained about pressure from corporations about upcoming stories. Pressure could take the "form of personal favors, such as expensive gifts, travel junkets or entertainment." According to Hubbard, some 23 percent of business editors had experienced cases where "as a matter of routine they were compelled to puff up or alter and downgrade business stories at the request of the advertisers."[95]

Numerous studies assert that business journalists, until recently, did not challenge fundamental issues about the economic order and instead sought to promote capitalism. Ernest Hynds, in a 1980 survey of newspaper editors, found that "more than half (57 percent) of the newspapers seek to foster the development of the free enterprise system through their business coverage. . . . Fewer newspapers reported doing exposes during the past year, and only 30% discussed how corporations wield power, More than a fourth (27%) ran exposés on a local business, 27% ran exposes on a state business, and 33% ran exposés on a national business."[96] Prakash Sethi, writing about the tensions between businesses and the press in the 1970s, observed these problems were not present in many smaller newspapers, which generally print the unfiltered corporate view. "Constrained by funds from hiring a sufficient number of reporters and heavily dependent on advertising, they are only too happy to accept press releases from the public relations department of various companies and print them as news stories," he wrote.[97]

Peter Drier argued that the news media held back on more aggressive coverage of business: "Much of it is simply boosterism—glowing stories of new investment plans, fawning profiles of corporate executives, summaries of quarterly and annual corporate reports."[98] We see this lack of integrity practiced by even its leading practitioners up until the modern era. Elite publications such as the *Wall Street Journal* failed to devote adequate resources to the savings-and-loan crisis in the mid-1980s and missed the story. Paulette Thomas, a former *Wall Street Journal* reporter, said the savings-and-loan beat "has never been a particularly high profile beat for any financial reporter over the years. And I think *The Wall Street Journal*'s Washington bureau has had a new reporter on this beat every year since 1981."[99] Myron Kandel, CNN's former financial editor, was hardly enthusiastic when he learned about his first business news job opportunity: "My first reaction was, 'Who wants to be in business news?'"[100]

STRACHAN SHAPES THE NEWSPAPER

Amid these historical trends and economic developments, *National Thrift News* sprang to life. Lindow and Glynn may have financed and launched the newspaper, but Strachan was the clear editorial voice of the newspaper. "He was the paper to some degree," Muolo recalled. Fogarty recalled Strachan's defining characteristics: "As a man, Stan was full of spirit and energy. He had a great zest for life. He loved jazz, he loved good food, he loved to talk—he loved the company of intelligent men and women."[101] Strachan's unusual personality played out in his management style. He had a formidable memory and he made decisions rapidly. Debra Cope, a former *National Thrift News* Washington bureau chief, recalled an unconventional job interview with Strachan, conducted at lunch during an industry conference. After some discussion, Strachan eyed a slice of cheesecake on Cope's plate. "Is she going to eat it?" he asked; Cope sniffed: "If it was from Junior's, I'd eat it." Strachan was impressed by Cope's knowledge of Junior's, the legendary New York bakery. "This woman knows her cheesecake!" Strachan exclaimed. "Let's hire her!"[102] Cope continued: "That's the kind of guy he was. He was very instinctive." Fogarty too said that Strachan hired him after a brief conversation, perhaps just three minutes.

Others painted a less flattering view of Strachan. Irwin Huebsch, *National Thrift News* advertising director in 1977, recalled that "Stanley is a volatile type that screams at everybody. He used to scream at me. When he was involved in getting the paper out, he was a real pain in the ass, to put it very mildly. . . . But nothing that doesn't go with his nature and temperament and the job. Nobody hated anybody. When it was over, it was over."[103] This unconventional style reflected Strachan's autonomy; he was, after all, co-owner of the newspaper. Fogarty recalled that Strachan that would arrive in the office around 7 a.m. In some instances, he would read an article in the *Wall Street Journal* about a hearing that day in Washington and then head out the door to the train station or airport. "Without any planning in advance, [if] he saw something that we should cover, he would jump" out the door and go to Washington to cover it, Fogarty said. "He did that frequently."[104]

By all accounts, Strachan created a culture of investigative reporting that ran counter to norms in the trade press, and at the time, also was unusual for many in business journalism publications. The basic factors that drove his in-depth reporting, a sense of outrage at industry abuses, is a common theme among investigative reporters. AuCoin's study of investigative journalism found "most, if not all, investigative journalism springs from a reporter's or a news organization's outrage toward some injustice, whether committed against the practice of journalism or against some segment of society."[105]

Strachan left a strong impression on his reporters that lasted years after his death. Several described how Strachan pressed them to dig deeper into a story. They all recalled his sense of idealism. "He would say, 'Where is your sense of outrage?'" Fogarty recalled.[106] Sichelman remembered asking Strachan for advice on how to frame a story. It involved a study that showed how lenders were making major errors on adjustable rate mortgages that were in the banks' favor and against consumers. "His response was, 'Get angry.' And 'Don't let them get away with that,'" Sichelman said.[107]

STRUGGLING THROUGH THE CRISIS

Strachan sought to adapt as the savings-and-loan crisis led to thousands of thrift failures and mergers, which decimated his core audience. The October 19, 1987, stock-market crash, known as Black Monday, represented an important cultural turning point in the 1980s. The Dow Jones Industrial Average lost about 23 percent of its value as the threat of falling corporate profits and rising interest rates threatened financing for debt-backed corporate takeovers and mergers. Investors panicked and dumped stocks. "The trends of the 1980s came to a head, and the result was a staggering loss, at least on paper, for investors," Charles Geisst wrote.[108] The 1987 stock-market crash, while damaging to investor sentiment, had limited economic damage and did not result in a recession.[109]

Kleege and other reporters recalled that *National Thrift News* struggled after the 1987 stock-market crash. It faced a variety of economic challenges as Wall Street firms reduced advertising as a cost-cutting move. By 1990, page counts in the newspaper fell to about twenty-seven pages from a high of ninety-two pages and circulation fell to 9,057, primarily because of the collapse of the savings-and-loan industry. "Eventually, I think the shrinking of the S&L industry caught up with the paper," Kleege said.[110] During these times, Strachan and *National Thrift News* investor John Glynn had "quite a few battles over the editorial budget behind closed doors," Muolo recalled.[111] Fogarty said the co-owners might argue with Strachan over budget issues, but they deferred to him in the end. Because money was tight and raises were lacking, some reporters began to leave in 1989 and 1990. Still, the paper maintained a steady editorial payroll of about thirteen journalists through 1993.

By June 1989, the industry's collapse was so profound that Strachan renamed the paper to *National Thrift and Mortgage News*. That was a year when some 327 thrifts failed, closed, or merged. He changed the name again to its current *National Mortgage News* in May 1990, a year when 213 thrifts failed. "As hundreds of institutions that were subscribers or advertisers perished week after week, NTN [*National Thrift News*] had to reposition itself at the same time it covered the repositioning of the staggered mortgage industry, whose traditional leader, the thrifts, now lagged mortgage banks and commercial banks in prominence,"

Fogarty wrote.[112] These name changes are not unusual in the trade press as publications evolve with their industries. M. B. Flynn noted, "When the street car, drawn by horses, gave place to the trolley car, propelled by electricity, the *Street Railway Journal* became the *Electric Railway Journal.*"[113]

As the savings-and-loan crisis subsided in the early 1990s, Strachan and his investors continued to look at ways to innovate, and they created a number of related publications such as *Resolution Trust Reporter*, a biweekly newsletter on the workings of the Resolution Trust Corporation, an entity created to help clean up the savings-and-loan collapse. Strachan and his investors were "a financial success" and launched a holding company, the Dorset Group, that contained a variety of mortgage- and housing-related publications, including *Problem Asset Reporter, Origination News*, and *Mortgage Technology*. The business had to evolve with the industry, and so these new publications "covered the new way business was beginning to be done,"[114] Fogarty said. Strachan did not just stick to print. *National Thrift News* experimented with video news reports in the mid-1980s to gain additional advertising revenue for its coverage of industry conventions.[115] Launching the new publications and using multiple communications channels, a practice in line with business models of today's digital newsrooms, helped the parent company of *National Thrift News, Dorset News*, diversify its revenue stream and enhance the company's brand in the marketplace.

LATE RECOGNITION

Although mainstream and general business news outlets largely ignored early and groundbreaking *National Thrift News* reporting on the Keating scandal, the newspaper's work eventually was recognized. *Columbia Journalism Review, Newsweek*, and the *New York Times* were among those celebrating *National Thrift News* work on the Keating Five case, albeit long after the newspaper published its exclusive stories.[116] *National Thrift News* won the George Polk Award for Financial Reporting—one of business journalism's top honors—for its 1988 savings-and-loan coverage. The Polk judges wrote

> *National Thrift News*, a weekly trade publication for savings executives, found a new market last year—print and broadcast reporters anxious to understand a national story that seemed to be growing faster than the national debt. The story—the demise of a significant segment of the savings and loan industry, initial government efforts to paper over the problem, and the ultimate realization that American taxpayers would absorb tens of billions of dollars of

bad debt—became front-page and top-of-the-telecast news months after it was covered in the pages of *National Thrift News*.

Throughout the year, and especially in a remarkably complete and readable report in October, *National Thrift News* alerted those closest to the crisis of its immense implications in an impartial, credible and thorough manner. *National Thrift News* has done itself proud and we are pleased to present it with the George Polk Award for Financial Reporting.[117]

It was highly unusual but not unprecedented for a trade publication to win a prestigious national journalism award. *American Banker*, for example, won Gerald Loeb Awards in 1981 and 1983, and the trade publication *Corporate Financing* won Loeb awards in 1970 and 1973.[118] Trade publications won Polk Awards six times between 1948 and 1987.[119] Strachan was awarded the New York Financial Writers Association's Elliott V. Bell lifetime achievement award in 1990 "for a distinguished career as a reporter and editor in financial journalism." Other winners of the Elliott Bell award included business journalists such as the *Wall Street Journal*'s Vermont C. Royster, television pioneer Louis Rukeyser, and personal finance columnist Sylvia Porter. The New York Financial Writers Association continues to award a Stan Strachan scholarship for journalism students.[120] Strachan reacted to this praise in a matter-of-fact manner. He told the *New York Times* in 1990, if his newspaper "wasn't way ahead of everybody else on this story, I'd be asking myself what was wrong. . . . We're supposed to see the trends and have the best connections."[121]

National Thrift News had an indirect impact on other aspects of the savings-and-loan crisis. Congressional investigators were influenced by *National Thrift News* reporting. Martin Lowy, in *High Rollers*, his recap of the S&L scandal, cited the newspaper's influence in the July 1990 U.S. Senate Judiciary subcommittee investigation led by former senator Howard Metzenbaum, an Ohio Democrat. "Most of what Metzenbaum's subcommittee found out—at who knows what cost to taxpayers—had been published in the *National Thrift News* a year earlier," Lowy wrote.[122] In 1996, Strachan reflected on the impact of the paper's Lincoln Savings coverage. "Four years after our stories appeared, a steady stream of 'knowledgeable' regulators and legislators told a Congressional hearing that they first learned of Lincoln's condition from articles in this newspaper."[123]

The paper's coverage also influenced financial news television broadcasts. Strachan began appearing on television in the late 1980s to discuss the savings-and-loan crisis and was a regular guest commentator on CNN. His appearance on this cable channel gave Strachan a prominent voice and an indirect impact on the public debate about the savings-and-loan crisis. At CNN, veteran broadcasters Stuart Varney and Myron Kandel were among Strachan's friends and admirers. "We had him on CNN frequently. He was so knowledgeable," Kandel recalled in an interview. Kandel, a pioneer in broadcast financial journalism, was impressed by the quality of Strachan's work and said he nominated him for a Pulitzer Prize.[124]

In the early 1990s, Strachan began to suffer health problems related to diabetes and a kidney condition. He sold the company in 1995 to Faulkner and Gray, a unit of Thomson Corporation.[125] On January 6, 1997, Strachan was admitted to St. Vincent's Hospital in New York after suffering a major stroke. He died the next day at the age of fifty-eight. Dozens of his current and former reporters and mortgage industry officials attended Strachan's shiva and funeral services. The family received a flood of condolence cards from journalists and leading industry figures, some 138 notes from people across the United States. One of Strachan's former reporters, Aleksanders Rozens, worked for *National Mortgage News* for less than two years but was moved to write a two-page typewritten letter describing the influence of his former boss. "Stan cared about printing news. You did not just re-write a press release, something most of today's media is content with. He demanded his reporters dig in and find out all they can about a story," he wrote.[126] Other notes were from top corporate executives such as Richard Parsons, then president of Time Warner; James F. Montgomery, chairman of Great Western Financial Corporation; Al DelliBovi, president of the Federal Home Loan Bank of New York; Peter Bakstansky of the Federal Reserve Bank of New York; Phil Roosevelt, editor of *American Banker*; and Angelo Mozillo, the former chief executive office of Countrywide Credit, who later became a controversial figure in the 2008 financial crisis. In a handwritten note to Strachan's wife and daughter, David O. Maxwell, former chairman of Fannie Mae, wrote, "It was always a treat to be with him—even when he was asking me hard questions."[127]

2

THE ENFORCERS

Like many trade journalists, Strachan held a basic belief that the industry he covered had some intrinsic social value. The savings-and-loan industry presented itself as offering a means of lifting up the working class though financing home purchases, the centerpiece of U.S. household wealth. "Stan was the defender of the whole idea of savings and loans being depository institutions that encourage homeownership," recalled Kleege.[1] And like many trade journalists, Strachan was deeply suspicious of anyone who broke the industry's norms in pursuit of personal aggrandizement. Keating was the antithesis of the savings-and-loan industry ideal, for example. Lincoln Savings became a financing vehicle for his speculative commercial developments, not a source of loans for middle-class people to buy homes. Lincoln made few home loans but bought millions in junk bonds. That deeply offended Strachan, Kleege recalled: "The whole Keating thing was a complete rejection of that ideal. So he was very adamant that this should be exposed, the perversion of original mission of savings and loan, to be a piggy bank for a real estate developer. That's why it was an important story to him."[2]

Strachan also was offended by the abuse of the political system. The five senators generally defended their conduct with Keating by describing it as constituent service, saying they were not doing anything unusual and they would do the same thing for any other major employer in their home states. Again, Strachan viewed the senators' conduct as a perversion of the democratic process. "Stan made a great effort to reassure us and our readers that was not a usual event. This was an unprecedented amount of pressure brought to bear on some bank examiners. It was a real violation of normal behavior," Kleege said. Other trade journalists have played a similar ethical enforcement role. Maryfran Johnson and *Computerworld* enforced the notion of fair play and competition in the technology industry. The magazine was critical of major players, such as Oracle's Lawrence Ellison, when it perceived a violation of those standards. Richard Korman of *Engineering News-Record* was offended by bullying in the construction industry; Whitney Sielaff at *National Jeweler* sought to expose corrupt gem dealers.

The actions of Strachan, Johnson, Korman, and Sielaff help us understand a little-appreciated but powerful role the trade press can perform as stewards of business ethics, being the "conscience" of a given sector of business. Put another way, they operate as enforcers of normative behavior in an industry, recording the industry's history and reporting on people who violate the standards of behavior so crucial for honest commerce. In this fashion, trade journalists again serve a critical function in capitalism. By enforcing a baseline of business ethics, they help the markets self-regulate and they police outliers. Think of the essential role news and information media perform for capitalism by helping with price discovery in the markets. Reporting on crooks and unethical business behavior represents an enforcement role that is crucial to self-regulation of the markets. Ida Tarbell's willingness to challenge the economic might of John D. Rockefeller helped reign in Standard Oil; Bethany McLean's early and incisive reporting paved the path for investor skepticism of Enron Corp.; Gillian Tett's writing about dysfunction in the global bond market previewed a systemic problem that contributed to the 2008 financial crisis.[3] Critical reporting not only helps expose bad players in the industry but it also highlights the misdeeds of people for state and federal regulators and private litigators. Put simply: trade journalists are the enforcers.

HARD NEWS SENSIBILITY

Although his reporting brought Keating to justice, Stan Strachan did not set out to be a crusader. Instead, he brought a hard-news reporting sensibility to his job and was willing to criticize his industry allies and sources if necessary. His colleagues and competitors described him as a solid, intelligent journalist, trying to do his job well. "It didn't start out as moral outrage," Muolo recalled. "He was trying to make a living but then the S&L crisis happened."[4] The *National Thrift News* reporting on Keating followed a tradition of interpretive journalism with roots in such pioneering publications as *The Economist*, *Fortune*, and the *Commercial and Financial Chronicle*. Strachan's reporting on the savings and loan crisis followed a classic pattern of the trade press performing a function of accountability journalism, which C. W. Anderson, Leonard Downie, and Michael Schudson defined as encompassing "traditional investigative reporting, but much more. It includes fact-checking political speech, digging into digital data, and aggressive beat coverage to reveal as much as possible about what is really going on in every aspect of American society—from national security, government, politics, business and finance to the environment, education, health, social welfare, sports, and the media industry itself.[5]

Accountability journalism thus is like watchdog journalism and stems from the normative ideal of journalism performing a surveillance function for the broader community good. Origins of this idea date back to the sixteenth and seventeenth centuries in Europe with the beginnings of ethical discourse in journalism. This grew into a concept of a "public ethic" for the emerging newspaper press during the Enlightenment era. "Journalists claimed to be tribunes of the public, protecting their liberty against government," Stephen J. A. Ward wrote.[6] Enlightenment-era political philosophers such as Jeremy Bentham and Immanuel Kant provided a valuable foundation by describing a "principle of publicity" that emphasized transparency and disclosure to keep political and economic institutions in check.[7] This was a key element of the watchdog and accountability ethic in journalism, the notion that publicity about politicians' activities can bring them to justice. "Kant conceived of publicity as a moral principle and legal norm, as an 'instrument' to achieve both individuals' independent reasoning and legal order in the social realm," Splichal wrote.[8] Edmund Burke and James Madison expanded on Kant and Bentham by envisioning the press as a Fourth Estate, an independent institution overseeing government.[9] Liberal political theory holds that a free and independent press is vital for protection of public liberties and liberal reform.

Driven by complaints about corrupt reporters and sensational articles, a general movement toward journalistic professionalism began at the end of the nineteenth century.[10] The first U.S. professional journalism society was founded in 1914 at DePauw University's Sigma Delta Chi, now the Society of Professional Journalists. Its first code of professional ethics was adopted in 1926. The movement led to the development of Fred Siebert's iconic "social responsibility theory" of the press, which described how the press served the political system, enlightened the public to facilitate self-government and served as a watchdog over the government.[11]

The Society of Professional Journalists' code emphasized avoidance of economic conflicts of interest,[12] a centerpiece of business journalists' ethical codes since that time. Some of the earliest evidence of a professional identity for business journalists came in 1890, when a business writer's association was founded in Detroit.[13] Various trade newspapers and magazines in 1906 established the Federation of Trade Press Associations, headed by James H. McGraw and John A. Hill of the McGraw-Hill publishing enterprise. It shaped the identity of the trade press and advocated for industry priorities, such as the reduction in postal rates for publications.[14] The National Conference of Business Paper Editors was founded in 1919. For business journalists, no industrywide ethical guidelines were established until 1963 with the founding of the Society for Advancing Business Editing and Writing, or SABEW.[15] This business journalist group has been a force for positive change by sponsoring professional development seminars. But an explicit no watchdog role for business journalists is included in the SABEW mission statement or code of ethics.

BUSINESS JOURNALISM SERVING THE PUBLIC GOOD

Researchers have documented how business journalism provides a significant public benefit by assisting regulators and others with identifying bad actors in the corporate world. A former top Securities and Exchange Commission official, Robert Sack, said about one-third of leads for accounting investigations emerge from the financial press.[16] This oversight role is valuable to the readers of the trade press. Top industry executives find the trade press to be a better source of information than the mainstream press. Dyck and Zingales found business journalism "pressures managers to act not just in shareholders' interest, but in a publicly acceptable way. This finding brings the role of societal norms to the forefront of the corporate governance debate."[17] Existing scholarship describes the strong impact of business journalism on corporate reputations.[18]

Some of the trade-press journalists interviewed for this project published works that led to significant reforms. One dramatic example involved reporting in 2012 by Fabey, the former naval reporter for *Aviation Week*, about troubled construction of the U.S.S. *Freedom*. Fabey's reporting coincided with a congressional inquiry into the U.S. Navy's Littoral Combat Ship program. Fabey discovered the U.S.S. *Freedom* was not seaworthy and had numerous faults that could have endangered sailors' lives. Fabey said the ship "was a death trap."

Amid the publicity, the Navy spent $42 million to repair the vessel. These stories led to the intense reactions from the U.S. Navy and the defense contractor

Lockheed Martin. Initially, Navy officials challenged key aspects of Fabey's reporting, suggesting he had fabricated material about the ship's problems. Fabey, however, had boarded the vessel in San Diego and had taken multiple photographs of the U.S.S. *Freedom*'s construction flaws, including a large gap in a stern door that allowed enormous amounts of water to pour into the ship when it was operating at high speed. "In this case, you have some stories that very probably . . . helped prevent the loss of hundreds of sailors' lives," Fabey said.[19]

According to Fabey, one Navy official threatened him and his publication with legal action if they published the photographs. Still, *Aviation Week* published details about extensive corrosion, leaking, and other manufacturing issues on May 9, 2012. Fabey then obtained a batch of confidential emails suggesting the Navy was trying to suppress damaging details about the U.S.S. *Freedom*'s sea trials. Eventually, the Navy switched course and agreed to cooperate with Fabey and allowed him access to see repairs to the ship. The Navy invited Fabey aboard to attend sea trials of the vessel. "They definitely had gone a long way towards fixing the ship," he said.[20]

The argument for hard news and accountability journalism was made powerfully by James Hamilton in his remarkable 2016 study called *Democracy's Detectives: The Economics of Investigative Journalism*. Hamilton made the case for societal benefits of investigative reporting: he found "that each dollar invested by a newspaper in an investigative story can generate hundreds of dollars in benefits to society from changes in public policy."[21] Hamilton has a glass-half-full outlook for journalism in the digital age. Computational journalism "can lower the cost of discovering watchdog stories and make it easier (and more profitable) to tell stories in personalized and engaging ways," he writes. "The same advances in technology and data that decreased newsroom revenues supporting investigative work hold the potential for advancing its future." Even though investigative and accountability reporting is expensive, Hamilton sees an opportunity ahead. "Investigative reporting is under-provided in the market, but new combinations of data and algorithms may make it easier for journalists to discover and tell the stories that hold institutions accountable."[22]

COMMUNITARIANISM

One important framework for understanding the interplay of journalism and its social impact is the theory of communitarianism. Former U.S. president Barack Obama, once a community activist, expressed communitarian ideals in his books and speeches, such as his call in *The Audacity of Hope*, to "ground our politics in the notion of a common good" and avoid identity politics to help better the broader society.[23] "Communitarians measure individual acts against the normative standard of their impact in creating a more just society," Philip Patterson and Lee Wilkins wrote. "Communitarianism asserts that social justice is the predominant moral value."[24] This framework traces its origins to Aristotle and his concept of politics, which is concerned with "the noble action or happiness of the citizens."[25]

Applying this to journalism, Stephen Ward wrote that communitarians "argue that neither liberalism nor any theory can be liberal among different views of the good and therefore, journalists should support their community's commitment to substantive values and conceptions of the good life."[26] Such an ethical framework fits nicely with business journalism, since it recognizes that businesses must align with broader societal values. "Viewed in this way, journalism cannot separate itself from the political and economic system of which it is a part," Patterson and Wilkins wrote.[27] Yet making the social good as the centerpiece of journalism is a significant shift from journalism's current normative foundations that emphasize objectivity and facticity. "Communitarian thinking takes social responsibility to the next level. It urges that justice, rather than truth, become the ethical linchpin of journalistic decision making. If justice becomes the fundamental value of American journalism, then the media—functioning at institutional level—have the goal of transforming society, of empowering individual citizens to act in ways that promote political discussion, debate and change."[28]

Communitarianism evolved as a response to the damage caused by liberalism, with its focus on individual rights over the community good. As such, the theory also departs from neoliberalism—the celebration of laissez-faire economics, deregulation, free trade—by challenging the primacy of the markets. "Communitarianism is a social philosophy that builds on the assumption that the good should be defined socially. This core assumption is in sharp contrast with liberalism, which assumes that each person ought to determine the good individually," notes Amitai Etzioni, a leader in the communitarian school.[29] Therefore, communitarianism can be an important lens for journalists to report on the markets and challenge some of capitalism's foundational assumptions. Etzioni said communitarianism emphasizes "the importance of society and its institutions above and beyond that of the state and the market, the focus of other public philosophies. It emphasized the key role played by socialization, moral culture, and informal social controls rather than state coercion or market pressures."[30]

MUCKRAKERS

These communitarian ideals can be seen in the work of the early muckraking journalists, the progressive-minded writers such as Ida Tarbell, Lincoln Steffens, Upton Sinclair, and Jacob Riis who wrote some of the toughest articles about businesses at the turn of the twentieth century. Their work reflected a broader view of liberal democracy in the nineteenth century where, as James Aucoin wrote, "Americans rejected the laissez-faire of social Darwinism, and with that rejection came a sense of responsibility for others in society."[31] Muckrakers grew out of two major trends, "a widespread alienation from authority" and a displacement of middle Americans from power at local levels of government and business. "The historical pendulum swung toward muckraking as two mutually reinforcing phenomena converged: the demand for information about societal ills from an alienated literate population of consumers; and a fiercely competitive national media that sought to supply it," wrote David Protess.[32]

Much of the muckraker's work was published in general interest magazines, such as *Harper's America* and *McClure's*. There was plenty to write about. A great consolidation of corporate power and wealth took place beginning in the 1880s, led by financier J.P. Morgan, industrialists John D. Rockefeller, Jay Gould, Andrew Carnegie, Cornelius Vanderbilt and others. This so-called "robber baron" era was a time of significant corporate mergers, with some 4,277 U.S. companies collapsing into 257 firms between 1897 to 1904.[33]

Muckrakers' targets were food companies, meat plants, oil and gas conglomerates or railroads, but as Chris Roush wrote, "The reporters and editors working on these stories did not consider themselves 'business journalists.'"[34] Perhaps they avoided the business journalism label since the genre lacked stature and was still an emerging specialty geared for narrow audiences. Tarbell's work and that of other muckrakers was well outside the established norms of business journalism at the time. She pioneered many investigative business journalism techniques in her influential series on Rockefeller,[35] such as research into affiliated corporations. Her reporting from 1902 to 1904 helped unravel Rockefeller's broad monopoly in the oil industry by documenting operations of his Standard Oil empire. No one had performed such detailed documentary work on a major business executive. Later, the U.S. Justice Department filed a landmark antitrust lawsuit against Standard Oil and the U.S. Supreme Court ruled in 1911 that Standard Oil was an illegal monopoly. Tarbell's reporting achievements in the early 1900s were even more remarkable considering her gender; discrimination was so embedded in society that women did not even have the right to vote.

The muckrakers' critiques of concentrated economic power resonated with basic American values, which Morton Keller describes as "hostility to the active, centralized state, deep commitments to social individualism and economic competition."[36] One of the major reforms to come out of the Progressive Era was the 1906 Pure Food and Drug Act which was inspired by investigative reporting about abuses in the meatpacking industry.[37] The corporate backlash against muckrakers and the Progressive era led to the rise of a new profession of public relations. J.P. Morgan, for example, adopted an aggressive public relations campaign in 1912 ahead of the Pujo congressional hearings on financial abuses in the market.[38] Other major corporations began using public relations strategies. As Schudson noted, "The public relations that developed in the early part of the 20th century as a profession which responded to, and helped shape, the public ... This had a far-reaching impact on the ideology and daily social relations of American journalism."[39] The "golden age of muckraking" came to a close by World War I, in part due to audience fatigue over the revelations of corporate abuse, the rise of Progressive candidates to national offices and a corporate backlash that led to "a withdrawal of corporate advertising from muckraking publications."[40]

Reporting by Strachan and the *National Thrift News* followed this tradition of muckraking and accountability journalism. Protess called it "the journalism of outrage." As in the muckraking era, Strachan lived during a period of distrust of institutions and a displacement of the working class. In the mid-1960s, public confidence in business and the government began to erode due to the Vietnam War and the Civil Rights Movement; in the 1970s, the U.S. working class began to experience a loss of manufacturing jobs partly caused by global competition. This societal turmoil helped fracture an elite consensus about the direction of the U.S. economy and provided an opening for a more assertive press. This assessment would be consistent with Lance Bennett's indexing hypothesis, which studies how journalists look to government officials and business leaders to define what is newsworthy.[41] In other words, during periods of societal turmoil, the press has more of an opportunity to set an agenda at variance with corporate priorities.

Other factors supporting investigative journalism in this era included important legal and legislative advancements in open records and protection of reporters' sources. Beginning in the 1960s, a formative period in Strachan's career, the U.S. news media began to express a more assertive voice in the wake of the declining influence of businesses. The rise of investigative journalism in the 1960s fits a pattern identified in the "muckraking model" of investigative journalism created by University of Maryland professor Mark Feldstein. Over time, muckraking journalism tends to rise and fall depending on the supply of media outlets, competition and reader demand, Feldstein wrote.[42] The supply, competition and demand were all present in the late 1960s and early 1970s. Newspapers such as the *Boston Globe, Newsday,* and the *Chicago Tribune* fielded permanent investigative teams and the program *60 Minutes* had debuted on CBS.[43] The audience generally supported the notion of investigative reporting. Weaver and Daniels cited three public opinion surveys in 1980, 1984, and 1989 that showed at least 90 percent felt investigative reporting was at least somewhat important.[44]

WATCHDOG AND SOCIETAL BENEFIT

Trade-press history reveals several strong examples of watchdog journalism that served the public interest, ranging from the work of Henry Varnum Poor on the railroad industry to William Buck Dana's editing of the *Commercial and Financial Chronicle*. One classic example was the reporting by *Engineering News* on the 1907 Quebec Bridge collapse, a disaster that killed seventy-five workers. An *Engineering News* editor and a writer conducted extensive interviews, performed engineering calculations, and discovered design flaws that caused the bridge collapse. Roger Burlingame wrote that the episode was a "telling illustration of the value of the technical press." The *Engineering News* articles challenged the established order in the industry. The tragedy, the *News* candidly stated, was an indictment of the entire profession.[45]

There is a history of watchdog journalism in the U.S. press as both a reporting strategy and business opportunity. James AuCoin wrote about the prevalence of watchdog reporting in colonial papers and the business opportunity for the Penny Press era in the 1830s.[46] Gerry Lanosga also found "a robust and steady tradition" of watchdog journalism, particularly at local newspapers.[47] Muckraking journalism in the early twentieth century, Marc Poitras and Daniel Sutter wrote, was not unfavorable for the survival of news organizations as it had no adverse effect on advertising or survival rates of magazines. "Our results imply that muckraking did not significantly impair advertising in the short-term or the long-term," Poitras and Sutter wrote.[48] Other academics are suggesting business journalism has a future providing hard news critical of the industry. Butterick writes, "To suggest that financial and business journalism should have a more critical function is not anti-business but can play an important role in building a new relationship with society."[49]

One of the earlier studies on trade journalism, by Julian Elfenbein in 1969, shows that business people find the trade press valuable for its interpretation and analysis of companies and events. General news can't just be repeated; trade-press articles must say how an issue affects them and their business, even if the news is not pretty. "The modern corporation needs a critical business press," Elfenbein writes. He compares the business press's watchdog role to the press's role in politics. "The modern corporation needs the free—that is, free to be critical—press just as much as the government does; it needs it as one of the fundamental checks and balances of a free enterprise economy."[50] Through this watchdog reporting, Endres argued, trade publications provide a public service to the industries they cover, in keeping with Siebert and his social responsibility theory of the press. Business reporting that holds companies to account can greatly influence corporate behavior by pressuring managers to behave in socially responsible ways, Dyck and Zingales write: "By selectively reducing agents' cost of collecting and evaluating information, the media play a major role in shaping the creation and accumulation of reputation."[51]

The *National Thrift News* staked out such a leadership position in its early issues. The paper's second issue, October 14, 1976, reported on discrimination in mortgage lending, a highly controversial issue for the thrift industry. A page-one story in November 1976 previewed Senate hearings on redlining, the practice of denying credit or business services to minority neighborhoods. Strachan wrote editorials about lending discrimination on December 9, 1976, and on April 14, 1977. Lending discrimination plagued the banking industry throughout the 1980s and still does to this day. This problem gained considerable national attention in 1988 after the *Atlanta Journal-Constitution* earned a Pulitzer Prize for its investigation of mortgage lending discrimination.[52] In addition, Strachan was a highly visible force in the industry, appearing more than one hundred times on CNN as an economic commentator from 1991 through 1996. His television appearances involved commentary on the mortgage market and broader economic and political trends, particularly on the economic policies of the Clinton administration. One theme in his CNN appearances was the topic of racial discrimination in mortgage lending. Strachan also appeared several times on CBS news programs such as *Face the Nation* and the *CBS Evening News*.[53]

The trade press, by its focused nature, is not intended to serve broad general interest news. Yet some portion of the trade-press coverage serves significant societal benefit. Look at the decision by *Aquatics International* to report on sexual misconduct by swimming coaches. Kendra Free, the former senior editor of *Aquatics International*, said she had observed periodic stories in local newspapers about swimming coaches accused of sexual assault. Yet none of the newspapers had sought to examine the broader trend. "In comparing with mainstream media, we were really one of the only organizations that did more of a big-picture look. The mainstream media, there might have been some stories about a local coach but, other than that, they didn't go into how it could be potentially impacting the entire structure of this sport,"[54] Free said. Free's article, "The Enemy Within," was awarded the 2011 Jesse H. Neal Award, one of the top honors in the trade press for reporting. Julie Triedman, former senior writer at *American Lawyer*, wrote about the bankruptcy of the Dewey and LeBoeuf law firm, the largest law firm bankruptcy in U.S. history at that time. The law firm's leaders had provided her misleading financial data about the firm's fiscal results, which *American Lawyer* wound up publishing in March 2012. Upon learning of the flawed figures, Triedman worked with her sources and obtained audited financial results and published a follow-up article in April 2012. These new details showed Dewey and LeBoeuf's finances were much weaker than what many of its partners and employees had realized. Dewey and LeBoeuf's leaders sought to discredit Triedman's reporting, yet she persisted and documented the unraveling of the firm, which closed its doors in May 2012. "In the face of relentless pressure from Dewey management, Julie persevered to get to the truth of the firm's financials," said Robin Sparkman, *American Lawyer* editor-in-chief.[55]

Some academic studies clearly point to a societal benefit resulting from watchdog business journalism. Consider the research of University of Michigan professor Gregory S. Miller, who studied 263 firms that had committed serious accounting violations. He found that in 29 percent of cases, the news media were first in reporting these accounting problems. He concludes that the business press fulfills an important watchdog function in detecting important accounting problems. "Consistent with dual role for the press, I find that business-oriented press is more likely to undertake original analysis while nonbusiness periodicals focus primarily on rebroadcasting," he wrote.[56] Paul Gao, an associate professor of finance at the University of Notre Dame, and his coauthors found that in cities where newspapers closed, citizens saw government costs rise from lack of oversight of municipal finances: "Disruptions in local news coverage are soon followed by higher long-term borrowing costs for cities. Costs for bonds can rise as much as 11 basis points after the closure of a local newspaper—a finding that can't be attributed to other underlying economic conditions, the authors say. Those civic watchdogs make a difference to the bottom line."[57]

Yet views among trade-press editors diverge on the concept of public service. For many publications, their core mission is to write for their industry and not the broader public. "We don't, generally speaking, think about the consumer when we are writing these things," said Prevor of Phoenix Media Network. Nevertheless, trade-press journalists can function as important intermediaries between the industry and the public, particularly in times of crisis, he added. Strachan, for example, was called by CNN several times to explain the inner workings of the savings-and-loan industry on the Lou Dobbs program, among others. Prevor said he is called by mainstream media outlets to discuss industry controversies, such as a food-safety crisis. In this fashion, he said, "An industry editor becomes an important person for communicating a broader story to consumers."[58] This is a paradox of the trade press; some editors view public service as a by-product of assisting their industry. They can expose flaws and bad behavior, but the primary focus is to help the industry to evolve. Other publications have a slightly broader view of their audience, such as *Computerworld*, which views its core readership as computer users, which could range from the individual hobbyist to a corporate information technology executive.

Trade-press editors representing many industries assert this leadership role. In the jewelry business, for example, Whitney Sielaff, former editorial director for *National Jeweler*, oversaw an investigation of corruption in gemstone processing. *National Jeweler* reported that more than 75 percent of rubies and emeralds were altered and filled with resins to improve color and clarity. Sielaff called for wider disclosure of the practice so consumers would not be duped into acquiring altered gems without their knowledge. The reporting won the 1998 Grand Neal Award from Connectiv, which describes the award as "the Pulitzer Prize of the business media."[59]

One compilation of important trade-press stories, *Journalism That Matters: How Business-to-Business Editors Change the Industries They Cover*, described how these niche publications can prompt change in their industries. Andre Shashaty, a reporter for *Multi-Housing News* in September 1988, provided the first report of an influence-peddling scandal at the U.S. Department of Housing and Urban Development involving lobbyist James Watt, the former U.S. interior secretary. The story was picked up by newspapers such as the *Washington Post* and led to reform legislation.[60] A 2003 report by *Government Computer News* described how Laura Callahan, deputy chief information officer at the U.S. Department of Homeland Security, inflated her credentials with a PhD purchased from a diploma mill. She was later suspended.[61] Trade publications such as *Variety, Broadcasting,* and *Women's Wear Daily* have been praised for their "often aggressive analysts of the industries they cover."[62] The publications received little public notice or credit for campaigning for better work and safety standards, for endorsing and in some cases helping form professional groups, and for publicizing innovations to make industry more efficient and profitable.[63]

Outstanding trade-press reporting is celebrated each year by the Jesse H. Neal Awards, sponsored by the Software and Information Industry Association.[64]

Since 2004, Connectiv and its predecessor organizations have sponsored the Tim White Award to recognize trade journalists who stand up to outside pressures and produce "independent, honest and ethical journalism."[65] The late White was the editor of *Billboard*, an influential trade magazine for the music industry and he was known for advocating musicians' rights, criticizing violence and misogyny in lyrics, and promoting undiscovered musical acts. While not a muckraker or a business journalist, White "kept the magazine that everyone depends on honest and independent and rigorous, while making sure that non-blockbuster music had a strong presence," critic Jon Pareles wrote.[66] One innovation was White's decision to revamp *Billboard*'s music charts by using computerized sales data that provided a highly accurate report about consumer buying habits and tastes, insights that ran counter to the industry titans' expectations. Chuck Philips wrote, "The new charts shocked the industry, showing that fans were often more fascinated by comparatively unknown rap, metal, alternative rock and country acts than pompous superstars."[67]

One of the Timothy White Award winners was Bill Sweetman, the senior international defense editor of *Aviation Week and Space Technology*. Sweetman was frequently quoted in the news media as an expert source on defense weapon systems. A search in LexisNexis shows he was cited by some thirty newspapers, including the *New York Times*, the *Independent* of London, and the *St. Louis Post-Dispatch*, as well as public interest groups such as Project on Government Oversight and even the House Armed Services Committee. One example of Sweetman's impact was his coverage of cost overruns for construction of the F-35 fighter, reporting which became a major story during the 2011 Paris Air Show.

Another Timothy White Award winner was Richard Korman of *Engineering News-Record*, who exposed bullying in the construction industry and a fraud in the surety bond business. After learning of a bullying complaint against a prominent New Orleans construction firm, Boh Brothers, Korman directed a group of interns to scour the Equal Opportunity Employment Commission files and build a database of cases involving men harassing other men. On-the-job harassment "has been such a perennial problem in the construction industry. We felt an urge to bring this to the public," Korman said. In pursuing this article, Korman envisioned a broader societal benefit from his reporting. "Business journalists are citizens participating in something bigger than themselves," Korman said. "We want E&R to represent the values of the construction industry. In order to have the moral authority, we have to have the values reflect the broader society."[68]

INSIDE JOB

One direct impact of the *National Thrift News*'s reporting culture and its willingness to challenge the industry was the publication of *Inside Job*, an award-winning book by Stephen Pizzo, Mary Fricker, and Paul Muolo.[69] It was one of the first books to argue that the savings-and-loan crisis was a national phenomenon, in contrast to the prevailing view among regulators and national journalists that it was a regional issue. *Inside Job* gained significant national publicity for its findings about the role of organized crime in the savings-and-loan failures. "At nearly every thrift we researched for this book, we found clear evidence of either mob, Teamster, or organized crime involvement," they wrote. "Only one conclusion was possible: The mob played an important role in the nationwide fraternity that looted the savings and loan industry following deregulation."[70] After the book's release, the Federal Bureau of Investigation invited Pizzo and Muolo to the FBI Academy in Quantico, Virginia, to lecture about their findings.[71]

The *National Thrift News* collaboration began when Pizzo, then editor of the weekly *Russian River News* in northern California, began to see broader linkages in his reporting about Centennial Savings and Loan, a failing thrift in the nearby town of Santa Rosa. Regulators seized Centennial in 1985 after an investigation of embezzlement and lavish spending, which included a San Francisco penthouse, a European chef on the payroll, and a private airplane. Centennial's failure at the time cost taxpayers an estimated $200 million.[72]

Pizzo and Fricker wanted to partner with a larger news organization to conduct a national investigation of organized crime in the thrift industry. Pizzo contacted the San Francisco bureau of the *Wall Street Journal*, and reporter G. Christian Hill met with Pizzo and Fricker to discuss their Centennial investigation. Hill examined their notes and files but he could not get his editors interested in pursuing the Centennial story. "No national publication did a good job uncovering the savings-and-loan scandal. With us, it was a question of territorial imperatives. The Balkanized structure of the bureaus didn't allow for national cooperation and coordination," Hill told Francis Dealy.[73]

Once the *Wall Street Journal* passed on a potential reporting partnership, an opening arose for collaboration with the *National Thrift News*. Strachan had been monitoring Pizzo and Fricker's reporting in the *Russian River News* and sent Muolo to northern California to discuss the Centennial case. The three soon agreed they had a national story and began pursuing leads from Texas to New York. Some of this reporting appeared in the *National Thrift News* as they pursued the book project. With *Inside Job*, the authors present an exhaustive, almost prosecutorial, report to back up their argument that fraud and corruption were significant factors in the savings-and-loan crisis. The book describes the dealings of twenty-two major characters and supplies the transcript of the Keating Five meeting with regulators on April 9, 1989. There are profiles of shysters and con men, such as developer Sid Shah in Sonoma County, California, businessman Don Dixon in Vernon, Texas, and Mario Renda of Long Island, New York. Kleege recalled watching as Muolo worked to document some criminal behavior in the industry. "He spent a week tracing a check that had gone from some gangster to a savings and loan," Kleege said. "It was an amazing piece of nose-to-grindstone journalism."[74]

The book won considerable acclaim. *Inside Job* was a *New York Times* bestseller and winner of an Investigative Reporters and Editors award. Warren Hinkle of the *San Francisco Examiner* wrote, "When it comes to understanding the eighties, *Inside Job* plays the same role that Upton Sinclair's *The Jungle* or Lincoln Steffens's *The Shame of the Cities* did at the turn of the century." Jonathan Kwitny, a former investigative reporter for the *Wall Street Journal*, said, "Stephen Pizzo is the person most responsible for exposing what many consider the worst financial scandal since the days of the robber barons."[75] Pizzo, Muolo, and Fricker spoke about their findings at journalism colleges, at public policy forums, and on television shows such as *Donahue* and the *McLaughlin Report*.[76]

The densely written and detailed account in *Inside Job* provides an indictment of the industry as well as financial deregulation. This is the book's enduring value. The political dysfunction in Washington, regulatory gaps, and neoliberal ideology so richly described in *Inside Job* blew up again, twenty years later, in the 2008 financial crisis, an even severer financial meltdown that triggered a major recession and put some 11 million people out of work. Students of contemporary financial crises can find valuable insight in *Inside Job* in its documentation of a dangerous mix of ideology and deregulation operating in a corrupt political system. Although Strachan wasn't involved in writing the book, he set in motion the collaboration of authors, all of whom praised the editor for his support. In that way, the book is one of the legacies of Strachan's newsroom.

3

THE DEVELOPER

Charles H. Keating Jr., a multimillionaire developer and banker, knew his place in the world and let people know it. By 1986, American Continental was the ninth-largest homebuilder in the United States. Keating had created thousands of new jobs, transformed the Sonoran Desert with new housing and retail developments, and brought some $1 billion in new investment into Phoenix between 1984 and 1986. American Continental shareholders saw the stock price soar 1,236 percent from 1981 to 1988. "We thought we were performing a public service as well as running a profitable business," Keating said in a 1987 interview. His vision as a developer was epic in scope, which Keating described in a 1989 press conference: "The regulators look at our construction sites and our planned communities, at our visions and dreams and see acres of raw dirt. We see homes, the entire gambit of educational facilities, entertainment, sports and recreational facilities, hospitals, neighborhoods, businesses, communities and cities growing and families, the basic unit of any society, stable and prospering."[1]

Keating's life was full of contradictions. The standard media portrayals of Keating rarely explored his complex character, a man who bought powerful politicians and yet helped feed the homeless. He spent lavishly: "Money was never an object," as one former employee said. Keating also was extremely generous to charities, particularly the Catholic Church and Mother Teresa, or Saint Teresa of Calcutta. He sought to project a folksy, family-oriented image as a hardworking man running a family-controlled company. Yet many described him as an autocrat, lashing out harshly at regulators, the media, subordinates—anyone who got in his way. Keating's arrogance and displays of wealth and power made him a public face of the savings-and-loan crisis. He was mocked by late-night television comedians, and his likeness was featured on a set of playing cards documenting the disaster. Judy Grande, former National Press Club president, introduced Keating at a journalist luncheon by describing him as "the very symbol of the hard driving, go-go entrepreneur . . . transforming a sleepy thrift institution into a financial juggernaut."[2] And after the revelations about the collapse of Lincoln Savings, Grande said, "One newspaper bestowed on him the title of the greediest man in America."

Keating became a symbol of 1980s excesses in his exploitation of a permissive business environment and the Reagan administration's deregulatory policies to build his American Continental Corporation and Lincoln Savings and Loan, a financial empire worth $5.5 billion. As described in this and subsequent chapters, Keating's temperament, political maneuverings, and business strategy resembled those of Donald Trump, particularly as their real-estate developments came under media scrutiny. Both used the threat of libel suits, political pressure, and bombastic rhetoric to intimidate reporters and editors curious about the impact of their large real-estate projects on local communities. Keating's political influence was well summarized in a 1989 *New York Times* report on the thrift scandal: "By all accounts, he was a frenetic and effective advocate for his business interests—here distributing campaign funds, there offering a former chairman of the Federal Home Loan Bank Board (FHLBB) a job or pushing the Reagan Administration to appoint one of his business associates to the bank board. Mr. Keating was for years almost ubiquitous in Washington and at the state and local level."[3] The following profile of Keating will demonstrate the depth and magnitude of his political and economic power and show the difficulty the small *National Thrift News* faced as it investigated Keating's corrupt political dealings.

KEATING'S ROOTS IN CINCINNATI

At six feet five inches in height, Keating's physical stature matched his imposing personality. He was trim and physically fit his entire life, the legacy of his early years as an All-American swimmer at the University of Cincinnati. He was born on December 4, 1923, in Cincinnati and served in the US Navy in World War II as a pilot. He didn't see combat, but his service was notable in one respect: Keating crashed his Hellcat fighter at a military airstrip in Vero Beach, Florida, during night training maneuvers. By one account, Keating had other priorities on his mind during the flight. He was in a hurry to land the plane and meet an attractive young woman for a date. With the Harry James big band blaring on the plane's radio, Keating did not hear the control tower warnings that he had forgotten to deploy the landing gear. Keating managed to escape without injury, but the plane was destroyed in the belly-flop landing. Keating's younger brother, William, saw the crash as evidence of his sibling's personality: "Charlie is impatient, aggressive, always on the move."[4] In one sense, the crash and destruction of the Navy plane represented the first time taxpayers would have to pay for Keating's reckless behavior.

After his stint in the Navy, Keating returned to the University of Cincinnati, where he earned his law degree. He brought great intensity to his studies: "Working to put himself through school, he graduated from college and law school in 1948—a feat he accomplished in just two and a half years."[5] Keating was an All-American athlete. He brought fame to the university with his swimming achievements. In 1946, he won the two-hundred-yard breaststroke at the NCAA Men's Swimming and Diving Championships, Cincinnati's first national championship in any sport.[6]

Keating grew up with a disabled father who had lost his leg in a hunting accident. Further, when Keating was only seven, his father, a dairy manager, came down with Parkinson's disease. "I had a father who was a total cripple. He used to sit in the front yard in a chair. We'd lift him and put him in that chair," Keating told Michael Binstein and Charles Bowden.[7] The elder Keating, also tall at six feet four inches, received $200 a month from a disability insurance policy; as his disease progressed, he was unable to do much more than feed squirrels in the front yard. Keating recalled of his father that "he had come out of the streets of Kentucky and he had done well—he didn't have any real money, but he maybe had ten or twenty thousand bucks in the bank. It wasn't uncomfortable. . . . No log cabins, we lived modestly but had ample means."[8]

After college, in 1949, Charles Keating married the former Mary Elaine Fette. Devout Catholics, the couple had five daughters and a son. In 1952, Keating started a law firm called Keating, Muething and Klekamp with his younger brother, William, in Cincinnati. William Keating later became a congressman from Ohio and chairman of the *Cincinnati Enquirer* and later chairman of the Detroit Newspaper Agency and owner of the *Detroit News*. He served as chairman of the *Associated Press* during the savings-and-loan scandal. In the 1960s, the law firm began work for Carl H. Lindner Jr., an aggressive corporate executive who became one of America's wealthiest individuals and an active patron of the Republican Party. Lindner was a pivotal figure in Charles Keating's life.

Working with Lindner led to his early success as a lawyer, his introduction to banking and finance, and his first serious brush with federal regulators.

Keating helped Lindner as he grew from his first business, United Dairy Farmers, a milk delivery company, to the acquisitions of grocery stores, insurance companies, and savings and loans. The eventual group of companies Lindner acquired became the financial conglomerate American Financial Corporation, with assets of $157 million by 1965.[9] From the early 1960s till approximately 1976, Keating's law firm "provided a broad range of legal services" to Lindner's American Financial Corporation, "providing advice and counsel on virtually all aspects of AFC's and its subsidiaries' businesses."[10] Keating's firm had Lindner as a main client through the 1960s and he formally joined Lindner as executive vice president of American Financial in 1972.

American Financial was a classic financial conglomerate, a creature of the rise of financial capitalism and its resulting ethos in American business. Financial capitalism places banks and other financial intermediaries at the center of the economy and emphasizes investment returns over other factors in production and other operational decisions.[11] A new ethos of "efficiency," a hallmark of financial capitalism, crept into boardrooms and CEO corner offices during this era. George P. Baker and George David Smith wrote that, under financial capitalism, the business community witnessed a wave of merger activity from 1963 through the 1970s that involved the creation of conglomerates. IIT Corporation, which acquired 350 companies between 1959 and the 1970s is a prime example.[12] Lindner held controlling interests in companies ranging from Great American Insurance Group, General Cable Corporation, the Penn Central Corporation, Hanna-Barbera Productions, Kings Island Company, the former Taft Broadcasting Company, the *Cincinnati Enquirer*, the Cincinnati Reds baseball team, Chiquita Brands International Incorporated, and the Provident Bank.[13] Lindner's group also included American Continental Homes, which Keating later would acquire and move to Phoenix.

Keating's first involvement with the banking industry and savings-and-loan industry began in 1966 through Lindner. Lindner and Keating acquired Provident Bank, "the first hostile takeover of a U.S. bank since the end of World War II."[14] This acquisition would put American Financial into the larger leagues of finance and contribute to the company's prosperity. American Financial would eventually own three savings and loans. By 1972, Lindner said that since 1959 American Financial posted annual earnings gains of nearly 30 percent each year.

The late 1970s marked the beginning of the corporate takeover era in US business history, a period when executives at firms such as Kohlberg Kravis

Roberts and Drexel Burnham Lambert became millionaires from the revolution in financial markets and the probusiness regulatory environment. During this era, the popular culture's attitudes toward wealth and capitalism changed significantly. A capitalist-friendly mindset was ascendant. Debt, which carried a stigma back to the years of Benjamin Franklin and Thomas Jefferson, enjoyed new popularity in part as a result of changes in demographics. The generation of debt-averse executives who grew up in the Great Depression began to retire; these business leaders had avoided debt after witnessing how financial speculation ruined families and communities during the Great Depression. The new generation of business executives in the 1970s and 1980s were more willing to take financial risks. This time period was marked by the rise of a "credit culture" throughout society; consumer debt tripled in the 1980s to $3.7 trillion. And executives such as Keating were "learning to love leverage."[15]

Through Lindner, Keating met the leading innovators in high finance, including the king of the debt market, Michael Milken of Drexel Burnham Lambert. Milken would help finance Keating's purchase of Lincoln Savings and Loan and would be closely involved in other dealings with American Continental. This trend in financial capitalism was aided by the dramatic growth of the US bond and credit markets. A bond market rally began in 1982, followed by a stock-market rally, both aided by the success of Federal Reserve Chairman Paul Volcker and his campaign against inflation. The bond market growth also was aided by globalization of finance and related innovations.[16] Milken brought a new vision to this "junk-bond" market, the term for risky high-yield bonds, seeing it as a way for new companies to access global financial markets and expand, particularly through mergers and hostile corporate takeovers. At its peak, there were 381 leveraged buyouts in 1988 and the value of deals peaked at $70 billion in 1989.[17] And one of Milken's major customers was Charles Keating.

SEC CASE

With Lindner, Keating had his first encounter with financial regulators. The Securities and Exchange Commission charged Keating and Lindner with using Provident Bank to make $14 million in loans to corporate insiders on preferential terms. The SEC charged Keating with making false statements and omitting key facts in reports to the agency about the insider loans and charged that his law firm "failed to carry out its professional responsibilities." Keating settled the SEC's fraud case in 1979 by accepting a permanent injunction against any future violations but did not admit wrongdoing. Lindner was ordered to pay $1.4 million to American Financial related to the loan transactions.[18] The *New York Times* reported that Lindner's payment was "believed to be among the largest cash settlements from an individual ever obtained by the commission" up to that time.[19]

This SEC fraud settlement would come back to haunt Keating. In 1981, President Reagan was considering whether to appoint Keating as ambassador to the Bahamas, where Keating had a second home. Senator Dennis DeConcini of Arizona, one of the Keating Five, sent a letter to Reagan supporting Keating's appointment.[20] The appointment fell though in wake of publicity about the SEC settlement.[21] Keating also was under investigation by the Federal Bureau of Investigation in 1956 and 1957 for possible fraud and espionage. Confidential files obtained by *National Mortgage News* in 1991 showed the FBI was close to bringing a case against Keating because of his legal work for Research Laboratories of Colorado, which was seeking business with the former Atomic Energy Commission.[22]

The SEC investigation of Lindner and Keating was consistent with a broader breakdown in ethical culture in the financial sector that began in the 1970s and grew in the 1980s. This new culture celebrated financial returns, and dysfunctional characters who were able to "make the numbers" gained market power and notoriety. One signature case involved Ivan Boesky and his financing of hostile corporate takeovers. He pleaded guilty in 1986 and was imprisoned on insider trading and securities fraud charges.[23] The Boesky case led to an investigation of Milken and Drexel Burnham Lambert, the pivotal player in the fast-growing junk bond market.[24] Milken, in turn, had significant junk-bond dealings with Keating and David Paul, owner of CenTrust Savings in Miami. For example, the FHLBB investigated Lincoln Savings in 1987 and found it had purchased shares in companies that were Boesky takeover targets. It also found Lincoln Savings had "almost exclusive use of Drexel Burnham Lambert as its broker."[25] CenTrust was actively trading junk bonds with Lincoln Savings in deals arranged by Drexel from December 1987 through June 1988. Milken and Drexel transformed CenTrust and other thrifts "into huge buyers of its junk bonds."[26] The *Wall Street Journal* and other publications devoted considerable staff and resources to covering the Milken and junk bond investigation, memorably captured in James Stewart's best-selling book, *Den of Thieves*, which described broad corruption in the financial markets. The period led to an explosion of news about white-collar criminal investigations, which were detailed in new business journals such as *National Thrift News*.

AMERICAN CONTINENTAL CORPORATION

As the SEC proceeded with its investigation, Keating and Lindner parted ways as Lindner decided to take his company back into private ownership.

Table 3.1. Charles Keating Jr. Timeline

Year	Event
1923	Charles Henry Keating Jr. is born in Cincinnati.
1942–45	Serves U.S. Navy as fighter pilot.
1946	Wins NCAA swimming competition.
1948	Graduates from University of Cincinnati and its law school.
1949	Marries the former Mary Elaine Fette; couple will eventually have five daughters and a son.
1952	Becomes founding partner of Cincinnati law firm Keating, Muething, and Klekamp.
1958	Organizes Citizens for Decent Literature.
1972	Carl Lindner Jr. names Keating executive vice president of American Financial Corporation.
1976	Resigns from American Financial and purchases an AFC subsidiary, Continental Homes of Arizona. Moves his family to Phoenix.
1979	Keating and Lindner settle Securities and Exchange Commission complaint over insider loans.
1984	Lincoln Savings and Loan acquired by American Continental.
1985	Federal Home Loan Bank Board imposes new regulations on thrifts, limits brokered deposits and direct investments.
1986	Federal thrift examiners begin lengthy audit of Lincoln Savings; Keating spars with FHLB chairman Edwin J. Gray.
	Mesa (AZ) *Tribune* "Keating Connection" exposé on Keating's political contributions, influence, and business dealings.
1987	Keating Five group of U.S. senators meets with federal thrift regulators over Lincoln Savings examination.
	Reporter Michael Binstein publishes exposé on Keating in *Regardie's* magazine, July 1987.
	National Thrift News publishes Keating Five story.
	Moody's downgrades ratings on American Continental long-term debt and preferred stock to reflect the higher risk, debt levels.
1988	Keating seeks to sell Lincoln Savings, without success.
1989	American Continental bankruptcy filing, April 13, 1989; regulators seize Lincoln Savings after declaring it insolvent.
	Federal regulators file $1.1 billion fraud lawsuit.
	U.S. Banking Committee hearings on Keating and Lincoln Savings collapse; Senate Ethics Committee opens probe of Keating Five senators.
1990	Keating indicted by a California grand jury on forty-two counts of criminal fraud associated with the sale of junk bonds. Keating is booked into Los Angeles County Jail.
1992	Keating sentenced to ten years in prison and fined $250,000 in California fraud case.
1993	Keating convicted in federal racketeering, fraud, and conspiracy case, sentenced to $12^{1}/_{2}$ years in prison.
1996	Keating wins appeal, released from prison after serving four years.

Sources: Michael Binstein and Charles Bowden. *Trust Me : Charles Keating and the Missing Billions.* New York: Random House, 1993; "Charles H. Keating." *Outlaws, Mobsters and Crooks.* New York: Gale, 2002; "Events Chronology: American Continental Corporation), Greater Arizona Collection, Arizona State University Library, Tempe, Arizona; Tom Furlong. "Developer with a Cause Battles on Many Fronts." *Los Angeles Times,* March 13, 1988; Jerry Nachtigal. "S&L Figure Keating Released from Prison." Associated Press, October 4, 1996; Jeff Shain. "Charles Keating Leaves Prison." Associated Press, October 3, 1996; Reporting by *National Thrift News, American Banker,* the *New York Times,* the *Wall Street Journal,* and the Associated Press, various issues and dates.

In August 1976, Keating resigned from American Financial and bought Continental Homes of Arizona, Incorporated, a failing homebuilding unit of the Lindner empire. Keating and his family relocated to Phoenix later in 1976.[27] His move coincided with the explosive growth of the Sunbelt, which made Phoenix a highly attractive location for an ambitious developer. From 1960 to 1970, the population of Phoenix grew 32 percent and then, from 1970 to 1980, by another 36 percent to 789,704 to become the country's ninth-largest city. It grew by another 25 percent in the 1980s, and the city reached nearly 1 million people by 1990. This growth and Keating's relentless work ethic combined to turn around American Continental from a money-losing operation into a successful company, and it emerged as a leading builder of single-family housing developments in Phoenix and Denver. "The guy was a brilliant and charismatic man. No one could ever take that away from him," said Michael Manning, the lead prosecutor for the Federal Deposit Insurance Corporation in the Keating case. "And had he stayed straight and just played by the rules that everybody else played with, even bent them a little bit, and not broken them, he would have been one of our state's leading and most well-respected businessmen."[28]

To finance his ambitions, Keating set out to acquire Lincoln Savings and Loan of Irvine, California, headquartered fifteen miles south of Disneyland. The conservatively run thrift was founded in 1925 and had twenty-five branches that primarily dealt with bread-and-butter home mortgage loans. Keating wanted Lincoln because California regulators had dramatically expanded the financial options for state-chartered savings and loans. With Lincoln, Keating could use the California thrift charter to finance commercial real-estate deals with access to a lower cost of funds, which would be the savings deposits backed by federal deposit insurance. In other words, Keating didn't want Lincoln for its existing business; he wanted Lincoln for its potential to exploit the promise of financial services deregulation. In 1984, American Continental bought Lincoln Savings for $51 million—by many reports, he overpaid for the thrift. Milken's Drexel Burnham Lambert financed the purchase by underwriting a preferred stock sale.[29] Soon after the Lincoln transaction closed, Keating began a series of ambitious commercial projects and corporate takeovers. He embarked on four significant deals that would eventually come back to haunt him: an investment the Upland, an Austin, Texas, real-estate project with former Texas governor John Connally; a $19.5 million purchase of Hotel Pontchartrain in Detroit; a new luxury resort in Scottsdale, Arizona, called the Phoenician, in partnership with Kuwaiti investors; and a major new city west of Phoenix called Estrella. He also used Lincoln to help finance a $132 million hostile takeover bid of Gulf Broadcast Corporation stock.[30]

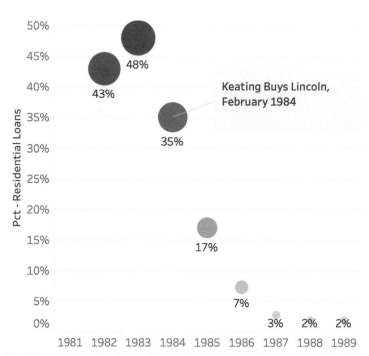

Lincoln Savings stops making housing loans. Under Keating, Lincoln Savings pursued specula-tive development loans, not traditional home mortgage business. Percentage of residential loans, by year. (Source: Office of Thrift Supervision, Lincoln Savings.)

Amid this activity, Lincoln's core business of making mortgage loans fell by the wayside. Under Keating's control, Lincoln made only a handful of home mortgages.[31] He used Lincoln's deposits to buy high-risk junk bonds as a way to finance construction of the Phoenician resort.[32] Keating steadily steered American Continental into finance. In 1978, American Continental started a mortgage company to assist its home-buying customers. By 1981, a Keating company began packaging these mortgage loans into a type of bond known as mortgage-backed securities, a move at the vanguard of housing finance at the time.

BUSINESSES SEES DECLINE IN TRUST

Keating's move to Phoenix and his operation of American Continental Corpo-ration came at a time when there was a broad cultural breakdown in the major economic, social, political, and cultural institutions in the 1970s.[33] The ascendancy of financial capitalism and an erosion of ethical standards helped account for the aggressive behavior of financiers. The basic cultural fabric of the financial services industry, and corporations at large, began to change, a shift marked by a more technocratic and transactional style of business, which was a hallmark of financial capitalism. This was a change from the long-term and personal style of business through relationships. Distance between employer and traders was growing, and between brokers and customers on Wall Street. According to economist Henry Kaufman, the change had serious implications for the long-term functioning of the financial markets: "Close relationships were being pushed aside by the increased volume of transactions in the open market, and by the profit that could be captured by trading, underwriting and merger activity."[34]

Such attitudes led to a decline in public opinion of business. In 1966, a poll showed 55 percent of respondents expressed a great deal of confidence in large corporations. The number dropped to 29 percent in 1973 and to 15 percent in 1975.[35] David Vogel wrote of issues facing corporations at the time: "Large corporations found themselves under intense public criticism: they were accused of promoting or condoning racial discrimination, neglecting the inner cities, supporting repressive regimes from Latin America to South Africa, despoiling the environment, and profiting from the war in Vietnam. Critics of business organized boycotts, protested at annual meetings, filed shareholder resolutions, and published exposés of corporate policies and practices."[36]

In the economy, a 1973 oil embargo by oil-producing companies and a decade of economic stagnation through the 1970s destroyed a rough perception of an affluent society and undermined a consensus about the economy's direction. The traditional remedies of Keynesian economics, such as increasing government spending to move the economy out of a cyclical trough, proved ineffective. Wayne Parsons writes that "during the 1970s, there occurred not only the break-up of the old economic consensus but also the build-up of the new information systems which increased the flow of information and the capacity of markets to function internationally."[37] The US economy faced a major inflationary shock, which stunted growth and job creation. The turmoil brought about by globalization of the economy led to a new wave of innovation throughout the financial markets, particularly in the foreign-currency and fixed-income arenas.

In the process, businesses lost their ability to control and frame the public agenda as they had in the past. While companies saw their power diminish, the US business press was ascendant. Reader surveys at the time showed a demand for more local business news, more stock-market news, and more news on government economic policy. In 1966, Timothy Hubbard surveyed 162 daily newspaper business and financial editors, and 81 percent said their readership's demand for business news had "increased substantially" since 1960.[38] Don Gussow described the mid-1970s as a period when "the consumer press really 'discovered' the appeal of business news for the general public and the revenue potential for advertising."[39]

The US news media experienced a period of economic prosperity, expansion, and innovation and found a more assertive voice in the wake of the Pentagon Papers and Watergate episodes, examples of journalists flexing their investigative reporting muscles. Some news organizations were able to profit from the market turbulence. Reuters created a news service to report on the global foreign-currency markets, which grew dramatically after collapse of the gold standard in the United States. Growth in the financial markets in the 1980s presented more opportunities, and money, for the news media to cover the business community. Damian Tambini described the period as "a golden age of financial journalism" in which a few players, such as the *Financial Times* in London and the *Wall Street Journal* in New York, "enjoyed a privileged monopoly provision as specialist business news providers. . . . Supported by 'tombstone' announcement[40] advertising by large corporate clients and steady sales, with little serious competition, times were easy."[41]

THE CULTURE OF AMERICAN CONTINENTAL CORPORATION

The 1980s were a decade, George Anders wrote, of "a legendary period of unchecked profiteering" on a par with the robber baron era of the 1880s and the stock speculation of the 1920s. According to Anders, the 1980s marked the end of a fifty-year period of economic egalitarianism and led to a greater concentration of wealth and power in the hands of the elite.[42] In the 1987 film *Wall Street*, actor Michael Douglas, as the iconic trader Gordon Gecko, declared "greed is good," a mantra for the go-go business era.[43] Multiple accounts of Keating's behavior in the 1980s would portray him as a kindred spirit to Gordon Gecko. Visitors noticed that America Continental's headquarters resembled the look and feel of a Wall Street firm. "American Continental's offices have a decidedly high-tech glow, with computer screens everywhere reflecting what is happening in the securities markets," the *Los Angeles Times* observed.[44]

While Keating ran his office as a fiefdom, he tended to cut loose and throw wild company parties and pull outrageous stunts. An internal company video, undated, showed Keating at a company event, lightly joking with a group of female employees assembled for his speech. Keating disparages the women's supervisors, saying "there are some things they don't do." He then reaches into his suit jacket and pulls out two stacks of money and throws it casually in the air. The workers laugh and Keating proclaims, "Dinner, ladies, dinner is on us."[45] Presumably, the women later would have to scoop up the stray dollars on the ground to pay for their meals.

Keating spent nearly $36 million in a four-year period operating a helicopter and three corporate jets, one of which was outfitted with polished teak and a custom sound system.[46] Keating's residences included a $2 million house in Phoenix, a $5 million house in Florida, and a home in Cat Cay, the Bahamas, where Senator John McCain once stayed as Keating's guest. Keating's epic resort project, the Phoenician, featured gold leaf on the ceilings, Italian marble, and some $25 million in artwork. Patricia Johnson, a former American Continental public-relations executive, told *PBS Frontline*, "There was no expense ever spared for any task that I could see. . . . Money was never an object."[47]

Employees described work inside American Continental as consuming, intense, and unpredictable. His employees may have called him "Charlie," but Keating was a taskmaster. "Charlie gives orders like a general, and his secretary blows a whistle whenever Charlie issues a new command."[48] He may have parted ways from Lindner, but Keating retained several of Lindner's key traits as he built what became American Continental. He paid his employees generously but they were given vague job descriptions. Some secretaries in 1988 were making $65,000, an amount worth $139,000 in 2018 dollars.[49] Employees also enjoyed catered lunches and unexpected bonuses and gifts. The American Continental offices were furnished with antiques. "A company limousine is available for in-town travel, company planes and a helicopter for longer trips," the *Arizona Republic* reported. Binstein and Bowden compiled numerous outrageous vignettes of Keating handing out spot bonuses to employees at drunken company parties or throwing furniture into swimming pools.[50] Keating micromanaged the operation and insisted on a dress code for employees.

The pace of business was frenetic. Deals multiplied and were pulled together quickly. Tom Frazer, an American Continental shareholder, told the *Arizona Republic* in 1987 that Keating "has a public company he can run like a private fiefdom." The newspaper described Keating as "a workaholic, impatient and demanding" but also "a brilliant businessman." As American Continental grew, so did the executives' wealth. Between January 1, 1986, and January 1, 1989, Keating and other insiders reaped $11.9 million through sales of American Continental stock.[51] Keating's net worth was estimated at $40 million in early 1987.[52] Keating sought to downplay reports of his wealth and spending in a 1990 interview: "I'm not extravagant in the sense that sometimes that it's been reported. And all of my officers and executives have worked hard."[53]

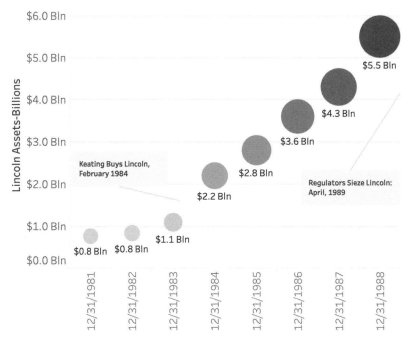

Explosive growth of Lincoln Savings.

Despite this harsh portrait, Keating was a frequent and generous contributor to social causes and a patron of the arts. He assisted friends and relatives beset by hard times with cash payments or a job. Keating generously supported Catholic causes and figures, such as the Mother Teresa and, in 1983, American Continental pledged $1 million to the St. Vincent De Paul Society for the next decade to help the homeless.[54] He expressed compassion for the less fortunate during a 1990 television interview: "I was crossing a Freedom Square the night before last here in Washington. And I saw meals being distributed to the needy on a lovely evening and the sociability of the situation was just heartwarming." Keating said the estimated $500 billion lost in the savings-and-loan crisis could have paid for a "hundred billion-dollar meals. It could be distributed to the poor of the world. That's say at five bucks a meal. You could see that every man woman and child in the United States of America for thirteen months you could feed them their evening meal a good wholesome, evening meal. For thirteen months."[55] A list of contributions by American Continental and its affiliates showed $1.1 million in donations to religious and social-welfare groups for the first five months of 1988. "We think that a business has an absolute obligation to the social welfare of the community in which it lives," Keating told the *Greater Phoenix Business Journal* in 1987.[56]

In this way, Keating and his patron Lindner both held onto some older ways of doing business, one in which family relationships and community philanthropy played a role. Lindner threw "legendary Christmas parties" that featured stars such as Frank Sinatra "and included gifts to every employee," according to a company obituary.[57] Lindner wrote checks to support the museums, schools, symphony, parks, mental health care facilities, and projects such as the National Underground Railroad Freedom Center. Lindner was involved in an urban redevelopment project in partnership with African American business leaders to rebuild Cincinnati's Avondale neighborhood after race protests in 1967 caused widespread damage. The goal was to provide "free enterprise opportunities" for the local African Americans, Lindner said.[58]

To mark his death, American Financial Group held a parade to commemorate and to celebrate the communities where Lindner had an impact. "Mr. Lindner was passionate about staying connected with the neighborhoods where he grew up, started his businesses and raised his family," the company said in a statement.[59] By contrast, there was no such parade through Phoenix after Keating's death in 2014.

PORNOGRAPHY AND POLITICS

Keating came into the 1980s with significant political, media, and legal experience built from his second life as an antipornography activist, where he chased down adult bookstore and movie operators. Through an activist group called Citizens for Decent Literature that he founded in the 1950s, Keating gained a public profile. The group was a formative training ground in politics that taught Keating to work the hallways of Congress while advocating against pornography and showed his willingness to use litigation, including lawsuits against publishers, to advance his agenda, two main tactics he also employed as a savings-and-loan owner.

Described as "a devout Roman Catholic," Keating founded Citizens for Decent Literature, later known as Citizens for Decency through Law, to assist "local police in arrests and prosecution of pornography cases."[60] The group eventually counted three hundred chapters and one hundred thousand members nationally.[61] Keating began testifying before Congress about obscenity in the 1960s and started a legal campaign against filmmakers and magazine and book publishers who produced obscene material. Keating filed numerous briefs with the US Supreme Court as it considered obscenity cases. In 1965, he bankrolled an antipornography propaganda film, "Perversion for Profit," which argued that sexually explicit magazines were encouraging deviant sexual behavior and promoting homosexuality.[62] Keating's pursuit of Larry Flynt, in conjunction with a Cincinnati prosecutor, help put the *Hustler* publisher in jail in 1976 on obscenity charges. Flynt, in his autobiography, recalled that Keating was heading "the most aggressive and well-financed anti-pornography movement in the country" and said Keating's group had six full-time lawyers to pursue cases and help prosecutors. "Before he f****d the savings and loan industry, Keating tried to prevent the portrayal of f*****g in magazines," Flynt wrote.[63] Keating's role in Flynt's outrageous life led to his being featured in the movie *People vs. Larry Flynt*, an account of Flynt's life story.[64]

Keating continued to help bankroll the Citizens for Decency through Law in the 1980s; the group, for example, received $350,000 in 1984 from Lincoln Savings.[65] Any media organization doing a cursory review of Keating's background would have seen the antipornography crusade as evidence of the banker's willingness to use the courts to advance an agenda. One internal American Continental memo provided some insight about Keating's reputation with the press and suggested his battles with pornographers caused some of the tension. In a September 16, 1986, memo, Mark A. Voigt of American Continental said he fielded a phone call from Chris Aaron, a reporter at the *Phoenix Business Journal*, who was seeking details on the company's landholdings. Voigt used the occasion to complain about Aaron's reporting on Keating and the Estrella project. "She indicated that she does not write the headlines and that Mr. Keating was a popular media target because of his stands on pornography," Voigt wrote. "She responded that Mr. Keating has made himself a target for many of the editors and publishers of many kinds of publications in Arizona."[66]

President Richard Nixon appointed Keating to the President's Commission on Pornography in 1969, further establishing Keating's role as a national figure in this field.[67] His activism served as an entrée into national politics. In 1978, Keating was an active fundraiser for the presidential campaign of Texas governor John Connally and briefly served as Connally's campaign manager.[68] Connally would later become a business partner when Keating invested in an ill-fated real-estate project near Austin, Texas, called Uplands. Keating was a reliable and generous contributor to Republican politicians and someone who espoused socially conservative principles, but he chafed at having his politics characterized as far right. "I'm not a member of the far right nor has my political activity nor my philosophy been consistent with the far right. I'm an independent minded voter. I vote for causes that I consider to be just and appropriate," he said.[69]

This background as an aggressive litigator for antiobscenity causes and a Republican activist formed the foundation for his battle with the Federal Home Loan Bank Board, or FHLBB, and his cultivation of the Keating Five group of senators. "We were impressed by his extensive lawyers and economists," William Black, an FHLBB lawyer, recalled. "We were utterly amazed, however, by his political power."[70]

KEATING-TRUMP PARALLELS

Keating's career and operating style bore considerable resemblance to Donald Trump in his career as a developer and evolution as a political figure. They shared a number of characteristics in their business operations, managerial style, political strategy, risk appetite, and even their rhetoric. Both were outliers in their fields, and as subsequent chapters will show, both relied on and reviled the media.

At their companies, both Keating and Trump surrounded themselves with family members, and their companies resembled family-run operations in many respects. Trump has employed his adult children in the Trump organization, such as sons Donald Jr. and Eric and daughter Ivanka. Ivanka and her husband Jared Kushner are unpaid senior advisers in the White House, albeit with considerable authority. The elder Trump also was raised in the family real-estate development business of his father, the notorious Fred Trump. The Trump organization had an informal structure. "We kind of run a little bit like a mom-and-pop in that sense," Donald Trump Jr. said in 2011.[71] Eric Trump, in a 2017 interview discussing the family business, said, "Is that nepotism? Absolutely. Is that also a beautiful thing? Absolutely. Family business is a beautiful thing."[72]

Like Trump, Keating had many of his children, who included five daughters and their husbands and his son, on the payroll. Overall, Keating and his family members extracted from American Continental $34 million in salary, bonuses, and proceeds from stock sales from 1985 to 1988.[73] Keating's son, Charles Keating III, was an executive vice president and director of American Continental, making $1.1 million a year, despite not having finished college. Michael Patriarca, head of supervision of the Federal Home Loan Bank in San Francisco, noted the younger Keating was a renowned swimmer but had worked as a busboy and a waiter previously and had "no relevant experience" for this executive position.[74] Like Trump, Keating was always quick to defend employment of his family in the business: "As far as nepotism, my family and I owned over fifty percent of that company. Our officers and directors owned another 15 percent to 20 percent. We had 25 percent—24 percent in the ESOP plan (employee stock option plan) which was to the benefit of all of our boys. We are a fairly privately controlled company. . . . I cannot think of any better people than my relatives. Every one of them worked hard, everyone was successful. Everyone produced enormous profits for that company."[75] In this 1990 interview, Keating expressed some awareness that his legal crisis and related criminal proceedings had placed a major burden on his family: "My family and I when we bought Lincoln . . . we were probably worth maybe $100 million dollars with fair market value back in 1983. And today, with the exception of the son-in-law who is an eye surgeon, we were all broke. We all have a combined net worth of zero."[76]

In their daily business operations, both Trump and Keating could be unpredictable. Many American Continental employees described "living with the daily fear of being fired by Keating." Binstein and Bowden document several instances of Keating randomly or suddenly firing people: "Charlie has such a short attention span. He likes chaos."[77] The anecdotes of the short attention span and mercurial behavior parallel one of the signature elements of Trump's *Apprentice* programs and, indeed, his conduct in the White House. Keating's staff could tolerate such behavior because American Continental's stock rose dramatically. Under Keating, the stock price of American Continental rose 1,236 percent from 46 cents a share in 1981 to $6.13 in 1988.[78]

In politics, both Keating and Trump abandoned political ideology when wooing politicians to advance their business interests. Between 1989 and 2009, more than half Trump's political donations went to Democratic candidates, according to a *National Public Radio* analysis.[79] The money helped advance Trump's transactions and projects. David Cay Johnston wrote, "Trump has often boasted (in the past and on the campaign trail) that he buys the friendship of politicians so they 'do what I want.'" In Chicago, for example, Trump made nearly $100,000 in campaign contributions to local politicians, nearly all Democrats.[80] He essentially cut off Democrats from campaign contributions from 2010 forward, according to NPR.

Overall, Keating expressed a more consistent political ideology than Trump, one that tracked his Catholic beliefs, particularly the opposition to abortion and pornography. Yet when it came to his business interests, Keating did not apply an ideological test. Keating donated hundreds of thousands of dollars to pro-choice politicians, such as California senator Alan Cranston, a leading liberal politician. Keating was asked on national television about the disconnect between his conservative views and support for Cranston. Without expressing irony, Keating replied, "This particular instance, I find all of those senators to be high minded public servants that have done an excellent job representing their constituency in the United States of America."[81]

RHETORIC

Keating and Trump both employed the optimistic rhetoric of the real-estate world, offering a vision of transforming a dusty frontier or a distressed urban location into an oasis of prosperity. In doing so, Keating and Trump were tapping into what Stephen Ward described as "a broad entrepreneurial ethos or ideology" of marketing and promotion within the real-estate development world.[82] The paradigm of the businessman as booster dates back to the founding of early US cities. "Such men thrived on growth and expansion. Where growth and expansion failed, they transferred their intense loyalties elsewhere and began over again," George Dangerfield wrote.[83] In a comment that captures the political expediency of both men, Dangerfield added, "The governments they devised were not ideological but functional, and they expected cooperation from government on any level."

Daniel Boorstin wrote about the peculiar "Booster Talk" of the early American businessman, a trait Keating and Trump inherited and internalized. "Much of what struck foreign observers as bizarre," he wrote, was the tendency of US businesspeople to engage in "a new linguistic confusion of present and future, fact and hope. . . . Statements which foreigners took for lies or braggadocio, American speakers intended to be vaguely clairvoyant. The American booster often was simply speaking in the future tense, asserting what could not yet be disproved."[84] Boorstin could be writing about the aspirational rhetoric about Trump's Taj Mahal or Keating's Phoenician. The few studies about rhetoric in the real-estate industry note the sense of excessive optimism bordering on delusion and a tendency to marshal one-sided arguments that minimize flaws in real-estate developments. Gwilym Pryce and Sarah Oates noted the tendency in housing advertisements to contain a combination of euphemism, hyperbole, and superlatives.[85]

This rhetorical tradition of property developers is in tension with the normative value of journalism "to seek truth and report it."[86] Truth has always been at odds with rhetoric. Aristotle's theory of persuasion involves working with the emotions of the audience, creating the right impression of the speaker's character and proving truth. "Persuasion is effected through the speech itself when we have proved a truth *or an apparent truth* by means of the persuasive arguments suitable to the case in question," he wrote (emphasis added).[87] Facts are important for your case, but to seal the deal with your audience, Aristotle wrote, "you must make use of the emotions."[88] Trump is an example of this phenomenon, as illustrated in his 1987 *Art of the Deal*: "The final key to the way

I promote is bravado. I play to people's fantasies. People may not always think big themselves, but they can still get very excited by those who do. That's why a little hyperbole never hurts. People want to believe that something is the biggest and the greatest and the most spectacular. I call it truthful hyperbole. It's an innocent form of exaggeration—and a very effective form of promotion."[89]

The notion of "truthful hyperbole" is a logical impossibility, as Jon Hesk of the University of St. Andrews noted.[90] Hyperbole, a rhetorical device dating back to ancient Greece and Rome, "is often translated as 'exaggeration,' and that's a fairly useful rendering of the technical rhetorical term. But the common Greek meanings of 'excess' or 'extravagance' also help us here," Hesk wrote. Such exaggeration was on view when Keating took calls on national television in 1990. He called the Phoenician "the best resort in the world" and described the twenty-thousand-acre Estrella development west of Phoenix in visionary terms:

> We had signed up Continental homes, which I'm sure is the best home builder in Arizona, to put subdivisions on it. We had custom lots out on the market, probably like a couple hundred of them sold, with builders coming in. We had brought Rubbermaid in, McKesson Robbins in as industry. Just the beginning of it. We anticipated through an economic development plan we had to put in a business a month in 1989. The thing was just started. We just brought the pig to market and the government stepped in and took it over. Wasn't anything wrong with Estrella.[91]

Not exactly. The Estrella development, while successful under later ownership, was "a disaster for taxpayers when Lincoln failed," Fogarty wrote. The US government accepted bids in the range of ten cents on the dollar for Estrella and sale of the Phoenician resulted in a $66 million loss, Fogarty wrote.[92] Sorting through the rhetoric and spin of Keating's statements, presented with such force and conviction, proved to be a major challenge for business journalists.

FIGHT WITH GRAY

Shortly after acquiring Lincoln Savings in 1984, Keating began to fight with the FHLBB over its attempt to dampen down speculation in the real-estate industry and its supervision of Lincoln Savings. The investigation and the board's attempts to reregulate the industry led to Keating's high-profile battle with Edwin Gray, the FHLBB chairman. The fight was a driving force leading to the Keating Five senators' meeting in April 1987 and revealed forces behind Lincoln's collapse.

In 1984, Gray moved to restrict direct investments in commercial real estate and other ventures after seeing that wild land speculation in Texas led to growing savings-and-loan failures, particularly the failure of Empire Savings and Loan and its speculative real-estate ventures near Dallas. Losses at Texas savings and loans became dramatic in 1985 during a crash of the state's oil market. For Keating, Gray's action undermined the whole purpose of the Lincoln Savings acquisition. The new rules restricted thrifts' direct investments in land, junk bonds, and corporate securities, all activities Keating pursued when buying Lincoln Savings. To Keating, these restrictions on direct investments were "suicidal."

"It is burning the house to roast the pig. That is what these regulations are," Keating testified at a 1986 congressional hearing.[93] The final rules were adopted in January 1985, less than a year after Keating closed on the Lincoln Savings purchase. The main problem with the new rules, Keating said, was "the government stopped the diversification before it got started."[94]

Keating's argument resonated with powerful officials in the Reagan White House. Gray's reregulation of the savings-and-loan industry was out of sync with the deregulatory agenda of the Reagan administration, which had cut federal red tape in industries such as trucking, airlines, and telecommunications. Gray soon was sparring with a powerful cabinet member, Treasury Secretary Donald Regan, later White House chief of staff, an advocate of deregulation. Gray, a longtime Reagan spokesman from California, lacked the depth of experience in the financial services field. He pushed to restrict the use of brokered deposits, a source of funding for thrifts. Gray and other regulators believed brokered deposits created incentives for shaky thrifts to stay in business longer than they should. They paid high rates to obtain this unstable funding source, which could be withdrawn quickly if better rates were available elsewhere. The move again put Gray at odds with Regan; brokered deposits were obtained from a national network of securities brokers, such as Merrill Lynch. Regan, a former Merrill Lynch chief executive officer, counted the brokered deposit business as one of his achievements. Gray was now attacking Regan's former business.

As this battle continued, Gray's opponents in the administration struck. In 1986, a story leaked to the *Washington Post* reported that Gray had let industry officials pay his travel and entertainment expenses, a politically damaging story for the regulator. Keating cited the episode in his campaign to discredit Gray, accusing him of being an unethical regulator in bed with the industry. Keating denied being the source of this damaging news leak: "For the record, neither Keating nor Lincoln 'planted' the news reports about Gray's alleged ethical misconduct."[95] But Keating harshly criticized Gray in public, accusing him of stifling innovation and new funding for the industry. "I thought then and I feel now that he (Gray) has contributed to more economic disaster and human misery in this country than virtually any American," Keating said.[96] "He's a Nazi task master that wants you to do what he wants you to do."[97] Although Gray accepted travel and entertainment from the industry, numerous post-mortems on the savings-and-loan crisis portrayed Gray sympathetically, saying he had made an error in judgment and was experiencing personal financial difficulties with his family living in California and Gray living alone in Washington, DC.

Keating believed Gray was conducting a personal vendetta against him and that Gray was leaking confidential information to the press about the troubled operations of Lincoln Savings. In a 1990 deposition, asked about the origin of this perceived vendetta, Keating recalled seeing Gray at a US League of Savings Institutions convention in Hawaii in 1985. Keating recalled Gray pointing at him across the room and saying something to people at a table, which Keating did not hear. Keating claimed an unnamed person later reported that Gray said, "I'm going to get that cocksucker and put him out of business."[98] Gray denied making the statement.

In 1987, Keating filed a formal petition to force Gray's recusal from any decisions involving Lincoln Savings and Loan, a bold step that betrayed Keating's anger and his confrontational relationship with the regulator. Keating cited several critical news stories with confidential details about Lincoln Savings and again asserted Gray had "personal bias and enmity towards Lincoln and Charles H. Keating Jr." and charged that Gray could no longer fairly rule on the Lincoln Savings dispute.

During the fight over direct investments, the FHLBB examiners in San Francisco began a detailed review of Lincoln Savings activities in 1986. Keating's aggressive business dealings, particularly Lincoln's accounting for its real-estate investments, came under scrutiny. Regulators were concerned about what they had found. By this point, the thrift was not being operated in its usual manner of extending credit for home mortgages. At the end of 1983, right before Keating acquired Lincoln, the thrift reported 48 percent of its assets were in residential loans. By the end of 1986, just 4 percent of assets were in residential loans.[99] In addition, documentation for major commercial loans and other developments was either missing or incomplete. The examiners found evidence of file stuffing and backdating of loan documents, both warning signs of banking fraud. The San Francisco examiners had not seen a thrift operated like this before.[100]

Keating went to considerable lengths to terminate the San Francisco examiners' audit of Lincoln Savings. He sought to intimidate lower-level employees such George Shiffer, an examiner with the San Francisco Federal Home Loan

Bank. Shiffer had sought to reject a 1986 application by Lincoln Savings to purchase a form of debt. American Continental hired a private investigator, Stephen W. Andrews of Andrews and MacKenzie Investigations of Northridge, California, to check into Shiffer's personal life, which included interviews with his roommates and neighbors.[101] American Continental was a frequent customer of private investigative services, and its files contained thirty-five pages of checks and invoices to two California private investigation firms. Few details of the reports remain.[102] The fight over direct investments foreshadowed the Keating Five scandal in many ways, one of which was Keating calling in favors from Congress to overrule Gray's decisions.

POLITICAL CONTRIBUTIONS

When Keating's challenge to the FHLBB didn't work, he went to Congress. Keating was close to House Speaker Jim Wright, the Texas Democrat, who supported a House resolution opposing FHLBB rules restricting thrifts' speculative investments. Wright and his top lieutenant, House Majority Whip Tony Coelho of California, were allies with leading savings-and-loan executives, who contributed generously to their political efforts. After thrift lobbyists complained about harsh federal regulations, Wright and Coelho stalled legislation to recapitalize the savings-and-loan industry's depleted deposit insurance fund. Instead, Wright and Coelho backed a watered-down bill in 1987, the Competitive Equality Banking Act, that reduced the FHLBB enforcement powers and delayed a refunding of the thrift industry's deposit insurance fund, the Federal Savings and Loan Insurance Corporation.[103] The pendulum began to swing back toward regulation with the election of President George H. W. Bush in 1988. By August 1989, Congress and the White House agreed to enact landmark banking legislation, the Financial Institutional Reform and Recovery Act, which was intended to clean up the savings-and-loan industry. The bill abolished the FHLBB and replaced it with the Office of Thrift Supervision.[104] It also created the Resolution Trust Corporation, a government entity that could acquire troubled mortgage loans and other assets of dying thrifts and repackage them for sale to investors.

A review of American Continental's files shows how Senator McCain, US Representative Charles "Chip" Pashayan of California, and others advocated on Keating's behalf. McCain, in a carefully worded July 1986 letter to FHLBB Chairman Gray, expressed concern about the board's new direct investment regulations without mentioning Keating or Lincoln by name. "I fear that the Board's regulatory program may, unintentionally, restrict industry profitability, increase the number of thrift failures and thus aggravate the current industry difficulties," McCain wrote.[105] A more explicit expression of power was seen in August 1986, when a group of leading House Republicans signed a letter expressing concern about the potential damage the direct investment rule would impose on the industry.[106] The letter's signatories would later have leading roles in the party in subsequent decades—Dick Cheney, Newt Gingrich, Bill Thomas, and Mike DeWine. The American Continental files contain an earlier draft of the letter, with just Pashayan's signature and with the business card of a lawyer for Leonard Bickwit Jr. of Miller and Chevalier, a major Washington, DC, lobby firm that represented Keating. Overall, Keating held some eighty meetings with twenty-five members of Congress seeking help to fight regulators, the *National Mortgage News* reported.

Well before the Keating Five senators' meeting, journalists reported on Keating's attempts to influence the regulatory and political process through campaign cash and use of powerful allies. United Press International's Gregory Gordon wrote about Keating's campaign contributions and his attempt to influence regulators in 1986.[107] *Mesa (AZ) Tribune* journalists Bill Roberts, Andrew Mollison, and others did early work on Keating's political influence in 1985. Binstein wrote an important exposé on Keating in *Regardie's* magazine and *Arizona Trend* in 1987.[108] American Continental's files also show Keating's activity in California and Arizona politics, contributing $9,000 to the Republican leader of the California State Assembly, Pat Nolan, in 1985 and contributing to Governor George Deukmejian's campaign. One ledger showed Keating's companies contributed $26,500 to California politicians in 1985 alone, and the California Democratic Party received $85,000 in 1986. The *Mesa Tribune's* 1986 investigation showed that from 1979, Keating or his associates gave $152,000 to McCain and DeConcini, $68,700 to Arizona congressional candidates, and $144,975 to Phoenix City Council candidates.[109] Keating was active on the Republican fundraising circuit. In October 1988, Keating wrote checks totaling $80,000 to the California Republican Party related to a fund-raiser for George H. W. Bush's presidential campaign. Comedian Bob Hope who was hosting the event in his home in North Hollywood, California, issued Keating's invitation to the fund-raiser.[110] Keating was eager to attend: handwriting on the telegram invitation read "mail ACC check overnight today!"

LOBBYISTS, CONSULTANTS

Keating used another strategy to pressure the FHLBB and Congress: hiring an all-star team of lobbyists and consultants. Key among them was Alan

Greenspan, then a top Republican economist and soon to be named chairman of the Federal Reserve Board. While on Keating's payroll, Greenspan wrote two letters to regulators and coauthored a major economic report arguing for Keating's Lincoln Savings to engage in higher-risk direct investments in real estate. "The new management has a long and continuous track record of outstanding success in making sound and profitable direct investments," Greenspan wrote to the Federal Home Loan Bank in San Francisco.[111] The risk and speculation arising from such direct investments, including a major land development southwest of Phoenix called Estrella, were factors in the Lincoln Savings failure.

Keating's influence was felt at the Federal Reserve Board, the Securities and Exchange Commission, the Treasury Department, and the FHLBB. Keating had hired a former SEC commissioner, Barbara Thomas, as a consultant, paying her a one-time fee of $500,000;[112] she also had a $250,000 unsecured line of credit from Lincoln at a favorable interest rate. Thomas sought to gather information from regulators about their investigation of Lincoln at a time when she was seeking a board seat at the thrift. Thomas was a former partner at the law firm of Kaye, Scholer, Fierman, Hayes and Handler, one of the main law firms representing American Continental, which sued regulators and threatened the *Phoenix Gazette* with a libel suit. Securities and Exchange Commission member Richard Breeden told Congress in 1989 that Thomas also called the agency's enforcement director in 1988 to ask about its investigation of Lincoln and volunteered "a favorable character reference" for Keating. In addition, Thomas called a senior FHLBB official for information about the Lincoln audit.[113] Thomas called FHLBB chairman M. Danny Wall twice. "She told them she knew and respected Keating and hoped they would give him a fair audience, and they said they would."[114]

KEATING'S MILITANCY SPOOKS INDUSTRY, INVESTORS

Keating's militancy on Gray and the FHLBB put him at odds with the US League of Savings Institutions, one of the main industry trade associations. League president William B. O'Connell sent an unusual letter on July 2, 1986, opposing George J. Benston, Keating's pick for an opening on the FHLBB. O'Connell, in a letter to Senate Banking Chairman Jake Garn of Utah, said Benston had "actively participated in a recent campaign to undermine the FHLBB and the FSLIC fund which it administers."[115] FSLIC was the Federal Savings and Loan Insurance Corporation, a deposit insurance fund for thrifts. The letter was a direct slap at Keating, who had hired Benston, a finance professor, and Alan Greenspan to conduct a study about economic problems with Gray's direct investment rule.

Keating's aggressive posture toward regulators then began to worry potential investors and business associates. On January 12, 1987, Moody's downgraded ratings on $240 million of American Continental long-term debt and preferred stock to the highly speculative category. The powerful rating agency said the company had a "high risk profile" for its loans, large amounts of leverage, and weakening equity levels. By midsummer 1987, Standard and Poor's followed suit, downgrading some $143 million of debt and preferred securities, citing the growing risks and weakening financial strength of American Continental.[116] The two downgrades to the speculative category would put the company's debts off limits for some pension funds that only invest in investment-grade debt.

In January 1988, Prudential Capital Markets refused to buy a debt offering from American Continental, in part because of the uncertainty about the FHLBB examination, according to a January 27, 1988, internal memo to Keating from ACC accountant Jim Upchurch.[117] The Prudential bankers expressed "difficulty in understanding the 'core' earnings of AMCOR (American Continental Corp.). . . . Even with additional collateral and possible credit enhancements, they weren't interested," Upchurch wrote. This passage means even sophisticated investors were puzzled by the basic operations and financial reporting of American Continental and would not accept common financial concessions to make risky investments more palatable. In April 1988, First Interstate Bank of Arizona rejected American Continental as a customer. In an internal memo to Keating, American Continental president Judy J. Wischer said the head of credit at First Interstate Bank Arizona "did not want ACC's or Lincoln's cash accounts (our checking accounts) because of the publicity of the FHLB exam."[118] Her memo suggests that regulators' concerns about Keating's real-estate speculation were shared by investors and potential business partners.

4

ADVERTISING AND CONTROVERSY

The rise of commercialism in journalism in the midnineteenth century set up a tension between press and corporate interests that persists today. The twin perils of business journalism involve a reliance on revenues from commercial advertising and a close contact with the businesses that are the source of advertising dollars. Advertising became a viable newspaper revenue source in the midnineteenth century, overtaking subscriptions and financial support from political parties, which bankrolled many newspapers in that era.[1] Advertising revenue shaped journalism in several ways, and historians continue to argue about its impact. Advertising influenced "newspapers' size, selection of stories, organization and personnel, and vulnerability to the economy," Delorme wrote.[2] In this era, "publishers began to sell their newspapers for less than it cost to produce them and to emphasize stories of more widespread interest."[3] Penny papers, embodied by the *New York Herald*, emphasized street sales and shifted away from an exclusive reliance on subscriptions.[4] The penny press was part of a broader movement, the growth of commercial-culture industries in the nineteenth century that included distribution of lower-cost books and magazines.[5] The penny press met the needs of what Michael Schudson calls a "democratic market society" created by the growth of mass democracy, a market ideology and new urban centers.[6] Advertising arose in part as a result of the growing urbanization of the U.S. population. The population growth was driven by immigration, which quadrupled from the midnineteenth century to the first decade of the twentieth century. By 1905, total revenues for the U.S. advertising industry were $45.5 million, double the level from 1890. Historian Frank Luther Mott called the early twentieth century the golden age of advertising: "It marked the beginning of an era in which advertising was not only to exert a great influence on American living but was also to work an important change in the publishing economics of all periodicals."[7]

Journalists as early as 1869 "worried about advertisers' power and attempts to manipulate the news."[8] Baldasty wrote that advertisers in the penny-press era sought to influence business news coverage and to seek free publicity and promotion from newspapers. They were often successful: "Business received much laudatory coverage in the late nineteenth century."[9] For example, newspapers printed news items called "puffs" or "local notices" to praise local advertisers or other products. "Industrialization changed the way in which commerce was conducted and made advertisers a major constituency of the American press," Baldasty wrote.[10] Silvio Waisbord wrote that as tales emerged of newspapers' favoritism toward advertisers, newsrooms began to differentiate between the editorial "church" and the advertising "state" inside news organizations.[11]

POLITICAL ECONOMY

To better understand this critique of advertising, commercial influence, and its application to business journalism, examine the political-economy-theory tradition of media studies, a powerful framework for analyzing the ties of journalism to business and the markets. The theory spells out important assumptions about how businesses influence news content and is critical to understanding why business journalism is dismissed and perhaps why the *National Thrift News* reporting on Keating initially was ignored. Describing the theory's broad outlines, Vincent Mosco writes, "In the narrow sense, political economy is the study of social relations, particularly the power relations, that mutually constitute the production, distribution and consumption of resources, including communication resources. . . . The political economist asks: How are power and wealth related and how are these in turn connected to cultural and social life? The political economist of communication wants to know how all of these influence and are influenced by our system of mass media, information, and entertainment."[12]

In media studies, the political economy theory's leading authors—Dallas Smythe, Edward Herman, Noam Chomsky, and Robert McChesney—contend that the power of corporations and government elites influences news media owners in multiple ways, resulting in weakened or suppressed reporting.[13] They argue that capitalism and corporate power offer significant financial incentives, create a hegemony of ideas, and thereby undermine press independence. Put another way, they argue that private interests trump the public interest. Commercial pressures, critics say, are even more pronounced in business journalism because of its origins and central role in the capitalist free-market system. These forces conspire to restrict the autonomy of journalists and mute challenges to powerful corporate and economic interests.

Political economy describes a link between economic ownership and dissemination of messages that affirm the elites' power in a class society. These ideas date to Karl Marx and his materialist theory of history. One of Marx's great intellectual contributions was his focus on the economic life of humans as central to society's formation and existence. Marx argues that the economy cannot be separated from history, an absolutely essential insight for business journalism and journalism in general. By linking the mode of economic production to the development of social relations and ideas, Marx asserts that individual decisions are influenced by an economic superstructure. Put another way, an individual's free will is constrained by the broader forces of capitalism and corporate ownership. In these and other ways, Marx says, economic and material forces shape individual consciousness: "The class which has the means of material production at its disposal, has control at the same time over the means of mental production."[14]

Marx's historical materialism, with its assumptions about individual agency, challenge contemporary desires for individuals to innovate and challenge corporate dominance. Marx asserts individual rights and aspirations are subordinated to broader economic priorities; the individual has interests imposed on him or her. From this viewpoint, Marx sees a predestination of class; the state and individual ruling classes assert common interests. In Mosco's words, Marx held the view "that people make history, but not under conditions of their own making."[15] These are valuable warnings, but here we see the seeds of Marx minimizing human agency, spirituality, and other aspects of individualism. Smythe built on Marx's insights and advanced a theory about the commercial media system treating readers as a type of commodity, an audience that can be bought and sold through advertising.[16] Baldasty describes this shift: "By century's end, editors and publishers saw their readers not only as voters but also as consumers, so they produced content that went far beyond the world of politics and voting. This vision of a 'commercialized reader,' if you will, naturally fueled commercialized news. . . . Advertisers operated with a vision of the press that valued the newspaper's ability to help them make money."[17]

Building on the work of Marx and Smythe, Herman and Chomsky's *Manufacturing Consent* asserts that governments and corporations exert their power indirectly—they don't rule by overt coercion but rule by consent. They argue the advertising model "served as a powerful mechanism weakening the working-class press" in the early nineteenth century as conservative business owners avoided advertising in radical publications. Herman and Chomsky write that hegemony is created through a "spontaneous consent" granted by the mass population toward a general direction in society. The public provides consent through the prestige afforded to the dominant group. Herman and Chomsky's propaganda model asserts that news is filtered through concentrated ownership and profit orientation of the dominant mass-media firms; that advertising is the primary income source of the mass media; that the media relies too much on government, business, and "experts" who are funded and approved by these primary sources and agents of power; and that the media is disciplined by "flak" from corporate and government interests.[18] Sparrow also saw a diminished role for individual reporters to assert the independence in their organizations, noting that news is a product of the organizational priorities, not the choice of individual reporters.[19] Herman and Chomsky's critique seems tailor-made for the trade press, in light of its reliance on industry for funding and information.

LIMITS TO THE THEORY

The political economy theory is a highly useful tool to critique modern journalism, yet the theory has its limits, and the *National Thrift News* case highlights its shortcomings. For one, the theory does not account for the behavior of the *National Thrift News* and other trade publications dedicated to pursuing investigative journalism. The *National Thrift News*, according to this theory, should not have pursued stories about powerful industry actors such as Keating or industry allies such as David Paul.

In this respect, this book contributes to a long-running debate in communications theory about commercialism and its influence on journalistic autonomy. Did the commercial turn in the nineteenth century compromise journalistic independence[20] or pave a way forward for a more professional and independent press?[21] The case of the *National Thrift News* provides a rather extreme example of how independent journalism can exist within a commercial marketplace. As will be discussed in subsequent chapters, the *National Thrift News* was able to produce this important reporting because of the newspaper's ownership: a journalist was part owner and able to take risks and set editorial priorities. At the same time, his strong grounding in traditional journalistic values allowed

Strachan and his reporters to proclaim and maintain their autonomy. Strachan won fights with his co-owners, who sought to cut staff during the depths of the savings-and-loan crisis, for example. Further, the *National Thrift News* succeeded because there was a demand in the market for this critical reporting, even a necessity for such reporting, as businesses sought to identify and avoid bad actors.

A strong argument exists that the commercial journalism model can support, rather than diminish, reporter autonomy. Advertising allowed the press to become financially separate from the state, Paul Starr argued. "From the founding of the republic, the federal government had given the press constitutional guarantees, postal subsidies and other benefits that enabled newspaper, book and magazine publishing to become economically as well as formally independent of the state and political parties," Starr wrote.[22] By the late 1800s, the press became a source of power in society and was able to provide independent commentary on events. Daniel Hallin said the increase in commercial value of newspapers allowed them to shake off government control: "The development of commercial media markets in the nineteenth century, according to the interpretation, permitted the differentiation of media from political structures, and their reconstitution as independent structures increasingly central to the process by which public opinion was formed."[23] Richard Altick shared this view: "Not until the nineteenth century was decades old would the increasing value of newspapers as advertising mediums allow them gradually to shake off government or party control and to become independent voices of public sentiment."[24] Newspapers financed through the private market would, in theory, make them independent and beyond authoritarian government press controls.[25] For this reason, Joseph Pulitzer viewed advertising as a pathway to journalistic autonomy. Starr wrote, "Pulitzer's equation—'circulation means advertising, and advertising means money, and money means independence'—captured the potential relationship between commercial success and editorial autonomy."[26]

Another weakness in the political economy theory involves its assumptions about individual agency, which in turn challenges the core of journalistic identity. After all, journalists envision themselves as autonomous from government and business interests. The concept of journalistic autonomy, reflected in the writings of Burke and Madison, remains a vital belief to this day. Many journalists interviewed cited this normative ideal of editorial independence as a bedrock principle.[27] Edward Epstein, in his analysis of autonomy, describes the reporter as an outsider,[28] a status that helps preserve autonomy, a concept enshrined in the Society of Professional Journalists' ethical code, which calls for journalists to be free from commercial and political ties.[29] Autonomy was central to the culture of the *National Thrift News* and a feature of Strachan's identity.

"Everybody understood Stanley was a maverick," recalled Ranieri, a prominent Wall Street financier and Strachan's close friend. "We would go to industry conferences and everybody knew Stanley would make up his own mind."[30] Strachan's numerous close connections with chief executives, brokers, and bond dealers meant he had to write about his friends. As the savings-and-loan industry began to fall apart, Strachan had to criticize friends and sources in his articles. "I remember my dad talking about having to write a story, a negative story about someone who was a friend," Strachan's daughter Hillary Wilson recalled. "He said it is hard, but you have to stand by your convictions, and this is the story and you can't shade it because you like the person who did something stupid."[31]

Strachan also made an impression on his staff by writing critically about his friends or important sources. "Stanley could like somebody a great deal and be very critical of him," said Ranieri. Strachan did not seek to write critically of his friends and business associates, but he didn't shy away from it, Ranieri said: "He didn't do it on purpose but it didn't stop him."[32]

One prime example, as described in more detail in a subsequent chapter, was Strachan's social relationship with David Paul, the former chairman of CenTrust Bank of Miami, who later was imprisoned on sixty-eight counts involving federal fraud in 1993. Before the prison sentence, Paul was one of Strachan's sources and the two socialized. Paul once invited Strachan and his family, along with others, to an afternoon on his yacht in Miami; Paul attended Hillary Strachan's bat mitzvah.[33] Muolo and Pizzo knew about Paul's friendly relationship with their boss as the two reporters uncovered evidence of corruption involving Paul. Strachan let critical stories of the CenTrust chief appear in the newspaper. "He was Stan's friend, but he didn't call me off on doing anything," Muolo recalled.[34]

In these instances, Kleege recalled, Strachan kept his main journalistic mission in mind. "He felt that he was a defender of the industry. And defending the industry means reporting that some savings and loan executive was being arrested and led away in handcuffs, you have to report that."[35] Fogarty recalled that Strachan "didn't let any business friendship get in the way of reporting negative things, if they were true."[36] Eugene Carlson, former communications director at the Office of Federal Housing Enterprise Oversight, called Strachan an "equal opportunity critic."[37] Such cases illustrate the vital nature of autonomy, a foundational element of the journalistic professional identity.[38]

This book argues that Strachan created a culture of autonomy that was critical for the newspaper's successful reporting on Keating and Paul. Business journalism history has other examples of strong, independent journalists who confronted powerful capitalists. Consider Ida Tarbell's remarkable investigative series on John D. Rockefeller's Standard Oil and its political influence, published in *McClure's* magazine. McClure estimated each of Tarbell's fifteen Standard Oil articles cost $4,000 in expenses and salary at the time.[39] It would be an extraordinary investment in reporting in any era; in 2017 dollars, $4,000 would be about $110,748 per article, meaning a fifteen-article series would cost about $1.7 million in current dollars.[40] It was an example of great journalistic courage prevailing in a commercial marketplace. The rising wealth and independence of journalism made autonomy possible in that era: "No publisher could have afforded that investment without the mass circulations then achievable under conditions created by cheap second-class mail rates, lower production costs, and a growing middle-class audience," Starr wrote.[41]

New research into media ownership models is showing some commercial media companies can, in fact, engage in civic-oriented journalism. Rodney Benson notes the distinction between media companies traded on the stock market and those that are privately held by wealthy individuals or families, which "are somewhat insulated from stock market demands for profit maximization."[42] The dual-stock ownership structure of the *New York Times*, the *Washington Post*, and the *Wall Street Journal*, for example, where the family owners for many years retained voting control, "has been widely viewed as at least partially responsible for the commitment to quality news at these leading national news organizations."[43] He calls for further research on "civil society media," or news organizations that prioritize democratic values over profit maximization. For these reasons, critics say the political economy theory's emphasis on the influence of capitalism is overly deterministic. As a result, it fails to account for the role of individual agency, or the power of individual initiative and action.

ADVERTISING CONFLICTS

The political economy theory, despite its flaws, helps inform a broad body of research concerned with the perils and conflicts of advertising and editorial content. Jay Black and Jennings Bryant described how newspaper editors traded a certain amount of editorial coverage in return for significant volumes of advertising.[44] In the 1920s, some business reporters developed reputations as "two-hatters," who sold advertisements and then wrote favorable stories about the same advertisers. It wasn't until 1934 that the *Wall Street Journal* banned advertising people from the newsroom and prohibited reporters from selling ads or trading stocks in companies they covered.[45] The *Columbia Journalism Review* noted that in 1973, the bulk of the business press still was "appallingly disreputable" with editors selling ads and ad salesmen editing stories.[46] Hubbard surveyed business newspaper editors and found they "seem curiously resigned to trimming their editorial sails to the edicts of the ad department."[47] A widely cited 1992 study found that 90 percent of newspaper editors surveyed said advertisers attempted to influence stories in their papers, 90 percent experienced economic pressure from advertisers because of their reporting and 37 percent capitulated to advertiser pressure.[48]

One classic example of corporate suppression of news content involved the tobacco industry. Blasco and Sobbrio described a link between suppression of news about the health dangers of cigarette smoking and magazines that accepted tobacco advertising. "Despite the overwhelming evidence on the dangerous effects of smoking available since 1954, U.S. media did not disclose this information for decades. . . . The fact that tobacco companies have been major advertisers seems to have played a key role in this cover-up," Blasco and Sobbrio wrote.[49] Ellman and Germano, Bagdikian and Baker, and even former *60 Minutes* executive producer Don Hewitt all described how tobacco companies' influence led to suppression of reporting on the health risks of tobacco consumption.[50] The tobacco companies employed economic pressure, such as advertising boycotts of *Mother Jones* magazine and *Reader's Digest*, or filed libel suits against news organizations such as ABC News.[51]

Similar episodes of corporate economic pressure involved pharmaceutical advertising. In one 1992 case, a large drug manufacturers withdrew advertising from *Annals of Medicine* after it published a study criticizing the accuracy of advertisements in medical journals.[52] Another involved a 1976 boycott threat of *Modern Medicine*, then owned by the *New York Times*, because drug makers were upset by a *Times* series on medical malpractice.[53] The financial services industry was another realm where advertisers influenced editorial content. Reuter and Zitzewitz examined mutual fund recommendations by personal finance publications and newspapers from 1997 to 2002 and found that "personal finance publications bias their recommendations—either consciously or subconsciously—to favor advertisers." Their study did not find such a correlation between advertising and content in either the *New York Times* or the *Wall Street Journal*.[54] This pressure is especially evident on smaller papers with less market power, which Soontae An and Lori Bergen found were more likely to compromise editorial integrity. These challenges are intensifying over time: "The line between news and advertising continues to blur," An and Bergen wrote.[55]

Advertiser influence dampens the willingness of leading business news operations to engage in critical reporting, Maha Atal wrote in her survey of six news organizations in the United States and the United Kingdom. She compiled a list of recent examples of advertiser influence in the suppression of critical news coverage: *Telegraph*'s downplaying or deleting of critical stories of HSBC at the bank's request; *BuzzFeed*'s 2015 decision to remove articles critical of brands such as Dove and Monopoly because Unilever and Hasbro had native advertising contracts at *BuzzFeed*; and *Gawker*'s move to delete a post for fear of blowback from advertisers.[56] Such cases "reflected a wider pattern of advertisers' growing power over newsrooms," she wrote.

OWNERSHIP

One of the central building blocks to better business journalism comes through the ownership structure. The academic literature clearly points to the problems of public ownership of media companies, a model in which profits are prioritized over the social benefits of accountability journalism. "What has been laid bare is what was only implicit before: that profits come first, and journalism second, that journalism can be served only to the extent that profits are already assured, that in any actual choice between the first dollar of profit and the next increment of journalistic quality the need for profit will prevail," writes Richard Tofel, general manager of *ProPublica*.[57]

As co-owner, Strachan could fight efforts from his investment partners to cut staff during the savings-and-loan industry's crisis and collapse in the late 1980s. The failure of hundreds of thrifts led to financial pressures at the newspaper. At one point, *National Thrift News* co-investor John Glynn pushed to lay off staff, which Strachan firmly opposed. "Stan basically said if you want me to lay off staff, I'll quit," Muolo said. The other owners backed off, fearing Strachan's departure would damage the newspaper.[58] The budget fight illustrated Strachan's autonomy and ability to protect his newsroom. This power is highly significant, particularly in light of the budget battles and cost-cutting pressures facing other newsrooms such as the McClatchy newspapers, Tronc, the former Tribune Company newspaper owners, or Alden Global Capital, the hedge fund that purchased the parent company of the *Denver Post* and subsequently laid off dozens of reporters.[59]

Examples are depressingly common showing how the for-profit media ownership model can be devastating to independent journalism. The Hutchins Commission, in its classic 1947 study of the media and democratic values, said corporate ownership of news organizations is a powerful force that can weaken the autonomy of individual reporters.[60] Victor Pickard and Josh Stearns wrote about the origins of the crisis facing U.S. newspapers and found it "has been exacerbated by a commercial media model that prioritizes profit imperatives over other concerns."[61] The shift from family ownership to corporate ownership in major newspapers and media companies began in the 1960s, as the *Wall Street Journal*'s parent company, Dow Jones, went public in 1963, followed by the Times-Mirror Company in 1964, Gannett Company and the *New York Times* in 1967, Knight Ridder in 1969 and the *Washington Post* in 1971. "The shift from private to public ownership made Wall Street a player in the newspaper business, making corporate concerns even more influential in media circles," Charles Lewis wrote.[62]

The corporate ownership and its emphasis on cost-cutting and high returns for shareholders, well in excess of returns for many Fortune 500 companies, led to consolidation and new debt burdens as companies sought to buy other media companies. "Efforts to consistently increase profits have led to massive job cuts in the U.S. newspaper industry, as well as the closing of newspaper bureaus in state capitals, Washington, D.C., and foreign countries, leaving a dangerous gap in coverage of state, national and international issues," Pickard and Stearns wrote.[63]

There are alternatives to the shareholder and hedge-fund ownership models, however. Numerous studies and interviews show that having journalists as media company owners will help shape the final news product.[64] Fabey, for example, said the culture of his former employer—*Aviation Week*, then was owned by McGraw-Hill—was crucial. At that time, McGraw-Hill had a number of veteran journalists in senior editorial and managerial positions who supported hard-hitting journalism and knew the reporting that made it necessary. "Most of the people who worked there had come up through a hard news kind of thing," he said.[65]

Another example of ownership supporting accountability journalism would be Pat McGovern, owner and founder of IDG Communications and publisher of *Computerworld*. Johnson, former editor in chief of *Computerworld*, recalled the extraordinary support from McGovern for some hard-hitting business reporting. In 2001, *Computerworld* reporter Craig Stedman wrote a series of stories about customer complaints concerning Oracle's database pricing practices. Oracle responded by pulling all its worldwide advertising from *Computerworld*'s parent company, IDG Communications, a move with a cost to the company "in the high six figures," Johnson recalled. The head of sales called her, angry that Stedman's reporting had cost the company such a lucrative client. A few days later, Johnson recalled receiving a personal note from McGovern, who praised Stedman's reporting. Johnson said McGovern had told her "congratulations on the outstanding series of stories that *Computerworld* is writing. You're out there working for our readers. There is no greater service." Johnson said McGovern's full backing in this case "was stunning. . . . He was such a great supporter of everything we did."[66]

The lesson from the episode was clear: "All of us were so secure in the knowledge that IDG wanted the very best journalism and they wanted us to be fearless in our reporting," Johnson said. Don Tennant, an award-winning *Computerworld* editor who replaced Johnson, echoed this viewpoint: "You can't help but be uplifted by that as a reporter."[67] McGovern's support and influence on the journalistic culture had an important impact on technology reporting; by one measure, three of the thirteen Timothy White Award winners came from McGovern's publications. McGovern seemed to take pride in the advertiser complaints as evidence the journalism was having an impact. "From time to time, I still get angry calls from advertisers insisting that I fire an editor and stop printing negative stories," said McGovern. "I ask them to send it to me in writing—and when they do, I publish it as a letter to the editor."[68]

This example aligns with academic research into workplace sociology, which shows the importance of ownership in defining corporate culture and values. "Corporate culture has been defined as the assumptions, beliefs, goals, knowledge and values that are shared by organizational members," according to a 1989 article by Shelby D. Hunt, Van Wood, and Lawrence Chonko.[69] "Though values, according to this view, are but one dimension of corporate culture, they have been theorized to be highly influential in directing the actions of individuals in society in general and organizations in particular." For example, Epstein wrote how journalists tend to align with their employer's viewpoints: "While undoubtedly there is some connection between what a newsman values and what elements of an event he chooses to emphasize or ignore, these values may come from the requisite of news organizations, rather than being deep seated individual beliefs or ideologies."[70]

PROFESSIONAL VALUES

Ownership can support professional norms and values that have enduring power in newsrooms and inspire important journalism. In some cases, reporters can use such journalistic values to win battles with publishers. Take the case of the *Los Angeles Times*, where protests by some three hundred journalists in

1999 helped defeat a revenue-sharing arrangement between the newspaper and the Staples Center sports arena for a special edition of the paper's Sunday magazine.[71] Journalists protested the crossing of the line between editorial and advertising. The *Los Angeles Times* reported the "arrangement constituted a conflict of interest and violation of the journalistic principle of editorial independence so flagrant that more than 300 Times reporters and editors had signed a petition demanding that their publisher, Kathryn Downing, apologize and undertake 'a thorough review of all other financial relationships that may compromise The Times' editorial heritage.'"[72] A similar newsroom rebellion broke out at the *Denver Post* in Spring 2018 over the decision by its owners, Alden Global Capital, to cut newsroom staff from around three hundred to about sixty. The *Post* staff in April 2018 printed a scathing critique of its owner, a full-page article headlined "News Matters—Colorado Should Demand the Newspaper It Deserves." In a related editorial, the newspaper wrote, "If Alden isn't willing to do good journalism here, it should sell the *Post* to owners who will."[73] At the *Wall Street Journal*, former editor in chief Gerald Baker faced a long-running insurrection in the newsroom from his personal ties to and defense of President Trump.[74] Baker found internal emails and statements from newsroom meetings leaked to the press, many of which "accused him of being too chummy with President Trump." He was replaced by *Journal* editor Matt Murray, a well-respected editor who rose through the ranks before Rupert Murdoch purchased the newspaper in 2007. Such instances illustrate the power of the journalistic ideal. "Professional norms have, over the last generation, significantly limited manipulations of news by owners seeking to push their particular political convictions or interests,"[75] Hallin wrote.

How are these traditional news values, such as editorial autonomy and separation from advertising, conveyed in the newsroom? It is an informal process, in which these editors serve as mentors and lead by example. Strachan's colleagues watched closely as the boss reported a story. "We who learned from him saw his persistence, his indefatigable energy when pursuing a lead," Fogarty recalled. "We saw, and hoped to learn, his attentiveness to fact and detail, his quickness in turning a story around and his facility with the language of journalism."[76] Besides setting the tone in the newsroom, Strachan's reporting allowed him to remain in close contact with the most important players on the beat. Industry officials described Strachan as a determined and prolific reporter. In 1992, after delivering a speech, economist David Olson recalled encountering Strachan. Olson recalled that Strachan grilled him for two hours after the speech. "All the questions were good and to the point.... No other reporter had ever penetrated as far or for so long," he wrote.[77]

Many of the trade-press journalists interviewed credited the mentorship and support of their immediate editors and backing of management as central factors in their ability to report their stories and engage in accountability reporting. "It starts with your immediate boss," Fabey said. Triedman said *American Lawyer* specifically looked for editors "who were grounded in strong investigative business journalism. [They] could have worked anywhere."[78] Blackwell said he did not learn the culture of *American Banker* from a handbook but instead by watching how former editor Barbara A. Rehm reported stories and interacted with sources. "She just commanded this instant respect," Blackwell said, adding she was "tough as nails." Blackwell recalled the support and lessons conveyed from his senior editors early in his career. In one example, Merrill Lynch complained about Blackwell's reporting on the firm's use of a legal loophole to avoid paying deposit insurance premiums. Merrill Lynch officials "became increasingly agitated by these stories. They were mad we were writing about it at all," Blackwell recalled. Eventually, the firm requested a meeting with Blackwell's boss to complain. Blackwell's editors backed their reporter. "I never had my bosses come to me and say we had to change coverage of this or change the phrasing of that," Blackwell said. "We kept running stories on it and they [Merrill Lynch] kept being angry."[79]

Kendra Free, a former senior editor with the swimming pool industry publication *Aquatics International*, commended her executive editor, Gary Thill, for his news experience and willingness to pursue investigative projects such as examining sexual abuse by swimming coaches. "Gary's goal for the magazine was to do one sort of big investigative piece each year," she said.[80] "His radar was always looking for these types of stories."

Several journalists described their transition from traditional, mainstream media to trade journalism and their gratification to see fundamental reporting values were honored in the specialty business press. Johnson recalled that "When I took the job at *Computerworld*, I really thought it was kind of a placeholder, and that within a year or two, I would be able to weasel my way into the *Boston Globe* and get a 'real reporter' job again. But I very quickly discovered at *Computerworld*, that it was very much a real reporter job and we were really [involved] in serious, in-depth covering the technology industry. And it was fascinating."[81]

Korman said he grew up in the Watergate era, so going to work for a trade publication initially was "a crushing disappointment." But when he arrived at *Engineering News-Record*, which then was part of the McGraw-Hill publishing empire, he saw "there was a tradition of investigations of construction failures, natural disasters and corruption."[82] Hanley Wood, the Los Angeles–based publisher of *Aquatics International*, set a clear tone for the magazine's editors and writers establishing its value of top-level journalism by encouraging them to submit their work for national journalism awards. "So there was that incentive to really do that kind of work," said Free.[83]

Sielaff, the former editor and publisher of *National Jeweler*, said he sought out reporters who had attended journalism school and had first spent one or two years on a daily newspaper, which he likened to a "Navy Seal boot camp." This helped filter out the people who did not care about reporting in the public interest. When such reporters saw the editor and publisher also cared about doing serious, independent journalism, a positive dynamic ensued. "With journalists, it's a matter of understanding that the person in that chair [the editor] cares," Sielaff said.[84]

ADVERTISING AT THE *NATIONAL THRIFT NEWS*

Former reporters and editors had mixed recollections about whether the critical coverage by the *National Thrift News* caused problems with advertisers. Few details are available about the *National Thrift News* finances through the 1980s, especially during the time when it was publishing its most controversial stories. No advertising records or correspondence was available to measure trends in the late 1980s and early 1990s. Extensive attempts to locate such records were not successful. Officials at Source Media, the current owner, said they could not locate the records because the newspaper had changed ownership before they acquired it. The former circulation and advertising staff declined numerous requests to discuss the business.

Some of the paper's most critical coverage came as the industry began to unravel in the savings-and-loan crisis. Muolo did not recall *National Thrift News* suffering advertising losses from its controversial journalism.[85] By contrast, Kleege and Ranieri said the critical journalism caused some advertisers to leave, but the extent of it was unclear.[86] Nearly all former *National Thrift News* journalists as well as industry officials described a paper resistant to pressure, but there was one unflattering account that alleges that Strachan failed to back up one of his reporters on a sensitive story. Former *Washington Post* banking reporter Kathleen Day, in her book *S&L Hell*, characterized Strachan as being cozy with industry officials and caving in to industry pressure in 1987 on a controversial story, even though it was accurate. The article in question was written by Debra Cope, then the Washington bureau chief for *National Thrift News*. Cope quoted a prominent thrift executive as saying the industry was preparing to ask Congress for taxpayer funds to bail out the thrift industry's deposit insurance fund. Reaction to the story was negative. Industry lobbyists sought to discredit the controversial story and push for a correction. Strachan ran a "clarification" to

Cope's story, even though another industry official confirmed Cope's account. Day contended Strachan faced pressure from major advertisers such as Michael Milken's Drexel Burnham Lambert.[87]

While unflattering, this episode is notable because it is the only one of its type to surface from more than twenty interviews and an extensive review of *National Thrift News* operations and history. Fogarty, the former news editor, did not recall the specific issues in this episode. He, Muolo, and others challenged assertions that *National Thrift News* bent to industry pressure. Generally speaking, the paper would publish a correction when warranted, but not just because something was "politically incorrect," Fogarty said. "Are you asking, 'Did we cave in to the industry pressure?' I would say the evidence of the Polk Award is we didn't."[88]

Historically, fearless reporting could result in advertisers boycotting newspapers. Delorme and Fedler, in their study on journalists and advertisers, write, "Dozens of journalists either experienced or knew of a boycott."[89] Tofel recounted how General Motors boycotted the *Wall Street Journal* in 1954 in a dispute over the paper's coverage.[90] Former *Computerworld* editors Johnson and Don Tennant both recalled adverting boycotts by powerful companies such as Oracle or Computer Associates International to protest their critical coverage.[91] These conflicts persist today[92] and in genres beyond business journalism. BuzzFeed, for example, was criticized in early 2015 for deleting posts under advertiser pressure.[93] Muolo and the other *National Thrift News* staff do not recall instances of advertiser boycotts. Kleege recalled when he first started at the *National Thrift News*, the paper did not have any advertising from Freddie Mac, the mortgage loan financier and a giant industry player. Kleege doesn't recall the nature of the dispute except "the paper had done some critical coverage" involving Freddie Mac. He said the *National Thrift News* won the 1988 George Polk Award not only for its particular coverage but also for the "great personal risk" that the stories would anger and alienate its industry readers.[94] Other journalists admired the *National Thrift News* willingness to take on its industry.

"They were fearless," recalled Christi Harlan, a former *Wall Street Journal* reporter who contributed to *National Thrift News* in the 1980s. "They were not afraid to take on the industry and the players who were buying subscriptions" to the paper, she said.[95]

The *National Thrift News* was willing to bite the hand that fed it. "We pulled no punches in our reporting and played no favorites, actions that were considered unusual, if not unique, for a trade publication," Strachan wrote.[96] Other longtime Strachan employees and thrift industry officials agreed. "Our stories cost Stan some longstanding friendships and shattered his faith in many whom he had highly respected," recalled Pizzo.[97]

Laib, writing about the trade press in 1955, said this is how a strong trade publication should function: "In principle the worthy trade journal is not afraid of antagonizing its advertisers and feels free to criticize the industry, individual companies or products—something company house organs and trade association bulletins rarely do."[98] Doing so is even more difficult in the finance and banking industry, where reporters face difficulty mastering issues of a complex and technical industry as well as significant political pushback from banks and other financial institutions involving critical stories.

TRADE-PRESS ECONOMICS

Broadly speaking, some trade-press titles are fetching a premium for their specialized content. In 2011, *Bloomberg* paid $990 million for Bureau of National Affairs, a highly respected publisher of trade newsletters dealing with taxes and regulations. McGraw-Hill in 2015 paid $2.2 billion in cash for SNL Financial in Charlottesville, Virginia, publisher of financial data and specialized banking newsletters. Berlin-based Axel Springer acquired *Business Insider* in 2015 in a deal valued at $442 million. *PoliticoPro, Axios, Bloomberg Government,* and *Business Insider Intelligence* are all examples of recent entrants into the high-end market of business and corporate intelligence. "There's an increasing demand for data, research and analytics in the financial and corporate markets," said Douglas Peterson, McGraw Hill Financial's CEO and a former Citigroup executive, told the *Wall Street Journal.*[99]

Overall, the trade press was a $27.8 billion industry in 2016, when you include revenues from events and conferences, digital and print advertising, and data sales, according to Connectiv.[100] That makes it about the same size as the U.S. newspaper industry, which reported $27.7 billion in advertising and circulation revenues that year. Some media executives see a clear opportunity to charge more money for insider details on business issues. *Axios* founder Jim VandeHei said in 2016 he was considering charging $10,000 for a subscription to his new business and political specialized publication. Other publications are charging thousands of dollars for their work: *Business Insider Intelligence* in 2016 was charging $2,495 for an "all-access membership." Axel Springer, parent of *Business Insider*, reported nearly 40 percent growth in membership at that time.[101]

Who is paying that kind of money for real-time business intelligence? One answer: corporate lobbyists. The corporate lobbying industry continues to grow dramatically; journalist David Cay Johnston said lobbying fees grew from

$100 million in 1975 to $2.5 billion in 2006, a growth rate ten times that of the economy over that period.[102] One veteran trade-press journalist argued that "paywall journalism" is thriving, especially in Washington, D.C., to serve the growing appetite for corporate lobbyists. "This sector of the Fourth Estate is booming, and its coverage of government has never been more robust," John Heltman wrote in the *Washington Monthly*.[103]

ADVERTISING AND TRADE PRESS

The conflict between advertisers and journalists was pronounced in the trade press, which lacked a diversified source of revenue. One of the few studies examining advertiser influence in trade-press editorial decisions focused on agricultural journalists.[104] "Our study offers clear evidence that advertiser-related pressure on farm magazine writers is a serious problem, although it is one not always recognized by those more seriously affected," Hays and Reisner wrote. They conducted a survey of farm journalists that found 64 percent agreed with the statement "Some media seem to bend over backwards to some of the commercial outfits to butter up sponsors, advertisers and the like."[105] Farm reporters and editors said advertisers attempted to win over journalists with gifts and free meals. Hays and Reisner, in an observation that speaks to the broader trade-press genre, wrote, "Farm magazines, like many other specialized publications, tend to have a somewhat narrow advertising base. The inherent danger of losing a single major advertiser that might be displeased by unfavorable editorial content necessarily weighs more heavily on the minds of farm magazine editors and publishers.[106]

Sielaff and other trade journalists were concerned about the persistent threat of advertiser pressure because of the narrow slice of industry the sector serves. "Trade journalism, which is a smaller world, [has] fewer players and fewer potential advertisers than consumer newspapers," Sielaff said. In Sielaff's experience, the top people running trade publications had backgrounds in advertising and not in editorial. "A lot of times what happens in that world is the editors really kind of take a back seat and are not protected," he said. "A lot of it is just kind of, pure up-and-up greed. . . . I hate to say it, but the model is set up that way. It rewards people for doing it that way."[107] In Sielaff's view, many trade publications lack "those safeguards that are inherent in the conflict between the business side and the editorial side. They are put in place much better, although in many instances they are not always perfect, in the consumer media."

Such a concern about advertisers influencing editorial decision was voiced in 1994 by John Emery, president of American Business Press: "We've been hawking advertising pages for too long, and with all the competitiveness among publications, frankly, we've been shooting ourselves in the foot. . . . Too often, we lock our editors in their offices and tell them to get magazines out, and not to offend anybody."[108]

This criticism was especially pointed for the trade press, which a 1990 *Columbia Journalism Review* derided as dull, "too cozy with the industries they cover."[109] Gussow described the trade press, with few exceptions, as "basically a hodgepodge. While improvements were made in the 1950s and 1960s, it was not until the 1970s that large numbers of business magazines took major steps to revamp their image and operations."[110] While trade-press editors and reporters claimed to believe in journalistic standards, "trade publications may not meet these standards when covering the business strategies and developments of the industries they serve," according to Ann Hollifield's 1997 study of the trade press. "Specifically, there is evidence that the trade media may be reluctant to write about the negative impact that industry-related expansion and development may have on individuals and society."[111] Blackwell at *American Banker* acknowledged this peril to reputation: "One of the things you run the risk of at a trade newspaper is being seen as a cheerleader for that industry."[112]

Sielaff had such an experience during his first stint as a reporter at *National Jeweler*. In 1992, he had uncovered a practice of some jeweler outlets misleading customers about the size and weight of diamonds. He had prepared a story about the misleading marketing: "The article was all ready. And it just got into this place where the publisher and the editor in chief were super worried about the ramifications of this article going through. This was a big company and what would they say? What would the diamond industry do? And ultimately that article never got published."[113]

Sielaff resigned. "I was very dismayed," he recalled. A few years passed and *National Jeweler* wound up needing a new editor. In 1996, he was offered the job of editorial director at *National Jeweler*, which he accepted. Under his leadership, the magazine won the Grand Neal Award from American Business Media, now Connectiv, and Sielaff won the Timothy White Award in 2005.

Sielaff's experience of having a story spiked illustrates the stigma of business journalism throughout the history of the field. Alexander Dyck and Luigi Zingales studied why journalists shy away from pursuing challenging stories about corporations and found numerous disincentives: threats of lawsuits; cost of gathering damaging information, especially in a buoyant market; and the risk of being ostracized by the company and therefore cut out of a regular information flow. Such risks are especially high for reporters who are first to uncover wrongdoing. "We have also argued that producing negative news is much more costly than producing positive news about a company," Dyck and Zingales wrote.[114]

Some publications enjoyed such a significant market reach that advertisers did not boycott them for long. Tennant said in each instance of an advertising boycott at *Computerworld*, the company staging the boycott would resume advertising usually within the next issue or two. That's because *Computerworld* simply was the place for advertisers to reach chief information officers and information technology professionals. Within this community, "everybody read *Computerworld*. . . . I never had advertiser leave that didn't come back," he said.[115]

Paul Miller, president and managing director of Informa Infrastructure Group, oversees publications such as *Transmission and Distribution World*. In Miller's career with the trade press, he viewed editorial autonomy as a business asset that helped sell advertising: "The more independent they are, the more they are able to attract an audience who trusts them. And the more they can attract a trusted audience, the more I can monetize that as a business person to put the right message in front of that audience at the right time. . . . I think independence is the foundation, the stone—it is the rock of the entire trade press business." Miller provided an example of a company, which he wouldn't identify, that pulled millions of dollars in advertising because a publication "wrote a story that highlighted some manufacturing challenges they were having." That led to an "aggressive call from the CEO to me." Miller asked the journalists about the story, who assured him it was correct. Miller contacted the angry CEO, and told him, "We're not retracting it. The story is correct. Our audience needs to know if they are going to be designing with your product that there may be some issues."[116] The company pulled its advertising for six months, but its competitors stepped in to fill that void. Miller said the company later resumed advertising, saying their withdrawal was "a big mistake."

REPORTER-SOURCE RELATIONSHIPS

The relationship between business journalists and corporations can be unequal in subtle ways. Gillian Doyle writes about how some business journalists, for lack of training and expertise, rely heavily on investment analysts at Wall Street firms as news sources to frame a narrative about business and market developments. "One business news editor explains that: Journalists certainly rely on analysts quite a bit to do the interpreting for them of the performance of companies and of economies . . . [and] for off-the-peg opinions and quick reactions to the things where we feel they are better briefed than we are,"[117] Doyle wrote.

The political economy critique also holds that business publications narrow the view of their readers to a smaller subset of elite business leaders and not to the general public, Davis writes, creating "a situation in which non-corporate elites usually lose out and certain corporate elites usually benefit." The reason is that business journalism is "highly dependent on information and advertising subsidies" and because the needs of sources, advertisers, and consumers are closely linked. Davis suggests that a "Financial Elite Discourse Network" has evolved in which "business news has been captured by financial elites. . . . [J]ournalists are highly dependent on the goodwill of city elites in their roles as sources, advertisers and consumers."[118]

FLIPPING INDUSTRY TIES

While Davis and other scholars view these industry ties as a barrier to good journalism, the *National Thrift News* sought to flip that notion and use such ties to produce good journalism. Fogarty, Strachan's successor at the *National Thrift News*, put it this way: "That kind of close engagement with the industry was how we got to those stories first because we were in there. Because of our sources and our method of attack, we got to know those things."[119] Other trade journalists, such as Julie Triedman of *American Lawyer*, described a similar method. "Because so few people outside the community that you are writing for really understand or are interested in every wrinkle of your business, people tend to talk to you. You do get scoops," she said.[120]

Kleege recalled how the *National Thrift News* was able to report on the taxpayer cost of the savings-and-loan bailout. At the time, federal regulators were asserting no such bailout was happening. Strachan devised a strategy to calculate the bailout cost through tax write-offs. The reporting was painstaking and illustrated how a trade journal can leverage its access to report on significant issues in the public interest. Kleege recalled that

> Stan got me access to this meeting, it was completely off the record. I couldn't even mention being there. It was some officials from the FSLIC [Federal Savings and Loan Insurance Commission, the former deposit insurance agency] made a presentation to some invited financiers on how to acquire a savings and loan and write off the losses on your taxes. . . . But four to five months later, we got someone to leak us some documents, which would have been impenetrable without having covered the meeting several months before. . . . We could add up what these were costing in lost taxes. That's a form of investigative journalism but it's also using your access

as a trade paper. You are close to industry and you've made relationships and someone is going to give you access to a meeting that you otherwise wouldn't be able to attend.[121]

Prevor, the food-industry editor, described a more nuanced set of challenges involving the intimate relationships between the industry and journalists. Prevor said he counts more than one hundred people in industry as close friends; many were invited to his wedding. "These are small ecosystems and people are going to have to work with these people over and over all through time," he said. Trade journalists need to be close to industry officials to gain insider knowledge. Without that, "you're not going to really know what is happening," he said. The downside is allowing that access to compromise editorial independence. "So it is important for people to maintain access and to maintain relationships and that leads to a certain degree of timidity," Prevor said. "You are always in danger of caring too much how they will think about you."[122] The ties between the media and industry are multilayered, as Piet Verhoeven found in his study of public-relations literature. Public-relations people and journalists often share professional networks and the media offices have an interdependency with public relations and marketing departments. His conclusion: "In reviewing 50 years of empirical research on communications between corporations and the media, one key word emerges: interdependence."[123]

Harry McCracken, former editor of *PC World* and now technology editor at *Fast Company*, said it is important to engage with industry officials and try "to hear things from their point of view and not to be a jerk about it." For McCracken, the journalist-industry relationship had a clear limit, that it should not "have an impact on the content in a way that readers would not like."[124]

Free, the former senior editor at *Aquatics International*, said the interplay between journalists and the sales team was quite close at her publication. Journalists would inform the sales team about stories and discuss who was and was not quoted in the articles. "We actually work closely with our sales team to keep them informed on stories that we are doing and who we are speaking with," she said. The goal was to "make sure it wasn't going to become something that was going to be such a problem that we weren't going to have a magazine anymore because we have no advertisers."[125]

Such interplay with the sales staff did not exist at *Computerworld*, according to Tennant and Johnson. They said their company adhered to a strict separation between editorial and advertising. Johnson said, "No editors or reporters ever talked directly to anybody about advertising." Triedman, the former *American Lawyer* writer, had a similar experience, saying she was not aware of advertiser threats of boycotts or complaints. "I was insulated from that so it was a wonderful place to be," she said.[126]

Fabey's initial reporting on the problems with the U.S.S. *Freedom* were met with intense criticism from the U.S. Navy and its prime contractor, Lockheed Martin. *Aviation Week* responded by taking Fabey's stories down from the free version of the website. Fabey was upset by this decision and said his senior management was not prepared for the blowback from the government and a powerful defense contractor. "So when the initial story came out, top leadership was blindsided," he said. Meanwhile, Lockheed Martin sought to ostracize him for his critical reporting about the troubled ship program. "Basically, I was disinvited from any function that they would have and all PR people were told not to give me any information," he said. Such an action was dramatic for a trade-press reporter. "In the trade press, I mean, information is everything. More so than the mainstream press, quite honestly."

"There was a discussion between me and my bosses, can you do your job anymore? To which I replied, 'Well, let me try,'" Fabey said. "That was the whole idea, I figured, they wanted to chase me out of my job."[127]

5

KEATING'S WAR WITH THE PRESS

In the American Continental Corporation archives at Arizona State University is a copy of the December 28, 1986, Sunday edition of the *Mesa Tribune*, a daily newspaper that once served the Phoenix area. The edition features one of the first in-depth investigations of Keating's political influence in Arizona and Washington. And this copy is marked with red ink, with handwritten comments, various underlined passages, and notations in the margins:

"Libelous"
"Lie"
"Wrong"
"Don't believe a 'close associate' or anyone said that"
"A statement out of 'whole cloth'"
"NOT TRUE"

The red ink handwriting appears to be Keating's, and some of the comments certainly reflect his public statements. For example, the article reported that "Keating has been demonical in battling child pornography for three decades." In handwritten red ink were the comments "Opposite" and "The pornographers are demonically [*sic*]." At another point, the handwriting read "Sue Gray @ FHLB."

This Sunday edition of the *Mesa Tribune* is a vivid testimony of the anger Charles H. Keating Jr. harbored toward the news media.

Although he had dealt with the news media as an antipornography activist and businessman for years, Keating was enormously thin-skinned when it came to his portrayal in the press. "We would have to be idiots to continue to take this massive defamation by the press," Keating said in a 1987 interview. "It's been murderous. We've all got families. We've got respect. We're not doing anything wrong. We're well within all the rules and regulations."[1] During his November 1989 House Banking Committee appearance, Keating sought to ban press coverage of his testimony. He even contemplated moving the headquarters of his $4.5 billion empire out of Phoenix in part because of tough press coverage.

A review of American Continental's archives shows extensive efforts by Keating's legal team to monitor and intimidate the press. From 1980 through 1989, the files reveal two libel suits, four lawsuits involving media leaks, and eight threats of libel or legal action against the media. Keating had a well-earned reputation for filing lawsuits and fighting his perceived enemies in court. As Keating proclaimed in 1989, he would "challenge in court those who would destroy us," a threat carried out against various news organizations over coverage of his business empire.[2] A 1989 *American Banker* article described Keating's ability to intimidate critics with lawsuits: "Mr. Keating refused to be interviewed for this article. Few who know him will allow their names to be used with their comments, saying they fear lawsuits or other reprisals."[3]

CORPORATE CONFLICTS WITH MEDIA: A NORMATIVE DIVIDE

Keating's antagonism toward the news media took place against a broader fight between corporations and the news media in this era. A major power struggle was at play between businesses and the press in the late 1960s and early 1970s. The struggle is rooted in a normative divide, the sharply divergent concepts that businesses and the news media have about disclosure of information. Corporations began to lose their ability to preserve privacy about their operations as new government regulations and aggressive public-interest groups asserted their roles. Vogel frames it as a power struggle over corporate information: "The right of privacy, like that of private property, is a major legal prop of corporate power. The public-interest movement wants the public's right to information about a variety of dimensions of corporate conduct to receive the same protection from the courts, administrative agencies, and the legislature that these bodies have historically accorded to the corporation's right to privacy."[4]

The struggle played out as the public-interest movement began to press for more government regulation and called for limits on industrial growth, a major change in the fundamental assumptions about the economy at the time. In the

1970s, groups such as the Sierra Club or Union of Concerned Scientists found sensitive corporate information and used it as a weapon against corporations in the court of public opinion. The public-interest movement aggressively used new tools such as the Freedom of Information Act or information released by new government agencies, such as the Environmental Protection Agency, to challenge the corporate agenda. In the process, public-interest groups gained a more prominent voice in the policy debates at the time. Drier writes, "Since the late 1960s, when public opinion polls began to report a dramatic decline in public confidence in big business, corporate leaders have discovered a convenient scapegoat—the news media. . . . The Santa Barbara oil spill, Hooker Chemical's Love Canal problems, and the Three Mile Island power plant incident were all technological accidents that became grist for journalists' mills."[5]

The business press entered the fight by picking up disclosures about corporate misdeeds as a basis for newspaper articles and television broadcasts. The practice marked a shift in business journalism, which previously had been largely accommodating to the corporate agenda. The news media was operating under a normative behavior of the disclosure to assist with the public's right to know, a foundational concept in democratic theory and discourse. The corporate view holds that such sensitive information can damage their ability to compete in the marketplace. These details can include important corporate assets or intellectual property; for this reason, the U.S. legal system contains a variety of protections for business information, such as copyright, trademark, and privacy and trade-secret laws. In some instances, disclosing corporate secrets can result in harsh penalties. A one-year prison sentence is possible under the Trade Secrets Act for someone who

> Publishes, divulges, discloses, or makes known in any manner or to any extent not authorized by law any information coming to him . . . information [that] concerns or relates to the trade secrets, processes, operations, style of work, or apparatus, or to the identity, confidential statistical data, amount or source of any income, profits, losses, or expenditures of any person, firm, partnership, corporation, or association; or permits any income return or copy thereof or any book containing any abstract or particulars thereof to be seen or examined by any person except as provided by law.[6]

Corporate privacy was a core issue in the litigation Keating threatened or brought against the press, the notion that journalists had published sensitive corporate information about the Lincoln Savings audit and threatened the thrift's ability to do business. As will be described, Keating sued the Federal

Home Loan Bank Board (FHLBB) six times between 1987 and 1989 to challenge the examination and seizure of Lincoln Savings.

BUSINESS COMPLAINTS ABOUT MEDIA

Keating certainly was not alone with his complaints about the news media. The power struggle between corporations and the press gained some broader attention in the mid-1970s as business leaders and even some journalists voiced the concern that business news coverage had become excessively negative. "We are fed a daily diet of authoritative ignorance, most of which conveys a cheap-shot hostility to business and businessmen,"[7] Henry Louis Banks, former editor of *Fortune*, wrote at the time. One review of CBS, ABC, and NBC news broadcasts from April 1977 to March 1979 showed 54 percent of the stories portrayed businesses in a negative light, and only 10 percent were positive.[8] Another survey of business leaders and senior editors found three broad complaints about the business press in the 1970s: the "economic illiteracy of most journalists, inadequate coverage and antibusiness bias among news people."[9] Another study comparing standard economic indicators between July 1988 and June 2002 to economic news coverage in the *New York Times* to ABC newscasts found a negative media slant:

> Economic news was framed as negative more often than as positive, and negatively framed news coverage was one of several significant predictors of consumer expectations about the future of the economy. The study supports the argument that media coverage, particularly the media's emphasis on negative news, may have serious consequences for both expectations of and performance of the economy. . . . In 1992, for example, Republicans argued that the media's focus on negative news about the economy misled the American people and influenced the outcome of the presidential election.[10]

Companies complained about what they considered unfair media coverage. One leader in the effort was Mobil Corporation, which spent $1.4 million in 1979 dollars on a national public-relations campaign to criticize the press and advance the energy sector's agenda. Mobil's aggressive public-relations efforts in the 1970s included full-page newspaper advertisements that decried "the myth of the crusading reporter." Corporate complaints about negative media coverage reached such intensity that in 1977, nearly one hundred senior U.S. corporate executives and journalists—including Merrill Lynch CEO, future treasury secretary Donald Regan, and *Washington Post* publisher Katherine Graham—gathered near Princeton, New Jersey, to air mutual grievances. Their deliberations, led by a group of Harvard and Columbia law professors, were captured in a 1979 book, *The Media and Business*, with an introduction by the current U.S. Health and Education and Welfare secretary Joseph Califano and *Washington Post* managing editor Howard Simons. Simons and Califano, in summarizing the session, which lasted nearly two days, described a litany of corporate complaints, such as sloppy, unfairly negative, and inaccurate business reporting by untrained journalists. The media representatives replied that businesses were acting without sufficient public scrutiny. Simons and Califano wrote, "Illegal campaign contributions, social accountability, health and safety, asbestos, thalidomide, the environment, the energy crisis, investment in apartheid—this is the stuff that fosters suspicion and discontent and investigative reporting. . . . Part of the antagonism comes from a growing awareness not just among journalists but the public at large of aspects of business which until a few decades ago were not questioned very often or very loudly."[11]

MEDIA CREDIBILITY PROBLEMS

The corporate attack was effective, since the news media experienced its own credibility problems during this era. The news media came under criticism for lack of accountability and ethical controversies such as conflicts of interests.[12] The literature about the press criticism and watchdog movement in this period described a mood of institutional arrogance among major media organizations, one compounded by the trend of increasing corporate ownership of large newspapers and television stations.

The tension between the press and businesses spoke to broader issues affecting the media climate at the time. One gauge of press and business tension was the formation the National News Council, a nonprofit entity that operated from 1973 through 1984 and reviewed complaints against newspapers, television, and other media outlets. Press coverage of the Vietnam War, civil-rights movements, and unrest at events such as the rioting at the 1968 Democratic National Convention in Chicago were events that drove the formation of the National News Council.[13] "The National News Council came into being at a time when the nation's news organizations—print and broadcast—were caught up in a storm of criticism over their performance, and at a time when they were thought who sought to stifle efforts to provide a free flow of information to the American people,"[14] the council wrote in its first report. The document cites complaints against the media such as conflicts of interest, payment to sources for information, and the effect of monopoly ownership on press freedom. Lobbyists and private businesses generated 41 percent of all complaints to the council.[15]

Other academic studies faulted business journalists in the era for engaging in a form of superficial "gotcha" journalism. They focused "on the micro aspect of conflicts of interest relating to single companies and neglect[ed] broader issues such as the role of business reporting in relation to market sentiment in general,"[16] Damian Tambini wrote. Other academics argued the business press was not exposing systemic problems and was therefore failing to fulfill a watchdog role.[17]

HENKEL

Against these broader trends in media and business relations, Keating became increasingly agitated and aggressive toward the news media. One prevailing theme involved media leaks from regulators, such as the transcript of the Keating Five meetings obtained by the *National Thrift News*. Keating sued to stop the leaks, arguing they were evidence of a vendetta by the regulators. The leaks represented a broader issue, however. They were evidence of a rebellion within the federal bureaucracy over the pace of deregulation. On one level, they showed how regulators, faced with a reduction of their power under the deregulatory agenda of a conservative White House, sought to assert control over a renegade savings and loan by providing damaging information to the press. In the case of Keating and the *National Thrift News*, this regulatory conflict would emerge with the FHLBB's efforts to rein in Keating and Lincoln Savings. The Keating Five senators' meeting was a prime case in point. A transcript of the five senators' meeting was leaked to the press, which allowed the media to report on the event, and the leaks later became a significant development in the savings-and-loan crisis. The leaks also affirmed the power of the press as a watchdog over society. Regulators, facing a reduction in their power, turned to another institution, the news media, to reign in a bad actor.

The Keating leak narrative began in the summer of 1986, when American Continental staff suspected FHLB officials were leaking confidential information about Lincoln Savings to the market. A Salomon Brothers investment banker informed Keating's associates that he heard a market rumor that Lincoln was having loan troubles with a New Orleans firm. American Continental suspected federal bank examiners were the source of the rumor, planted as a way to retaliate against the company for its high-profile opposition to the FHLB's direct-investment regulation, which sought to prevent thrifts from making risky investments in businesses, commercial real-estate developments, and junk bonds. Keating was a leading opponent of this regulation, since it would undermine his business model for Lincoln Savings. Keating hired an outside law firm, Kaye Scholer, which formally complained to the FHLBB in September 1986 and requested an investigation.

As problems mounted between Lincoln and its regulator, Keating began to explore how to blunt Chairman Edwin J. Gray's influence on the FHLBB and get the agency to delay or abandon the direct-investment rule. Keating pushed for developer Lee Henkel to fill the opening of departing board member Donald Hovde. Henkel was an Atlanta lawyer whose development company borrowed more than $69 million from Keating's companies.[18] Keating attorney Michael B. Gardner, in an August 28, 1985, memo, spelled out how such a nomination would help reduce Gray's influence on the FHLB: "Instead of trying to sack Gray, who unquestionably is a disaster but still a 'nice guy' to the Reagan inner-circle, our efforts should focus primarily on getting the White House to take a less controversial (and therefore highly desirable) remedial course of action: identifying and nominating a (Donald) Hovde replacement that would be acceptable to you and other enlightened industry leaders."[19]

What follows is an examination of the Henkel media coverage, a precursor of the Keating Five story and an early example of Keating's attempt to bend the regulatory process to serve his ends. Keating's reaction to the Henkel coverage marked a significant escalation in his fight with regulators and his pursuit of the press. This content analysis helps measure the depth and extent of beat reporting about alleged regulatory corruption prior to the Keating Five meeting. The analysis also suggests which newspapers were paying close attention to Keating and his tactics.

National Thrift News first reported on Henkel's ties to Keating on August 11, 1986, and mentioned the conflict in three subsequent articles that year. The *National Thrift News* linked Henkel's politics to the deregulatory trends: "Both Lee Henkel, former Atlanta attorney and real estate developer, and Lawrence White, a New York University economics professor, are said to favor broader deregulation of the industry than does Mr. Gray."[20] Overall, the name "Henkel" was mentioned in seventeen of thirty-three *National Thrift News* articles, or half of the stories captured in a search from January 1, 1986, to April 16, 1989. Henkel was mentioned in seven of thirty-one articles in the *American Banker*, in five of fifteen articles in the *Wall Street Journal*, but just in two of ten articles in the *New York Times*. Henkel was mentioned in a single *Associated Press* dispatch in this period, noting the controversy with his Keating connection. The *American Banker* first mentioned Henkel and Keating in a December 30, 1986, story; the *New York Times* carried its first report on Henkel on February 17, 1987, by publishing a dispatch from the *Associated Press*. It was the *Wall Street Journal's* December 1986 coverage of Henkel and his conflicts of interest that infuriated Keating and marked a significant escalation in his fights with regulators and the press.

The *Wall Street Journal* articles reported on financial ties between Keating and Henkel, who later proposed a regulation to ease the direct-investment regulations that would benefit Lincoln.[21] The article further intensified the clash with Gray. Henkel denied the conflict-of-interest allegations, but he later resigned in 1987 in the face of a Justice Department ethics inquiry. In 1992, Henkel was banned from the U.S. banking and thrift industries in a settlement with the U.S. Office of Thrift Supervision for his unethical conduct in relation to the failed Lincoln Savings.[22]

Keating described the *Wall Street Journal* coverage as "damaging, scurrilous, libelous" and feared it could weaken demand for a $200 million bond issue by American Continental. Keating began to marshal a significant legal counterattack by arguing the bank board staff was guilty of criminal violations for leaking confidential examination information to the *Journal*. The federal Trade Secrets Act bans federal employees from disclosing sensitive records such as ongoing bank examinations.[23] Keating said he planned to hire another prominent outside law firm, Sidley Austin, and have them pursue "an investigation, full-blown by the proper authorities of the United States government to inquire about this breach of trust by the Bank Board."[24] Keating discussed the possibility of personal lawsuits against bank board officials, which were later filed in 1989. Keating's outside law firm again complained to the FHLBB about press leaks, attaching coverage by the *Wall Street Journal, Washington Post*, and *Mesa Tribune*, which reported Keating's contributions to Arizona politicians and the Henkel episode in a significant series on December 28, 1986.[25]

KEATING, TRUMP, AND MEDIA LAWSUITS

Keating's attack on the press was a strategy similar to one employed by Donald Trump, another businessman who came to prominence during the rise of an adversarial business press in the 1970s and decline in public trust in businesspeople. Like Keating, Trump used the courts to intimidate and stifle reporters, a strategy he continued to pursue as president. By one count, Trump issued forty-three threats and filed five libel suits since the early 1970s.[26] In 2018, Trump's lawyers threatened author Michael Wolff and publisher Henry Holt with a libel lawsuit over publication of *Fire and Fury*, Wolff's controversial insider account about the first year inside the Trump White House. In denouncing Wolff, Trump spoke to broader issues about press freedom. Trump told reporters, "The libel laws are very weak in this country. If they were strong, it would be very helpful. You wouldn't have things like that happen where you can say whatever comes to your head."[27]

Journalist David Cay Johnston recounted one such threat from Trump as he was researching his book, *The Making of Donald Trump*. According to Johnston,

Trump told him, "I know I'm a public figure but I'll sue you anyway."[28] In another instance, Trump in 2006 sued journalist Timothy O'Brien, author of the 2005 book *TrumpNation: The Art of Being the Donald*, for $5 billion in damages, claiming defamation. The dispute? O'Brien reported Trump's net worth was somewhere between $150 million and $250 million, not the $5 billion to $6 billion that Trump had claimed. Trump unsuccessfully sought a court order to force O'Brien to reveal his sources. Trump and his lawyers also tried to prevent the *New York Times* from publishing excerpts from O'Brien's book, arguing it "contained glaring falsehoods." The *Times* published the O'Brien reporting anyway. In all, Trump's legal fight with O'Brien stretched over five years before a New Jersey appellate court dismissed Trump's charges.[29] Writing about the case, the conservative *National Review* observed, "Those who think Trump is a 'winner' ought to take a close look at *Donald Trump v. Timothy L. O'Brien*. Because Trump didn't just lose the case. He was humiliated."[30]

Despite the loss, Trump said he achieved a goal. "I spent a couple of bucks on legal fees, and they spent a whole lot more. I did it to make his life miserable, which I'm happy about," Trump told the *Washington Post*.[31] Some thirty years earlier, Keating's lawyers expressed similar sentiments when considering a libel suit against the *Mesa Tribune* over its December 1986 investigation of Keating: "Nevertheless, a libel suit strong enough to withstand a motion to dismiss may cause the *Mesa Tribune* some discomfort."[32]

Like Trump, Keating used his economic power to file lawsuits and bully reporters and regulators as he pursued his expansion of Lincoln Savings and his real-estate empire. Keating at one point had retained eighty-two law firms and, by 1987, had spent $50 million fighting regulators.[33] Keating raised the specter of "fake news," the signature political mantra of Trump, in a 1987 libel lawsuit against the *Mesa Tribune*, saying it published material "for the purpose of giving wide exposure to manufactured and untruthful news" about Keating.[34] Even regulators said Keating's reputation for litigation put them in edge. Gray, the FHLBB chairman, told Congress later that his agency's lawyers were afraid to take action against Lincoln Savings earlier because "they did not want to risk losing in court."[35] In litigation, Keating was willing to take significant risks, such as challenging the integrity of a prominent federal judge assigned to one of his cases. The *American Banker* reported in September 1989 on Keating's unsuccessful attempt to disqualify U.S. District Judge Stanley Sporkin in Washington, D.C., from his case because of Sporkin's prior employment at the Securities and Exchange Commission and his involvement in an enforcement case against Keating.[36]

Such libel suits were a growing concern for journalists investigating the savings-and-loan crisis. Mario Renda, a deposit broker based in Long Island,

N.Y., filed a $90 million libel suit against the *American Banker* in 1983 after a story about Renda's involvement in a midwestern bank swindle.[37] Guaranty Savings and Loan Association sued *Virginia Business Magazine* for $3 million, asserting a story on the thrift crisis was "grossly misleading and defamatory."[38] Foothill Financial Target of Utah sued KSL-TV of Salt Lake City for $11 million, contending two stories started a run on its deposits. Ohio Savings Association sued Business First of Columbus over an April 15, 1985, article about five troubled Ohio savings and loans, saying they were near insolvency. The magazine prevailed when a state appeals court ruled in its favor.

Libel suits have been a constant worry and deterrent to investigative journalism. Roush wrote how libel suits were a factor in the demise of muckraking journalism.[39] One of the highest-profile libel suits of this era involved the case of former Mobil president William P. Tavoulareas brought against the *Washington Post*. At issue was a November 1, 1979, front-page story that said Tavoulareas had set up his son, Peter, then twenty-four, as a partner in a shipping firm with a multimillion-dollar management services contract with Mobil. Tavoulareas initially won a $2 million jury verdict against the newspaper after a trial that included testimony by Bob Woodward, who had edited the story. Tavoulareas, however, lost the case on appeal, and the appellate overturning was upheld by the U.S. Supreme Court in 1987.[40]

The mere threat of a libel lawsuit presents a clear illustration of the conflicting norms of business journalism and the corporations they cover. The close relationship between the business press and companies unravels when businesses issue legal threats. Journalists said that when companies confront them with legal threats, it challenges their basic existence as independent and autonomous purveyors of information. The risk to a journalist's reputation of buckling to a threat is significant. "If someone figured out they could bully you into changing your coverage or withdrawing your coverage, it's a death spiral from which you will never recover," Blackwell said.[41] A libel suit threat shuts down the typical give-and-take that is part of the relationship between business journalists and companies. "If we feel like there is some merit to your argument, then we can make adjustments. The second you threaten me, I can't do anything or I won't do anything because you have effectively locked me into a situation where I am seen as responding to a threat," Blackwell said.

KEATING AND THE PHOENIX MEDIA

To understand the intensity of Keating's fights with the press and his obsession with news leaks from regulators, examine his relationship with the local news media in the Phoenix area. The *Phoenix Gazette*, the city's former afternoon newspaper, experienced firsthand Keating's willingness to throw hard punches and devote considerable legal resources to challenging articles that criticized his real-estate projects. In April 1980, Keating had a New York law firm send a letter to the *Gazette* threatening a libel lawsuit over a March 19, 1980, article about a minor dispute at one of his subdivision projects. The offending article was "Homeowners Teed Off about Sale of Golf Course." The article reported on a dispute involving Keating's Continental Homes and a golf course and recreational facilities at its Bellair development. The newspaper received three other letters from American Continental lawyers in April and May 1980. Preceding the letter was a four-page memo to Keating from American Continental counsel Robert Kielty describing problems with the *Gazette* story. The file containing the correspondence had copies of legal statutes and relevant case law on libel in Arizona and a report on Continental Homes advertising purchases in the *Gazette* in 1980. The *Gazette* later published a correction about its characterization of Keating's 1979 settlement with the Securities and Exchange Commission.[42]

Keating and his staff were close students of the news media and its operators. A 1980 American Continental internal memo provided the background of Eugene C. Pulliam, owner of Phoenix Newspapers, which published the morning *Arizona Republic* and the evening *Phoenix Gazette*. The author of this memo is unknown, but it was written to American Continental general counsel Kielty. The memo said the *Republic* and *Gazette* newspapers have "been extremely aggressive on what they consider to be land fraud issues. In fact, they have been given to excess on the subject. They are rarely if ever sued and if sued they are somehow in the wrong, very little if anything is said about it. In fact, they appear to thrive on destroying people by using the printed word." "My recommendation would be to proceed cautiously and calculate each step extending its recourse to the farthest possible conclusion before engaging this media in war,"[43] the memo said.

Keating and his associates had sympathetic contacts in some of the newspapers. American Continental had a tipster within the *Mesa Tribune* newsroom who provided a heads-up about an impending investigation of Keating prior to publication.[44] Keating also had a tipster in the *Detroit News*, who gave advance warning about an impending story in February 1988 criticizing Keating's connections to Senator Don Riegle, according to an internal memo.[45] This tipster had called *Detroit News* chief executive officer William Keating, brother of Charles Keating. "Had not a friendly reporter phoned Bill Keating to basically express sympathy and to say 'They were out to get Charlie,' this new level of attack might well have gone undetected," according to the memo.[46]

The next round of libel threats against local media involved several stories about Keating's companies building artificial lakes in his desert developments around Phoenix. These lakes were filled with drinking water, angering many residents who felt it was a waste of a precious resource in the Sonoran Desert. *Arizona Republic* columnist Gail Tabor captured the mood, describing Keating as "too busy destroying our groundwater supply and turning the desert into one big artificial lake."[47] The backlash built to such a level that the Arizona State Legislature in 1986 considered but rejected legislation to ban the practice. The Arizona Senate passed the artificial lake ban, but Keating's lobbying was a factor in the legislation's defeat in the Arizona House of Representatives.[48] A September 4, 1986, editorial in the *Arizona Republic*, "Builders Ignore Conservation," challenged Keating's practice of building the artificial lakes. In what appears to be Keating's handwriting, the editorial is marked with the words "Lie, Lie Lie."[49] In a subsequent letter to the *Arizona Republic* complaining about the coverage, the anger of Keating's legal team was palpable.

"Instead of lambasting Keating and telling its readers that Keating is endangering Arizona's general economy, Phoenix Newspapers Inc. should have pointed out that Keating was responsible for the infusion of $1,000,000,000.00 worth of direct investment in Arizona's economy in the past two-and-a-half years," Philip T. Goldstein wrote to the *Republic* editors.[50] Keating and his lawyers played hardball. They demanded a correction from the *Arizona Republic* and sent threatening letters to people quoted in the September 1, 1986, story about artificial lakes, including an employee of the Arizona State Department of Water Resources. "Did you in fact make this statement to The *Arizona Republic* reporter?" A. Melvin McDonald, an outside attorney for Keating, wrote to Dennis Kimberlin of the Arizona Water Resources Department.[51] A similar letter threatening legal action was sent to Sue Lofgren, chair of the Groundwater User's Advisory Council, a citizen's group. The *Republic* issued a correction on October 10, 1986, revising its calculation on water lost from evaporation in Keating's lakes. The annual evaporation from lakes in Keating's developments would serve the water needs of 7,700 people, not 35,000, as originally reported.[52]

Citing this case, *Phoenix New Times* columnist Michael Lacey mocked Keating for his tendency to file libel suits, adding this "seemingly innocuous" article by the *Arizona Republic* led his legal team to overreact by sending threatening letters to a state worker and a citizen quoted in the story. Lacey, calling Keating the "Godzilla of desert development," said Keating "blames the press for not being loved enough. . . . You're not just a public figure, you're an out-of-this-world spectacle."[53] Keating's lawyers threatened a weekly newspaper, the *West Valley View*, with libel in November 1986 over a story about artificial lakes on Keating's Estrella Ranch development. *West Valley View* editor Vin

Table 5.1. Keating News Media and Litigation Leaks

Date	Event
1970s	Keating wages anti-pornography legal fight against *Hustler* publisher Larry Flynt
1980	Keating threatens libel action against *Phoenix Gazette* over coverage of a housing development. No suit filed.
Oct. 1986	Keating threatens *Arizona Republic* with libel suit over coverage of artificial lakes at developments. Newspaper prints minor correction; no suit filed.
Nov. 1986	Keating threatens the weekly *West Valley View* newspaper with libel in November 1986 over a story about artificial lakes on Keating's Estrella Ranch development; no suit filed.
Jan. 1987	Keating attorneys ask Justice Department to investigate Federal Home Loan Bank board media leaks. FBI opens preliminary investigation in February. No charges brought; case closed 1989.
Feb. 1987	Keating files $11.8 million libel suit against *Mesa Tribune* over column about airplane noise at a proposed development. Case dismissed four months later.
July 1987	Keating sues Federal Home Loan Bank board for leaking corporate information to the news media. Suit withdrawn in a month.
Sept. 1987	Keating files $35 million libel lawsuit against *Arizona Trend* magazine; a Michael Binstein article had questioned Keating's solvency. Suit settled for two free advertisements.
1987	Keating drafts civil racketeering lawsuit against Binstein, seeking $75 million in damages. Case never filed.
June 1988	Keating, *Phoenix Gazette* court fight over reporter Leslie Irwin's cassette tape of regulator interviews. Keating loses case.
May 1989	Keating drafts $20 million libel suit against contractor Arthur Eugene Whitson over statements on KPNX broadcast. Suit never filed.
Oct. 1989	Keating sues FDIC, FHLB official Darrell Dochow, others, alleging libel, claiming he started a bank run on Lincoln.

Suprynowicz addressed complaints about unfair news coverage, saying his reporter was threatened with arrest if he continued to speak to people on the Estrella Ranch development site. "This left us dependent on other sources for our information," he wrote.[54]

The American Continental archives show how quick Keating was to anger and willing to file lawsuits against his perceived enemies. Keating contemplated a $20 million libel suit in May 1989 against contractor Arthur Eugene Whitson, who complained during a KPNX television interview about nonpayment of $2.5 million for work on the Phoenician hotel, according to a draft complaint in the American Continental Corporation archives.[55] During the television interview, Whitson made one incorrect reference to Keating's 1979 Securities and Exchange Commission (SEC) case, saying "when he left Cincinnati, he was under indictment." In fact, the SEC brought civil fraud charges, which Keating settled without admitting or denying wrongdoing. A transcript of the KPNX broadcast shows the announcer correctly characterized the SEC case. On the basis of this one statement from Whitson, Keating drafted a libel complaint, but there is no record the case was filed.

Keating sued the *Mesa Tribune* for libel in 1987, seeking $11.8 million in damages over a column by executive editor Max Jennings about airplane noise at a proposed Keating development called The Crossings. Keating claimed the article caused a renegotiation of a property sale. The libel case didn't last long. Five months after it was filed, Maricopa County Superior Court judge Rudolph J. Gerber dismissed the libel lawsuit, ruling Jennings's column was protected speech under the U.S. Constitution.[56]

The lawsuit came after the *Mesa Tribune* published an extensive investigation of Keating and his political connections on December 28, 1986. The series, "The Keating Connection," covered a full page of the newspaper's Sunday Perspectives section and contained eight articles that described Keating's business empire, his contributions to local and national politicians and his attempt to pressure the FHLBB to back off on its audit of Lincoln Savings. "In several senses, Charlie Keating is a man of obsession. Whatever crusade he undertakes is followed to the ultimate overstatement," *Mesa Tribune* reporter Bill Roberts wrote.[57] Keating underlined this passage and wrote in red ink, "absolutely a false interpretation."

Keating and his staff had been closely monitoring Roberts and the *Mesa Tribune* reporters as they worked on the series. They even had an informant in the *Mesa Tribune* newsroom. Virginia Novak, an American Continental corporate counsel, wrote to Kielty that "our friend" at the *Mesa Tribune* called to inform them publication of a major investigation of Keating was eleven days away. "It will focus in on CHK [Keating] specifically regarding political contributions (i.e., the buying of Arizona) and the story is about buying at auction and flipping it at exorbitant prices." This person passed along some details about the article's main author, Roberts, describing him as "basically a pretty nice guy and is usually fairly reasonable." Roberts had interviewed Senator McCain for the story and "McCain said he was sick of people dwelling on the negative aspects of Charlie and that they should focus on the good things he has done in the community."[58]

Keating sought to pressure the newspaper not to publish the stories. Phoenix attorney Philip Goldstein, who handled many of Keating's media cases, sent a threatening letter to the *Mesa Tribune* a week prior to publication. The letter offered a quote from Thomas Jefferson that the newspapers should focus on "true facts and sound principles only." Goldstein's letter concluded, "Our client wishes to avoid any future controversy with your publication."[59]

Publication of "The Keating Connection" set off a flurry of legal activity behind the scenes at American Continental. The company archives contain a seventeen-page legal memorandum describing possible legal claims against the *Mesa Tribune* for the series. The memo said any such libel suit should be filed in Arizona state court, which is "likely to be a forum with a sympathetic court and jury." The unidentified author concedes that Keating could be considered a public figure, which is a central defense newspapers raise in libel suits. It also concedes that commentary by editor Max Jennings probably is protected speech under the First Amendment.

"For the reasons outlined above, the ultimate chance of a successful fully litigated judgment in a libel case files against the *Mesa Tribune* is slight. In addition to the possibility of simply losing a suit against the *Tribune*, the filing of a libel claim may alienate not only the *Tribune* but other members of the media. Moreover the risks of creating additional negative reporting are substantial, particularly if the lawsuit is not combined with a strong positive public relations campaign,"[60] according to the memo. In the end, Keating and American Continental did not sue *Mesa Tribune* over "The Keating Connection" series but instead sued the newspaper over Jennings's editorial column about airplane noise at The Crossings, a case Keating quickly lost.

FBI PROBE

In January 1987, the Sidley and Austin law firm asked William Weld, then assistant attorney general, to open a criminal investigation into media leaks at the FHLBB. "Someone at the Bank Board is deliberately leaking information whose confidentiality is protected by statute," Rex E. Lee, a Sidley and Austin attorney, wrote to Weld. Lee had significant political connections in Washington; he was a former law clerk to Supreme Court Justice Byron White and a former U.S. solicitor general from 1981 through 1985.[61] A month later, Weld agreed to such an investigation, saying he requested that the FBI agents launch a preliminary probe and coordinate with Justice Department attorneys in the Public Integrity section, which examines government corruption.[62] Lee followed up with the head of the Justice Department's Public Integrity Section on June 9, 1987, offering a list of names that the FBI agents could interview on the leak case.

Through a Freedom of Information Act request, I obtained documents describing the FBI probe that showed an initial flurry of activity, followed by a lull before the agency dropped the probe in 1989 without bringing any charges. The FBI team appeared to take the leak investigation seriously at first, interviewing

FHLBB staff on five occasions, from March 25, 1987, to May 8, 1987, and gathering at least six document requests. "The focus of the San Francisco inquiry was to determine where the information that appeared in the two news articles was reported within the bank board and who had access to that material," according to one of the FBI documents.[63] The articles would have been the December 24, 1986, *Wall Street Journal* article on Henkel and the December 28, 1986, *Mesa Tribune* exposé of Keating's political connections. By the end of May, however, the Justice Department apparently ruled out staff at the Federal Home Loan Bank of San Francisco, writing that "any further investigation or interviews conducted in San Francisco would be unproductive." The FBI stirred to action after *Regardie's* magazine published a highly critical article on Keating and Lincoln Savings in July 1987, an episode described more fully later in this book. An unnamed FBI agent wrote, "it was his opinion from what he had seen that any information leaked to the press was disclosed at a high level." A subsequent interview with an unnamed FHLBB board member in October 1987, however, was inconclusive. The documents show that by April 1988 FBI agents believed that "there is no known leak of confidential information," and the case was formally closed in November 27, 1989, "based on the above and the fact that no known violation ever occurred."[64]

KEATING'S COMPLAINTS ABOUT MEDIA

Fed up with the bad press in Phoenix, Keating threatened to leave the city in 1987 and take his multimillion-dollar corporation with him. In a February 1987 interview with the *Greater Phoenix Business Journal*, Keating complained the political climate in Phoenix "is not as hospitable as it needs to be for a developer to operate at a profit" and that his company was subjected to a "constant admonition and lashing." He added, "But when you look like a black-hearted knave because of the constant beatings you get from people who see things differently than I guess you do, you know, I'm willing to change and switch to doing other things."[65] Keating said the company would not be buying any new land in the current climate. "I don't have a lifelong ambition to be a developer or anything else in an environment in which we're not wanted. . . . [W]e would have to be idiots to continue to take this massive defamation by the press," he said.[66]

In an earlier letter to the editor, Keating made a similar threat to leave Phoenix: "I am not sure the economic welfare of the people of Arizona is best served by our decision to work our way out, but only time will tell. We hope we will be missed. We love Arizona," Keating said.[67] Keating later claimed the newspaper got it wrong and that he would be staying after all. Other developers considered

Keating's comments about a negative business climate in Phoenix to be highly unusual. "I can't imagine anyone in the real estate business abandoning this area," said J. Fife Symington, then a commercial real-estate developer and later governor of Arizona, told the *Greater Phoenix Business Journal.* "Despite the give and take on the political side, there are tremendous opportunities here. You also have to adapt and change and you don't always get your way."[68]

By the mid-1980s, the press was replete with commentary about Keating's fraught relationship with the news media. Even with routine coverage, Keating didn't cooperate. The *Greater Cincinnati Business Courier,* for example, sought to reach Keating for a 1987 article about Keating taking American Continental into private ownership. Keating couldn't be reached for comment and Kielty, American Continental's legal counsel, said, "the company doesn't speak with the press."[69]

Keating's complaints about the media and this threat to leave Phoenix drew some measure of support from the business community, in keeping with the broader cultural fight between businesses and the media. Keating received a number of letters urging him not to leave Phoenix, praising his charitable deeds and the work of American Continental. Paul E. Danitz, vice president of Phoenix Broadcasting, wrote to Keating in early 1987 that it is "painful to acknowledge the loss of one of Arizona's class organizations."[70] Brian Richards, president of the Phoenix office of the home builder Richmond American, said Keating had made a "very substantial contribution to this community over the past decade."[71] Joseph A. Adams wrote to Keating, "Each of us in the development community has had to bear the burden of unfair treatment by the press—the misquotations, poor research and sourcing, lack of confirmation, misrepresentation and misplaced emphasis. Admittedly, none have been as severe as American Continental."[72] Phoenix businessman Ronald H. Warner, owner of a leading furniture and interior design store, told Keating "how much you are appreciated as one of the great citizens in our community."[73] Joseph Schaffer, public-affairs officer of the Heard Museum in Phoenix, praised Keating in a letter to the *Arizona Republic* in 1984: "Less newsworthy, less glamorous, perhaps, but no less important is Keating's generally unpublicized support of the arts in Phoenix."[74] Keating "sets the guideline that everybody tries to at least meet. Other developers try to keep up with him," Robert Burns of Burns International told the *Greater Phoenix Business Journal* in 1987.[75] Even the *Arizona Republic* acknowledged Keating's talent, describing him as "brilliant—the word used repeatedly by Keating's friends and foes alike."[76]

In what turned out to be a recurring tactic, Keating in 1987 offered to extend an olive branch to the news media. "I'm getting sick and tired of the old policy I had of sitting there and taking it all the time and not letting you see for yourself," he said. "I don't know if I'll be any better off but I figure it's worth a try."[77] This campaign for media openness had its fits and starts; the 1987 initiative came after he lost the libel suit against the *Mesa Tribune* and had issued a number of legal threats to other local publications. Keating also sought to burnish his public image and flooded the Phoenix airwaves with commercials. "If you are over 25, you can hardly drive to and from work without hearing the spots," the *Arizona Business Gazette* reported. "He is spending an estimated half million dollars in just 13 weeks to say what he wants to say in the media without some nasty reporter being able to edit, change or mangle his words."[78]

Keating reversed course in April 1989. He called a press conference to discuss a lawsuit against regulators related to the American Continental seizure but did not take questions. He read a prepared statement to reporters and then "left a meeting room at a resort hotel and got into his limousine without answering questions. . . . The session had been billed as a press conference, but Keating spokesman Mark Connally said Keating had been advised on legal grounds not to answer questions."[79]

After the devastating House Banking Committee investigative hearings in 1989, Keating launched his most ambitious and audacious media outreach campaign. The national media blitz began in May 1990 with Keating appearing live on a nationally televised call-in program on C-SPAN, on May 8, a marathon session during which he fielded calls from around the country for one-and-a-half hours. On May 9, he spoke at a National Press Club luncheon and took questions from the media for nearly thirty minutes, an event also broadcast nationally. At this point, he seemed like he had little to lose.

"We are broke. They took everything away from me when they took the Lincoln," Keating said at the National Press Club event. "And I'm not complaining. I guess that's part of life today. And we're going to do everything we know how to recover what we considered an unlawful seizure."[80]

Keating explained his reasoning for the new détente with the press: he was tired of being labeled as a symbol of the savings-and-loan crisis. "The question of hey, 'Is Keating responsible for a $500 billion-dollar debacle? Am I the cause of the whole thrift thing?" Keating asked the ballroom full of journalists.[81] He decided to speak up because "the information became so inundating, such a flood tide" with allegations ranging from Keating burying cash in his backyard to wiretapping regulators. He soon returned to his theme that regulators had unfairly smeared his reputation. Keating, in essence, was begging for a second chance from the media.

"They have a very facile way of pinning the blame on (me) and of feeding you all this information. And all I'm saying is, I don't blame you for printing it. That's what you're getting. It's your business in the media to print. But at this point I am trying to tell you my side of the story. And I do appreciate the fact that you're letting me do it," he said. "Whether you like what I am telling you or not, I am telling you the truth and I'm appreciating the opportunity."[82]

For some, Keating's outreach was not persuasive. Callers to the C-SPAN program were unsparing. "I am so appalled by this man I learned by watching this program. Mr. Keating is a crusading anti-pornographer, an alleged devout Catholic and an ardent right to lifer and in my opinion, in my fifty-three years of living, I have never ever ever seen a more amoral person in my entire life," a caller from Newton, Massachusetts, told Keating.[83]

The next day, when Keating appeared at the National Press Club, the reception was frosty. Judy Grande, then president of the National Press Club, gave a blunt introduction: "Charles Keating, former all-American swim team member and University of Cincinnati Hall of Famer, is blamed for the $2.5 billion collapse of the Lincoln Savings and Loan, the largest thrift failure ever. Allegations that he mismanaged and looted Lincoln to finance speculative real-estate ventures have mired him in a thicket of lawsuits. One newspaper bestowed on him the title of the greediest man in America."[84]

With those words, Keating grimaced and bowed his head. Grande continued painting the harsh portrait of the man standing next to her: "Mr. Keating also is in the center of what has been called a textbook example of political influence peddling. Ethics probes are focusing on a handful of senators who intervened with federal regulators on Mr. Keating's behalf after he gave them hefty financial contributions. Every state in the union gets only two U.S. senators. But Charles Keating had five working for him."

Keating then stepped to the wooden podium, smiled tightly, and said, "Believe it or not, I've really looked forward to this." His remarks were met with nervous laughter. Keating soon shifted gears and lectured the journalists about regulatory abuse and arbitrary real-estate appraisal standards and sought to debunk claims he had put money into offshore accounts or committed arson at a California savings-and-loan regulator's office. Keating also apologized to the elderly bondholders and claimed he was trying to ensure they would be repaid after the bankruptcy.

He made an extended defense, arguing that inexperienced savings-and-loan regulators were mismanaging the millions of loans and properties seized in the S&L failures. He argued the Phoenician hotel and the Estrella community were high-quality projects that would realize their value if given sufficient time. "Nothing wrong with those assets. It's the way those assets are being handled that's leading to the destruction," he said. He called for national leaders in finance such as Walter Wriston, the legendary former CEO of Citibank, to take control of the S&L cleanup.

"There need not be any money lost in the Lincoln. And I think with proper financial direction, there need not be a fraction of that $500 billion lost everybody is predicting," he said. "This is one of the most ridiculous, obscene situations in the history of America. And I just hope that, sooner or later, somebody will listen—if on no other basis than the fact that it can't be Charlie Keating that caused a $500 billion debacle."[85]

Then, at the conclusion of the event, Keating struck a defiant tone: "I expect that it might work out," Keating said of his pending court battles. "And if it doesn't, you know," Keating chuckled and looked at the podium, "I'll do it again." He then recited the opening lines of *Invictus*, a poem by William Ernest Henley, about defiance and perseverance in battle.

"'Out of the night that covers me, dark as pit from pole to pole. I thank whatever gods may be, for my incomparable soul,'" Keating said. "And that's the way I'll live. I'm not afraid of the future and I don't think my family is. . . . We'll talk to you as long as you listen. We'll talk to everybody else and we'll be talking in the courtroom. And we're just doing our dead level best."

BINSTEIN LEGAL BATTLE

In July 1987, Keating sued the FHLBB, accusing it of leaking confidential examination records to journalist Michael Binstein for his reporting in *Regardie's*, the former Washington, D.C., magazine known for investigative journalism, and *Arizona Trend* magazine. Binstein had obtained some three hundred pages of sensitive and confidential bank examination records about Lincoln Savings, which he used for a detailed and highly critical report in *Regardie's*, suggesting Lincoln was headed for bankruptcy.[86] Binstein's article said, "What follows is a rare look into the inner workings of a federally insured financial institution. The window is the most sensitive and secret variety of information produced by federal regulators: the bank examiners' reports. . . . Regardie's gained access to more than 300 pages of secret reports, memos, correspondence and other documents from the Federal Home Loan Bank Board."[87]

Binstein would publish a similar story in September in *Arizona Trend* magazine.[88] Keating, already complaining about media leaks, immediately sued the FHLBB, charging the staff with leaking documents to the reporter. He later remarked the FHLBB was "a prime example of leaking information that had no business being made public. . . . This was a general melee with respect to the information availability to the media."[89]

Keating's reaction to the Binstein articles marked a major escalation in his war with the press. In addition to the leaks lawsuit against the FHLBB board, Keating filed a $35 million libel case against Binstein and *Arizona Trend* magazine in September 1987. Keating and his legal team contemplated an even more dramatic third step: a civil racketeering lawsuit against Binstein, alleging he used "stolen documents to write materially misleading articles about Lincoln that were published in national magazines." The draft lawsuit alleged Binstein and government employees were "inflicting severe economic harm on a private party" and Binstein sought to gain economically from the reporting. The draft lawsuit sought $75 million in damages, but there is no evidence it was ever filed.[90]

Binstein published the exposé in *Arizona Trend* because he could not convince his employer, investigative journalist Jack Anderson, to publish a Keating investigation. Anderson's libel insurance premiums had skyrocketed and he could not afford another lawsuit.[91] In addition, Keating had retained the same law firm that was representing Anderson in libel cases; Jack Anderson's libel lawyer, David Branson, worked for the firm of Kaye, Scholar, Fierman, Hays and Handler, according to Howard Kurtz.[92] This was one of the main law firms Keating used to sue the Federal Home Loan Bank over media leaks in 1987 and threaten the *Phoenix Gazette* with libel in 1980. Anderson cited the legal conflict in deciding not to publish Binstein's exclusive material on Keating. "We did not break the big stuff because we were represented by Keating's lawyer," Anderson told Kurtz.[93]

Keating's rapid legal action generated press coverage, but detailed follow-up on the specific allegations in Binstein's reporting was sparse. *National Thrift News* reported on the suit on July 27, 1987, reporting that it had filed a Freedom of Information Act request for the documents cited in Binstein's article, a sign it was playing catch-up. The *National Thrift News* article cast Keating in a critical light, describing him as engaged in a "personal battle" with Gray, and said the "politically active and conservative" banker pursuing a high-profile "battle for deregulation."[94] The *National Thrift News* article fulfilled a trade-press normative function by providing readers details about a significant industry development, regardless of who reported the material first. The article also served a watchdog function by framing Keating's lawsuit in the broader context of a regulatory battle. Keating's leak lawsuit was withdrawn a month later, but it still had an impact. *National Thrift News* reported that two days after Keating's lawsuit, FHLBB chairman M. Danny Wall issued a memo to all staff warning them of disciplinary action against leakers.[95]

Keating and *Arizona Trend* settled the libel case in October 1988; a copy of the confidential agreement was obtained in the American Continental archives at Arizona State University.[96] *Arizona Trend* agreed to publish an "update" that said its description of Lincoln's financial condition was based on preliminary documents. *Arizona Trend* agreed to print two free advertisements for American Continental in its January and February 1989 editions. The agreement said Lincoln encouraged the magazine to write an article about the Phoenician resort.[97] Even though the magazine essentially prevailed in the case, Keating successfully delivered his message. "That's the terror of the libel suit," Binstein told Kurtz. "The message gets telegraphed to people who cover the S&L industry: If you want to write about Charlie Keating and Lincoln, it'll cost you $150,000. That's the admission price."[98]

Kurtz reported that Charles Bowden, the editor of *City Magazine* in Tucson, considered printing a version of Binstein's work, particularly the transcript of the five senators' meeting. Bowden recalled the urgency of the story.[99] Bowden dropped the story after he received a letter from Keating's lawyers, noting that Binstein had "illegally obtained confidential documents, full of unnamed errors." Bowden recalls his magazine getting "a call from its libel insurer, and the editors are told if they're thinking of writing about Charlie Keating their insurance is in jeopardy."[100] Bowden told Kurtz, "The magazine's major investor lost interest in freedom of the press and heroic journalism, and the story died."[101]

A rare photo of Strachan without a beard. Possibly during the 1960s during his tenure at *American Banker* newspaper. (Source: Strachan personal papers, courtesy Hillary Wilson.)

Strachan speaks at May 1, 1989, National Press Club forum on media failings on the savings-and-loan crisis. (Source: C-SPAN. "Where Was the Press During the S&L Crisis?" Video. Washington, DC: C-SPAN, May 1, 1989. http://www.c-span.org/video/?7307–1/press-sl-crisis.)

Front page of the coverage of the Keating Five story by *National Thrift News*.

Front page of *Mesa Tribune* Perspective section investigation of Keating marked up with red handwriting, angry comments about the reporting. Handwriting believed to be Keating's. (Source: Image made by author during research at Arizona State University Archives. "American Continental Corporation Records circa 1971–1993." Greater Arizona Collection, Arizona State University Archives, Arizona State University Library, Tempe, Arizona.)

Detail of marked-up *Mesa Tribune* with red handwriting, angry comments about the reporting in *Mesa Tribune*. Handwriting believed to be Keating's. (Source: Image made by author during research at Arizona State University Archives. "American Continental Corporation Records circa 1971–1993." Greater Arizona Collection, Arizona State University Archives, Arizona State University Library, Tempe, Arizona.)

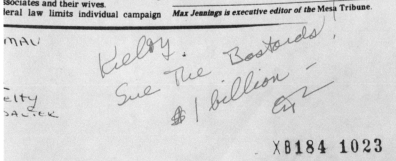

Detail of red handwriting, "Kielty Sue the Bastards!" about the reporting in *Mesa Tribune*. Handwriting believed to be Keating's. (Source: Image made by author during research at Arizona State University Archives. "American Continental Corporation Records circa 1971–1993.")

Stan Strachan and friend Lewis Ranieri, a senior Salomon Brothers bond trader and market innovator. Date unknown. (Source: Strachan personal papers, courtesy Hillary Wilson.)

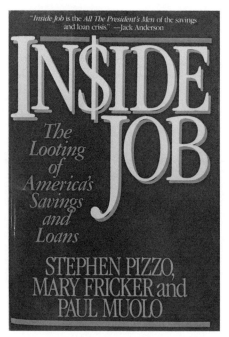

Cover image of best-selling book by *National Thrift News* journalists on the savings-and-loan crisis.

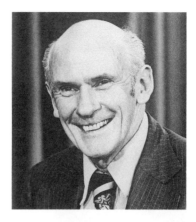

The Keating Five Senators (clockwise from top left): Dennis DeConcini, Democrat of Arizona; Alan Cranston, Democrat of California; John McCain, Republican of Arizona; John Glenn, Democrat of Ohio; Donald Riegle, Democrat of Michigan.

Charles Keating being sworn in before the U.S. House Banking Committee on November 21, 1989. (Source: Associated Press.)

Stan Strachan speaking at Mortgage Industry Forum, 1996. (Source: Strachan personal papers, courtesy Hillary Wilson.)

6

MEDIA AND THE KEATING FIVE

Stan Strachan, fresh back from a trip to Washington, D.C., walked into the *National Thrift News* newsroom in the summer of 1987. "I remember when he came back, it was late in the afternoon, I remember him coming into the newsroom saying, 'I got it,' holding up his hands with this piece of paper," Muolo said.[1] Strachan called Muolo, Kleege, and Fogarty into his office for a meeting about the document, which would prove to be politically explosive. This document would contribute to the downfall of Keating and tarnish the careers of five U.S. senators. Strachan had obtained a transcript of an April 9, 1987, private meeting where five senators had sought to pressure federal regulators to curtail enforcement actions against Keating's troubled Lincoln Savings. *National Thrift News* correspondent Pizzo later remarked the transcript was so detailed it appeared to be from a tape recording.[2] The degree of accuracy raises the possibility someone in the meeting was wearing a wire. Keating had given an estimated $1.3 million to the campaigns of the five senators: Republican John McCain of Arizona and Democrats Dennis DeConcini of Arizona, Alan Cranston of California, John Glenn of Ohio, and Donald Riegle of Michigan, who later became chairman of the Senate Banking Committee. Keating's ability to get not one but five U.S. senators to intervene in a regulatory dispute was unprecedented in the banking realm.[3] "I can tell you for a fact there aren't any of the largest banks in the country who can get two senators in a room together to argue with its regulator about the examination. I think that this meeting was an example of some extraordinary political influence, the likes of which I'd never seen in my career," said Michael Patriarca, former head of supervision at the San Francisco office of the Federal Home Loan Bank Board.[4] What follows is an analysis of the media coverage surrounding the Keating Five scandal, a detailed review of sourcing, narratives, and sentiment in 460 articles published by the *Wall Street Journal*, the *New York Times*, the *American Banker*, the *Associated Press*, and the *National Thrift News* from 1986 to 1990. This analysis measured how *National Thrift News* reporting differed from mainstream business publications and how media narratives changed before and after the April 13, 1989, bankruptcy of Lincoln's parent company and regulators' decision to seize the thrift.

MANY CLUES

National Thrift News may have broken the story about this crucial meeting, but there were abundant clues for other news organizations to pursue about Keating, his political meddling, and his escalating conflicts with regulators. By mid-1987, Keating's fight with regulators and his battle over media leaks was well documented in the *Wall Street Journal*, the *New York Times*, and other major publications. For example, in November 1986, United Press International described how Keating had contributed $150,000 to politicians, such as Senator John McCain, who were opposing the Federal Home Loan Bank Board's direct investments regulation.[5] In Arizona, a December 1986 *Mesa Tribune* series detailed Keating's influence and campaign contributions to Arizona politicians. The *Wall Street Journal* and its coverage of Keating and Henkel made waves in late 1986. The *New York Times* on May 25, 1987, wrote a 1,744-word story warning about Keating, "California's Daring Thrift Unit." In July 1987, Michael Binstein's exposé on Keating was published in *Regardie's* that enumerated Lincoln's serious financial problems as determined from regulator records. Keating's litigation against the Federal Home Loan Bank Board gained significant press coverage, such as a 722-word article in the *Washington Post* on July 29, 1987.

Word about the unusual meeting at which five senators pressured federal regulators on behalf of a single thrift circulated in newsrooms before *National Thrift News* published it. Binstein approached *National Thrift News*, pitching a story about the Keating Five meeting, Kleege said. Binstein had tried to sell it to the *New York Times* and some other media outlets, but they were not interested, Kleege recalled.[6] There was concern Keating would sue the media outlets that would publish the story.[7] But, in addition, "They didn't think it was that important," Kleege said. "That was something the general press didn't recognize." Strachan also passed on Binstein's pitch, saying *National Thrift News* staff needed to get such a story on its own and not rely on a freelance writer.

An analysis of Keating coverage in five major news organizations, along with interviews and other accounts of the savings-and-loan crisis, leads to a stark conclusion. Mainstream business journalists failed to report on a significant event that foreshadowed the failure of Lincoln Savings and Loan, the bankruptcy of American Continental, and the fate of hundreds of elderly investors who purchased $250 million in bonds in the failed enterprise.

THE SCOOP

With the transcript in hand, Strachan directed his reporters to contact their sources and confirm as much they could of the transcript's contents from the people present at the meeting. For the next several days, Muolo, Kleege, and Strachan reported out the story. Strachan and Kleege wrote the 2,362-word story, with Muolo working on a sidebar story about problems with Lincoln's accounting firm, Arthur Andersen.[8] They called all the senators and then called Keating. "We were pretty nervous when we did the call with Keating," Muolo recalled. "I don't remember being nervous with the senators. I do remember being nervous with Keating's people." Kleege agreed that the stakes were high: "It was sort of a tense moment. Everyone was very engaged in it; we thought it was a really big story and important." Kleege described the interview:

> What we did, which no one else did, was to actually call all of the senators and Keating. And we basically had the whole thing on the record without the document. . . . We had a long phone conversation with Keating—there were four or five of us standing around a speakerphone. And on the other end, Keating would take the question and put us on hold and ask his lawyers what he should say. . . . Everyone was taking notes. People were suggesting questions when we were put on hold.
>
> And his [Keating's] viewpoint was what he had done was perfectly appropriate. He was a big employer in these senators' states. He was a visionary, and he was building projects for the future and needed to have some leeway from the regulators and he had the access to do it. . . .
>
> We knew that Keating had been litigious and had threatened to sue reporters who wrote stores that he didn't like. So we felt it was important to give him his say and to show him what we were about to publish. . . . It was sort of a high-pressure thing.

Muolo said he didn't remember Keating saying much during the interview, with American Continental attorney Robert Kielty doing most of the talking. The senators' interviews were less intense. Kleege recalled that the senators' aides revealed important nuances and differences in viewpoints in the source transcript. "If you read the story, there are a few [points] where the source disagreed with interpretation the senators want to put on it," Kleege recalled. For example, McCain was quoted on the transcript as saying he would "mediate" a dispute over a loan appraisal. "And the notes made it sound like he was offering to be a go-between and come up with some different number on the loan for the Phoenician. His interpretation is that he was making a suggestion that that ought to be done," Kleege said. "The message was you can't take shortcuts with these kinds of stories. You've got to make the calls. You can't just rely on the anonymous source."[9]

The reporting complete, Kleege and Strachan wrote the page-one story for the September 28, 1987, edition. It began as follows:

> Five U.S. Senators last April intervened in the regulatory examination of Lincoln Savings and Loan Association, pressing for more liberal appraisals on the thrift's real estate investments, National Thrift News has learned.
>
> In an unprecedented display of Senatorial effort on behalf of a thrift institution, Sens. Alan Cranston, D., Calif., Dennis DeConcini, D., Ariz., John R. McCain, R., Ariz., and John Glenn, D., Ohio, pressed examiners to be "fair" to the thrift. They noted that Charles H. Keating, Jr., chairman of Lincoln's parent, is engaged in a long, highly publicized battle with the Federal Home Loan Bank Board over investment regulations.
>
> Also attending a meeting in Mr. DeConcini's Capitol Hill office, was Sen. Donald Riegle, D., Mich., a member of the Banking, Housing and Urban Affairs Committee, whom Mr. DeConcini had invited as a kind of expert witness.
>
> The conference included four representatives of the San Francisco Federal Home Loan Bank, which is responsible for supervision of Lincoln, based in Irvine, Calif.
>
> An industry source said the dispute between Mr. Keating, who runs American Continental Corp., Phoenix, and the regulator centers on $167 million in additional loss reserves the FHLB wants Lincoln to set aside for loans and investments on which the appraisals are in dispute. . . .
>
> The two-hour meeting on the influential Mr. Keating's problems was interrupted twice so the Senators could vote on a bill to provide help for the homeless.[10]

The article reported the regulators raised the possibility of criminal charges against Lincoln: "Mr. Patriarca reportedly said the FHLB officials intended to file charges against Lincoln with the Justice Department.

"NTN was unable to confirm with Justice Department officials in Washington, San Francisco, or Los Angeles, that any such referral has taken place. It is generally their policy not to comment on investigations."

Strachan "knew it wasn't usual for five senators to go to bat for one savings-and-loan executive," Kleege said. To provide context about the meeting, Strachan called around to his regulatory sources, including former Federal Reserve chairman Paul Volcker, to put Keating's actions in context. "The word was it just never happened. Our news story used the word unprecedented," Kleege said. The article also reported Keating's political contributions to the senators. An aide to DeConcini said while Keating had contributed $40,000 to the senator, "it was unfair to suggest that the Senator had the contributions in mind when he contacted the regulators on Lincoln's behalf. He said Mr. DeConcini was providing the 'constituent service' for which he is known," the article said. Keating contended he had a constituent connection to the five senators: to Cranston because of Lincoln Savings, based in southern California; to McCain and DeConcini because American Continental was based in Phoenix; to Riegle, because Keating's Hotel Pontchartrain was in Detroit; and to Glenn because of the developer's business dealings in Ohio.

On the topic of campaign contributions, Strachan wrote an editorial, "Money & Politics," to accompany the September 1987 Keating Five exclusive. He wrote that the meeting was an abuse of the regulatory process by a wealthy donor and evidence of the need for campaign finance reform. It spelled out Keating's attempts to buy influence in the regulatory system through the senators and his proxy on the Federal Home Loan Bank, Lee Henkel. It called for strict limits in campaign contributions. "And we think businessmen need to play a role in politics. But that participation should be limited to exchanging views and providing information," Strachan wrote.[11]

The timing of the *National Thrift News* story was even more extraordinary because of the hostile legal climate at the time. The week of publication, Keating filed a $35 million libel case against *Arizona Trend* magazine for its exposé of Lincoln's troubled finances. This was after he sued the *Mesa Tribune* in a $11.8 million libel action in February 1987. "There was concern that Keating was a litigious kind of person and he might sue," recalled Kleege.[12] Fogarty said any legal concerns were mitigated by the solid reporting on the story. "I remember that we weren't very much concerned about libel since truth is a perfect defense and we had definitive source material from the actual meeting with the Senators," Fogarty said.[13] The reporters also were very careful to give Keating a chance to respond to all the issues raised in the story. "We didn't blindside him with the story. He knew before we published what we were going to publish and we gave him a chance to respond," Kleege said. It was noteworthy that Keating did not sue *National Thrift News* after the Keating Five story.

In fact, Kleege recalled that after publication of the story, he visited Keating at the American Continental headquarters in Phoenix. Some months after publication of the Keating Five exclusive, Kleege was in Phoenix interviewing other savings-and-loan executives and decided to call Keating to keep the lines of communication open. "He was fairly gracious," Kleege recalled. Keating gave the reporter a gift, a cassette tape of a stand-up comedy routine. Kleege thought the gift was awkward. "I can't remember who the comic was," Kleege said. "It was probably very clean because he [Keating] was an anti-porn crusader."

By many measures, reporting of the Keating Five meeting was an explosive political story. The Senate Ethics Committee later investigated and found "substantial credible evidence" of misconduct by Senator Cranston for his intervention on Keating's behalf. The other senators received less severe rebukes, but their political reputations were damaged.[14] For McCain, the Keating Five meeting haunted him for the rest of his political career; he faced criticism for his role during his presidential runs in 2000 and 2008. The *Wall Street Journal* described the personal impact on McCain: "Sen. McCain ruefully observes that during five years he spent as a prisoner of war in North Vietnam, 'even the Vietnamese didn't question my integrity.'"[15]

Strachan knew the staff produced something special: they had the story copyrighted to force competing news organizations to credit *National Thrift News*. The copyright effort was somewhat in vain, however, since their extraordinary piece of journalism was ignored in many respects. Despite all the earlier attention to Keating, the *New York Times*, the *Wall Street Journal*, *American Banker*, and other major newspapers would have very little follow-up on the Keating Five exclusive for the next year and a half. One exception was the *Los Angeles Times*, which matched the *National Thrift News* report with an item inside its business page the day after the story broke.[16] The *Washington Post* in May 1988 mentioned the Keating Five meeting briefly in the fourth-to-last paragraph of a broader story about the brewing political risks of the savings-and-loan crisis. The *Detroit News* in 1988 reported about the campaign contributions to Riegle from Keating and his associates.

The *Wall Street Journal* and the *New York Times* didn't mention the Keating Five meeting in their news pages until mid-1989. A database search revealed that the *New York Times* made its first reference to the Keating Five senators meeting on July 9, 1989, in the twenty-first paragraph of an article describing Keating's political influence, twenty-two months after the *National Thrift News* article. Both the *Associated Press* and the *Wall Street Journal* made their first reference to the Keating Five meeting, according to the database search, on April 14, 1989. The Associated Press named the five senators and the overall donations from

Keating in a story about Lincoln's failure.[17] The *Journal* mentioned the senators' meeting in a one-sentence item in the American Continental bankruptcy story, which did not identify the five senators.[18] The *Journal* referred to the meeting in an article later in the week and in a two-sentence item on May 26, 1989, in the paper's closely read "Washington Wire" column that reported federal investigators were examining Keating's political donations in wake of Lincoln's collapse.[19]

The Keating Five coverage began to shift in April 1989 after regulators seized Lincoln Savings and American Continental filed for bankruptcy. After Lincoln's failure, the *New York Times* mentioned the Keating Five episode in forty articles, the *Wall Street Journal* in thirty-seven articles, and the Associated Press in sixty-three articles. Indeed, some 40 percent of the total articles in this study were published in the second half of 1989. The heavy coverage illustrated the inherent newsworthiness of the Keating Five meeting. It also showed the gravity of the mistake in initially overlooking the story. "It wasn't until nearly two years later—in July 1989—that the Keating Five became a major national story," according to the *Columbia Journalism Review*.[20] The *New York Times* on July 9, 1989, published a major analytical article spelling out Keating's influence and the Lincoln collapse, which stitched together the Keating Five meeting and Keating's influence on various regulatory agencies.[21]

In June 1989, the *Wall Street Journal* intensified its coverage of the Keating Five, publishing a scathing and remarkable editorial on June 13, 1989, "World's Greatest: Senatorial Shills,"[22] which described the plight of the elderly investors who lost millions buying American Continental bonds. The *Wall Street Journal* published the office telephone numbers of Senators Cranston and DeConcini and urged the defrauded investors to call. The editorial mentioned the work of other newspapers but failed to credit *National Thrift News*. Still, the *Wall Street Journal*'s editorials were commendable for distilling the thrift bailout into terms that an average family could understand: "A lot of members of Congress still don't want taxpayers ever to learn who bears responsibility for the S&L crisis that will cost each American family at least $4,000."[23]

American Banker first mentioned the Keating Five meeting in two sentences on May 24, 1988, referring to "five congressmen" interceding on Keating's behalf with Federal Home Loan Bank Board chairman Gray. The article noted the event "gained widespread publicity" even though it was the first reference in the newspaper since the *National Thrift News* exclusive some eight months earlier. The item was in the eleventh paragraph of a story about Keating winning his battle with the San Francisco Home Loan Bank.[24]

After breaking the Keating Five story in September 1987, *National Thrift News* followed up in the next issue with an important story about major accounting irregularities at Lincoln. On October 12, 1987, *National Thrift News* reported the Federal Home Loan Bank Board was investigating allegations that Lincoln's accounting firm, Arthur Andersen, was engaged in "file stuffing" to cover up improper loan underwriting practices. Arthur Andersen's actions foreshadowed one of the major charges in litigation Keating would face after Lincoln's collapse.[25]

In banking, signs of improper accounting can indicate deeper fraud and mismanagement. One of the central fights between Keating and the bank examiners involved Lincoln's optimistic property appraisals of bank-financed projects. Keating complained regulators were imposing unrealistic accounting and appraisal standards that devalued his loan portfolio. He argued regulators didn't understand the growth and market dynamics in the booming Phoenix real-estate market, which was a topic of some detailed discussion during the five senators' meeting. A spokesman for Senator DeConcini said, "The general impression [among the senators going into the meeting was] that appraisals, at least in some instances, were considered by knowledgeable people to be ridiculously low."[26]

Subsequent analysis showed such loans were inflated and actual property values were far less than the market rates.[27] Well ahead of the other media, *National Thrift News* raised allegations of improper accounting in its September 1987 Keating Five story. The newspaper reported that Arthur Young, an accounting firm working for Lincoln, was being accused of improperly advocating for Keating and that an Arthur Andersen accountant was being investigated for fraudulently handling accounting records.[28] There were significant conflicts of interest. A top official at Arthur Young defended Lincoln's accounting practices in letters to Senator McCain, among others.[29] That official, Jack Atchison, Arthur Young managing partner in Phoenix, later joined American Continental as a vice president. Beyond the accounting, the newspaper kept reporting on major developments, such as a March 21, 1988, report that Senator Riegle was returning $76,100 in campaign contributions from Keating and his employees.[30] It cited press coverage by Detroit newspapers as prompting Riegle to return the money.

National Thrift News staff was deeply disappointed the mainstream news media failed to follow up on its September 1987 exclusive. Reporter Mary Fricker, a *National Thrift News* contributor, recalled speaking to an editor on the Associated Press business desk in September 1987 to alert them about the Keating Five exclusive in *National Thrift News*, but the Associated Press editor passed on the story, and then accused her of having a conflict of interest, saying she was just trying to promote her book. "I was stunned," she recalled.[31]

Strachan, appearing at a May 1, 1989, National Press Club forum on the savings-and-loan crisis, faulted his colleagues for the lack of follow-up on the Keating Five story. He said such a political intervention in a bank examination "literally had never happened before. But most reporters had accepted that this was run-of-the-mill political business, for five senators to intervene in the examination of a savings and loan institution."[32] Strachan said journalists were accepting government denials about the story. "When reporters from other papers called about the story, they were told by the spokesman for Federal Home Loan Bank Board, this was not at all unusual," Strachan said. "The press could have been a little more aware of what was happening there and a little less trusting of officialdom. I think that's been a major problem."[33]

Strachan may have not known it at the time, but the Federal Home Loan Bank Board, then run by deregulatory advocate M. Danny Wall, was conducting an active campaign to deflect negative media coverage about Keating. Karl Hoyle, spokesman for the Federal Home Loan Bank Board, revealed in a 1990 deposition that he was working with two senior American Continental attorneys, Robert Kielty and James Grogan, to convince other news organizations not to follow up on critical reporting about Lincoln Savings, particularly the Binstein revelations. "We spent a lot of time with the staff of ACC trying to kill stories we felt were inappropriate relative to Lincoln/ACC," Hoyle said. He elaborated:

> I have spent weekends, evenings at places and gone on trips with Mr. Kielty and Mr. Grogan relative to articles, that resulted from articles Mr. Binstein wrote, and also discussed those with Mr. Wall, trying to not have information that resulted from articles [repeated by other news organizations]. . . . I spoke with editors, I had Mr. Wall speak with editors. We indicated this [Lincoln Savings] was an open institution, that information of this type would be detrimental to an open institution, that it was information in our opinion that was largely inaccurate, and we did not feel that it was appropriate that it should be printed.[34]

Here, Strachan's criticism of the press coverage was on the mark: "We've been much too quick to accept the official version of things."[35]

REGULATORY COVERAGE BEFORE LINCOLN CRASH

The mainstream news media's decision to ignore the Keating Five story is especially puzzling in light of earlier coverage of the developer's regulatory battles. Keating and his fights with Gray and the Federal Home Loan Bank were a regular topic on the savings-and-loan beat. As described in the previous chapter, there was considerable coverage of Keating's push to get former business ally Lee Henkel on the Federal Home Loan Bank Board. The following review of Keating's activities before the crash of Lincoln Savings only highlights the extent of the mainstream media failure in covering the Keating Five story.

Overall, *National Thrift News* and the *American Banker* both covered regulatory developments in the industry more closely than the *New York Times* and the *Wall Street Journal* in the crucial period prior to Lincoln's seizure, from January 1, 1986, to April 12, 1988. The coverage was in keeping with the trade press's normative behavior of closely covering its target industry. Prior to regulators' seizure of Lincoln, *National Thrift News* mentioned Keating and Lincoln Savings in 36 percent of all articles reviewed in my content analysis, the highest percentage for any of the newspapers, suggesting *National Thrift News* was following Keating earlier and more closely than the competition. At the *American Banker*, 34 percent of its Keating articles came prior to the government seizure of Lincoln; the *Wall Street Journal*'s was at 16 percent; the *New York Times*, 11 percent; and the Associated Press, 2 percent.[36] *National Thrift News* and *American Banker* nearly doubled their coverage of Keating after the seizure, publishing sixty-one articles each in the April–December 1989 period. The intensity of coverage at the two other papers is dramatic after the seizure: the *Wall Street Journal*'s coverage rose nearly fourfold, the *New York Times* coverage sixfold.[37] Nearly all the *Associated Press* national coverage followed the Lincoln collapse.

One notable story prior to Lincoln's collapse was the attempt by Keating to manipulate the regulatory process by offering a job to Gray, his main federal regulator. *American Banker* reported the story on October 7, 1986. *National Thrift News* had similar information on August 11, but it was buried at the bottom of an article and not as fully developed as the *American Banker* report, which properly treated it as an extraordinary political development. Here was one example where *National Thrift News* missed the opportunity to fully develop the political context around an issue. Such lack of political or social context is a common critique of trade journals.[38] Like the Keating Five event, major news media was slow to pick up on the Gray job-offer story. The database search shows the *New York Times* first mentioned the Gray job offer seven months later, on May 25, 1987, and the *Wall Street Journal* first mentioned it three years later, on November 8, 1989, as part of Gray's congressional testimony.

LINCOLN'S DEAL WITH WALL

For a short period, Keating gained an upper hand in his fight against the Federal Home Loan Bank Board. Gray faced intense political pressure from the Reagan White House after he began to reregulate the savings and loans. This was ironic since Gray was a longtime Reagan loyalist who served as a spokesman for Reagan during his years as California governor. Soon, Gray was sparring with a powerful cabinet member, Treasury Secretary Donald Regan, later White

House chief of staff, who was a forceful advocate of deregulation. Keating's relentless attacks on Gray, combined with Gray's hostile relationship with the White House chief of staff, took their toll. Gray departed the Federal Home Loan Bank Board in June 1987, to be replaced by a deregulatory advocate, M. Danny Wall, a former aide to Senator Jake Garn, an Idaho Republican and a member of the Senate Banking Committee. Wall brought a new industry-friendly message to the agency. At this point, Keating had won a major victory; he had helped remove a critical regulator from power and bought extra time.

Wall's tenure at the Federal Home Loan Bank Board was dramatically different. He quickly settled a lawsuit Keating filed over the agency's protracted examination of Lincoln Savings. Wall's action kept Keating in the savings-and-loan business for nearly another two years. In an unusual development, Wall ordered an internal investigation of Keating's complaints about the regulatory examination. In May 1988, Wall assigned the national staff of the Federal Home Loan Bank Board, which he directly supervised, to take over the Lincoln examination from the regional examiners in San Francisco. The change stalled aggressive regulation by the San Francisco staff, who were prepared to recommend seizure of Lincoln. Journalist Jill Dutt wrote of the shift of supervision to the industry-friendly Washington office, "The bank board buckled under the pressure. Rather than acting on an April, 1987 recommendation of its regional regulators to seize control of Lincoln, the regulators took the unprecedented step of transferring regulatory oversight and conducting its own investigation of Lincoln from Washington, D.C."[39]

These decisions by Wall drew significant criticism in the fall 1989 congressional hearings about the Lincoln Savings failure, since the actions kept Lincoln Savings open and further increased the eventual cost of the taxpayer bailout. William Black, a former Federal Home Loan Bank attorney who pushed to close down Lincoln, told Congress, "If our recommendations had been followed, the taxpayers . . . would have suffered dramatically smaller losses."[40] Other regulators agreed Wall had made a bad decision. The chairman of the Federal Deposit Insurance Corporation, L. William Seidman, said that his agency would have moved to close Lincoln Savings in March 1986—three years ahead of the Federal Home Loan Bank Board's action.[41] Richard Breeden, then chairman of the Securities and Exchange Commission, said Wall's agreement to keep Lincoln in business gave Keating and Lincoln Savings a strong legal argument to resist an emerging SEC investigation.[42] *American Banker* noted in the sixth paragraph of a May 24 story that industry analysts regarded the decision to move the investigation to the Washington office as "a strong rebuff" of the San Francisco Home Loan Bank Board examiners.[43] The *Wall Street Journal* on May 23 called the development "a major victory for Lincoln and a defeat for regional thrift examiners in San Francisco and that Lincoln would not have to write down the value of its real estate investments." This real-estate accounting detail was missing from the *American Banker* article.[44] The *New York Times* noted the real estate detail and the unusual nature of the settlement in its brief May 23 story.[45]

The newspapers, except for *National Thrift News*, treated the May 1988 settlement announcement as a significant news story. A newspaper database search did not reveal a *National Thrift News* story that mentioned the settlement until June 27, more than a month after the announcement.[46] This omission was striking because it was an important development in a saga the newspaper had documented thoroughly up to this point. The paper's lack of coverage stands in contrast to the emphasis other news media outlets placed on the event—as well as subsequent historical accounts of the Keating affair. *American Banker* previewed such a settlement on May 10, citing an American Continental filing with the Securities and Exchange Commission and then reported the details on May 24.

LINCOLN SALE

Unlike the Keating Five episode, the national news media payed close attention as Keating sought to sell Lincoln Savings in late 1988 and early 1989. The episode was further evidence that Keating was a newsworthy figure and illustrates the mainstream media failure in the Keating Five coverage.

The failure to sell Lincoln Savings represented Keating's final call; it led to the American Continental bankruptcy filing in April 1989 and the decision by regulators to seize Lincoln Savings. Reporting by the five new organizations about the attempts to sell Lincoln show the most consistent and skeptical beat reporting of the four newspapers, which generally provided context about Keating's background and his fights with regulators. *National Thrift News*, however, did not report as many articles about the attempts to sell Lincoln Savings, a story that was central to the collapse of the Keating empire. The content analysis showed *National Thrift News* coverage was lacking, behind the competition and out of step with the trade press norms of closely following a major industry development. By contrast, the *American Banker* was early to report about the likelihood of a sale on July 3, 1987, some eighteen months ahead of the competition. The July 3 article reported that Keating was upset with his ownership of Lincoln and clearly suggested Lincoln would be for sale at some point.[47] Other newspapers covered the details of Keating's attempts to sell Lincoln, beginning in December 1988. The *Wall Street Journal* carried six articles addressing the Lincoln sale; the *New York Times* carried five; the *American Banker,* five; *National Thrift News,* four; none appeared on the Associated Press's national feed.

One major story came on March 2, 1989, when the *Wall Street Journal* reported that Lincoln was under a fraud investigation by the U.S. Attorney's Office in Los Angeles.[48] This story, coming as Keating was struggling to sell Lincoln to outside buyers, could have killed the sale. Keating filed for bankruptcy six weeks later. The article quoted an unnamed source as saying a pending offer for Lincoln "is a dead duck. Frankly, I don't see it ever coming back together, because of the financing. And the economics of the transaction never made sense."[49]

CORPORATE-GOVERNMENT SOURCING

The robust media coverage of the Lincoln sale raises other questions. Why was there more consistent beat reporting by three newspapers on this topic and not by the others? One reason could be the stories of the sale were pegged to an official source, a company announcement, as opposed to the Keating Five senators' meeting or tales of regulatory intrigue that required source development.

The content analysis revealed a significant shift in sourcing after Lincoln Savings was seized. Prior to Lincoln's failure, all news organizations relied significantly more on corporate sources, but afterward government sourcing became dominant. In the review of five news organizations' articles, a code was assigned to each named source. For example, a quote from a Keating spokesman was assigned a code for American Continental; House Banking Committee Chairman Henry Gonzales was assigned a legislative code; a Federal Home Loan Bank Board press release was assigned a regulatory code. These codes were tabulated using the MaxQDA qualitative analysis software and visualized in the Tableau data visualization software. Controlling for the number of articles, corporate sourcing fell by half after the crash of Lincoln Savings, whereas government sourcing nearly doubled. The result would be consistent with Bennett's indexing hypothesis, which holds that official sources tend to frame news narratives.[50] The shift is understandable in that the Keating tale moved from a corporate-centered drama to a regulatory and legislative story after the failure.

The *Wall Street Journal* had the highest ratio of corporate sources per article, followed closely by *National Thrift News* with Associated Press having the least. In the period from January 1, 1986, to April 13, 1989, the *Journal* had about 2.7 corporate sources per article and *National Thrift News* had 2.5 corporate sources per article. The comparison is distorted in that *National Thrift News* carried twice as many articles in this period as the *Journal*.[51] Viewed from another perspective, *National Thrift News* outhustled the competition with its sourcing, speaking to more analysts, industry officials, congressional aides and citing more legal documents than the competition, especially in the critical period before Lincoln's failure. For example, in the period leading to the Lincoln crash, the newspaper had 49 percent of the legislative sources, 42 percent of the legal and court sources, 59 percent of the industry sources, and 70 percent of the analysts cited among all five news organizations. The statistics are, of course, also distorted since *National Thrift News* published more than the other news organizations. Yet it makes the point that the newspaper was fulfilling its normative role as a trade journal, using its close contact with the industry to advance its news coverage.

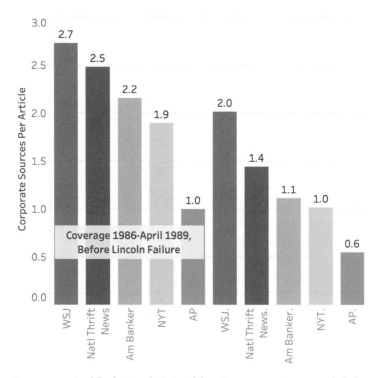

Corporate sourcing falls after Lincoln Savings failure. Corporate sourcing per article, before and after failure of Lincoln Savings, 1986–90.

NEGATIVE MEDIA PORTRAYAL OF KEATING

Before the collapse of American Continental and the seizure of Lincoln Savings, the newspapers generally did not provide a positive portrayal of Keating. I measured negative portrayal by four themes: descriptions of adverse regulatory action, violations of bank industry norms, manipulation of the political or regulatory process, and guilt by association.[52] The *New York Times* was the most severe, portraying Keating in a negative light in 60 percent of its articles in the period from January 1, 1986, through April 12, 1989. *National Thrift News* and *American Banker* portrayed Keating negatively in about a third of their precrash articles, and the *Wall Street Journal* had a negative portrayal in about 20 percent of its articles. The public record had ample evidence about Keating's unsavory background. *American Banker* noted in 1986 that Keating had settled fraud charges with the Securities and Exchange Commission seven years earlier in relation to his dealings with Provident Bank in Cincinnati.[53] During this January 1, 1986, to April 12, 1989, period, many of the negative portrayals involved Keating's attempt to manipulate the political or regulatory process for his own ends.

The critical tone in the *New York Times* began on May 25, 1987, with a 1,744-word article, "California's Daring Thrift Unit," which described Keating as a risky outlier in the industry, or "one of the most prominent examples of a new and controversial breed of savings and loan institution. . . . [T]he new breed sees thrift units as a low-cost source of funds that can be used in potentially more lucrative—and often riskier—investments."[54] Other examples of negative portrayals included a discussion of a pending federal criminal investigation.[55] The newspaper described Keating as outside the norms of the industry, noting on December 21, 1988, that he "aggressively expanded the institution," which "brought intense scrutiny from the Federal Home Loan Bank Board of San Francisco."[56] A February 25, 1989, article reported Keating was "one of the most aggressive proponents of using federally insured deposits for activities that, while generally permitted by California's liberal regulations, are deemed too risky by many regulators."[57]

The portrayal of Keating turned negative in all five news organizations after April 13, 1989, when American Continental filed for bankruptcy and regulators then seized Lincoln Savings. Many of the negative references were due to the bankruptcy and the regulators' action. In turn, these developments showed Keating was outside the banking industry's normative values of safety and soundness. In the postcrash period, the *New York Times* again led the five news organizations, with critical portrayals of Keating in 80 percent of the articles

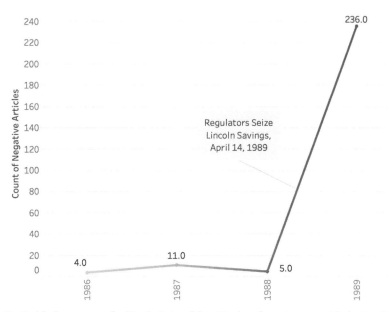

Keating's bad press surges after Lincoln Savings failure. Number of negative news articles by Associated Press, *New York Times*, *Wall Street Journal*, *American Banker*, and *National Thrift News*, 1986–89.

evaluated after April 13, 1989. The *Wall Street Journal* had negative references in 59 percent of articles evaluated; for the *American Banker*, 64 percent; Associated Press, 60 percent; and *National Thrift News*, 49 percent.[58] Another finding: the mentions of Keating directly speaking in all the news organizations fell by 71 percent after the Lincoln collapse; one reason could be that he limited his public comments because of pending litigation.

After the American Continental bankruptcy, the *Wall Street Journal* published negative portrayals that were often in colorful terms: "An angered Charles H. Keating Jr. put on a show for reporters yesterday, blaming regulators for forcing American Continental Corp. into bankruptcy-law proceedings and seizing its Lincoln Savings & Loan Association unit last week. Using his harshest fighting words, the arch-conservative chairman of American Continental took a gunslinger's stance and vowed to do battle in court with his enemies—in this case, thrift regulators led by the Federal Home Loan Bank Board in Washington."[59] Like the other news organizations, the *Wall Street Journal* associated the collapse of Keating's thrift with an estimated \$2 billion taxpayer bailout.[60] The term *bailout* was used forty-seven times in the *Wall Street Journal*'s reporting; it referred to *seized* or *seizure* thirty-five times. The only item coded as positive toward Keating in the April 13–December 31, 1989, time period was Keating's June 22, 1989, letter to the *Wall Street Journal* that spelled out his defense and rebuttal to the newspaper's critical coverage.[61]

CONGRESS INVESTIGATES KEATING

U.S. House Banking Committee chairman Henry Gonzalez, a Democrat from Texas, launched hearings on the Lincoln Savings failure in the fall of 1989 with two goals in mind.[62] He sought to make a dramatic case against deregulation by focusing on Keating's abuses. And he wanted to get rid of Wall, the Federal Home Loan Bank chairman who had eased up on the regulation of Lincoln Savings. The hearings led to a surge of Keating coverage: Lincoln and Keating appeared in 199 news items in October and November in the five news organizations, or about 42 percent of the total articles in this study. This hearing presented the news media an opportunity to tell the complex savings-and-loan story in a more accessible fashion. Gonzalez and his staff developed a narrative about Keating, Lincoln, and the regulators that was made for easy consumption in Washington, especially via television: he called the collapse of Lincoln a "mini-Watergate."[63]

These hearings helped solidify the Keating Five narrative, making it a shorthand reference for the savings-and-loan scandal. The *Wall Street Journal* first used the "Keating Five" term in an October 16, 1989, editorial that said, "the lack of attention to the Keating drama was astonishing in light of the magnitude of the savings-and-loan disaster."[64] There was no mention of the fact that *National Thrift News* broke the story two years earlier. The "Keating Five" term appeared in the *New York Times* news coverage on November 5, 1989.[65] *American Banker* first used the "Keating Five" term on November 16, and *National Thrift News* first printed the term on November 27, the last of the four newspapers to adopt the phrase.

Highlights of the hearings included the following:

- October 17 testimony from William Seidman, the Federal Deposit Insurance Corporation chairman, who said he would have closed Lincoln Savings in 1986.
- October 26 testimony from San Francisco Federal Home Loan Bank regulators, who said Chairman Wall had prevented them from closing Lincoln Savings.
- November 7 testimony from Gray, who described his private meeting with Cranston, DeConcini, Glenn, and McCain and the pressure to

ease up on Lincoln. Securities and Exchange Commission chairman Richard Breeden criticized the accounting firm Arthur Young for its optimistic assessment of Lincoln's property values.

- November 21 appearance by Keating, who declined to testify, citing his Fifth Amendment protections against self-incrimination. Chairman Wall defended his supervision of Lincoln. A group of elderly investors who lost millions investing in American Continental bonds testified about their financial hardships.[66]

A direct comparison of themes in the hearing coverage was slightly skewed from the fact that the *American Banker*, the *Wall Street Journal* and the *New York Times* published daily editions and the Associated Press published continuously, but *National Thrift News* published weekly or semimonthly during this period. The comparison also would suggest the small *National Thrift News*, with a 1989 circulation of about nine thousand, would be outgunned by the daily circulation *American Banker*, more than double its circulation with about twenty thousand, the *Wall Street Journal*'s circulation of about 1.9 million, and the *New York Times* circulation of 1 million.[67] Yet in consideration of its resources and publishing schedule, *National Thrift News* was competitive in a measure of total word count, having published 26,673 words on Keating in October and November, second only to the 31,187 words published by the *New York Times* during this period.

Keating coverage in the *New York Times* during these two months illustrated the enormity of the story, as one of the nation's leading general newspapers published thirty-seven articles from nine reporters on the topic, according to the search. The Associated Press carried eighty items on its national wire, some of which were daily updates of developing stories. A review of the coverage also demonstrated the writing and reporting talent of the journalists covering the story, such as this November 1, 1989, article by Brooks Jackson, an investigative reporter for the *Wall Street Journal*: "In a riveting day of hearings before the House Banking Committee, the examiners described finding shredded documents, a mysterious Panamanian subsidiary, millions of dollars funneled into a Swiss bank, and a complacent attitude by Mr. Wall's deputies, one of whom was portrayed as acting more like a public-relations man for the thrift than a federal regulator."[68]

Keating was not the only casualty of the House Banking hearings. Wall was forced from office shortly after his testimony. On November 14, 1989, the *Wall Street Journal* was the first to report that President George H. W. Bush had signaled his lack of support for Wall.[69] Wall announced his resignation the following month. *Wall Street Journal* editorial writer John Fund wrote one of the earliest and toughest articles about Wall's complicity with the savings-and-loan industry, reporting in far greater detail than other news outlets.[70] The article detailed the political power of the U.S. League of Savings Institutions, the lobbying arm for the savings-and-loan industry, as it pushed for deregulation and the expansion of deposit insurance. It described a campaign by industry lobbyists to cultivate Wall, "who is largely self-taught on banking matters and had a reputation for not being skilled with numbers," and reported about his "reputation for taking all-expense paid junkets" as a Senate aide.

ELDERLY INVESTORS

Another regulatory issue involved an abuse of individual investors, many elderly, who purchased American Continental bonds through Lincoln Savings offices. American Continental sold some $250 million in bonds through twenty-nine Lincoln branch offices in California; the sale was controversial because the bonds lacked federal deposit insurance but were sold from the Lincoln branches, particularly to elderly investors, who would expect something sold from a bank to carry federal protection against loss.[71] The "swindled elderly" narrative was an important step for the Keating story to move from the business page to the front page. This narrative would become prominent in the congressional hearings, which humanized a story about banking, a topic difficult to portray on television or in general-interest newspapers. As Martin Mayer wrote, "Because the disaster could be personalized, television began paying attention."[72] The *Wall Street Journal*, particularly its editorial writers, seized on this topic and wrote several biting and vivid articles about the plight of the elderly investors. This development represented a critical turn in the mainstream news media's coverage against Keating.

American Banker raised concerns about the Lincoln Savings bond sales on February 23, 1987, two years ahead of *National Thrift News*. *National Thrift News* began to aggressively cover the story immediately after American Continental's bankruptcy. The reporting on the Keating story in the two trade publications contrasts significantly. *American Banker* found significant material, such as the bond sale yet did not always follow through with reporting on the implications of the events. *National Thrift News* had its misfires as well (such as weak coverage of the Lincoln sale), yet it tended to follow stories more aggressively. For example, a *National Thrift News* article on April 24, 1989, detailed the fate of some twenty thousand bondholders who stood to lose their savings. It also cited regulators' concerns about misleading marketing of the investments.[73] It devoted a significant feature story on May 8, 1989, to focus on the elderly investors, noting that Keating's company had been charged with "bait and switch."[74] The article reported that "An 80-year old Southern California woman who was legally blind was chauffeured by officials of American Continental Corp. to a branch of its S&L affiliate here after being persuaded into investing $30,000 in what was now considered worthless unsecured debt, said an attorney here."[75] In a July 24, 1989, article, *National Thrift News* then pointed out the irony that Senator Cranston, an aggressive Keating advocate, was seeking to help Keating's victims, the elderly bondholders left holding worthless American Continental bonds.[76] A related story described an investor lawsuit against the California Department of Corporations for allowing sale of the bonds in the first place.[77] The newspaper editorialized on the topic on August 14, 1989, with the headline "Too Late, Sen. Cranston?"[78]

Such coverage fulfilled journalism's normative watchdog function and the trade-press normative values of criticizing industry abuses. Like the Keating Five story, it was an instance in which *National Thrift News* served both its core industry audience and a general audience. *National Thrift News* displayed energetic beat coverage of this elderly bond sale issue, but the stories were dense, with a technical industry term, "sub debt," used throughout to refer to subordinated debt, the formal classification of the American Continental bonds sold through Lincoln Savings branches. One example of this dense financial insider writing was an April 24, 1989, headline: "Lincoln Challenges Takeover; Sub Debt in Danger"—an example of a trade publication using jargon and technical language and failing to translate the issues for an average audience.[79]

The *Wall Street Journal* addressed the plight of the individual bondholders on April 17, 1989, and it published an editorial on June 13, 1989; the *New York Times* first mentioned them on August 1, 1989. The *Wall Street Journal's* April 17, 1989, article described "some 25,000 small investors . . . were left to fret over what now may be $200 million of worthless paper. The switchboard at American Continental's Phoenix, Ariz., headquarters was flooded with calls from irate noteholders."[80] The *Journal's* editorial page was hard-hitting, linking the elderly bondholders' losses to Senators Cranston and DeConcini and their ties to Keating. The newspaper called Cranston and DeConcini the "World's Greatest: Senatorial Shills."[81] The *New York Times* was the last of the four papers to explore the story. The newspaper published an extensive report on the elderly bondholders in late November, a report pegged to the revelations from the House Banking Committee hearings.[82] It followed up on November 24, 1989, noting that the California attorney general had launched a criminal investigation of

Lincoln for misleading marketing of the bonds.[83] The Associated Press's coverage of the elderly bondholders centered on their congressional testimony.

As a postscript, some elderly bondholders received assistance from some of the Keating Five senators, such as Cranston. In the case of McCain, they received an apology. William Lerach, a San Diego attorney, was the lead counsel on the main class-action lawsuit against Keating. He represented several elderly women who had lost their savings in the Lincoln Savings collapse. One was Ramona Jacobs of Glendale, California, who had invested $11,000 in American Continental bonds, planning to use the funds to buy a van for her disabled daughter. Lerach brought Jacobs and two other women who lost funds in Lincoln to Capitol Hill in January 1990 to confront the Keating Five senators. Cranston met with them and pledged his assistance. McCain brought the group of women into his personal office. Instead of sitting behind his desk, McCain stood as Lerach introduced the victims and recounted their hardship. Patrick Dillon and Carl Cannon, in their biography of Lerach, recounted the scene: "McCain looked pained. Then dropping down—Lerach swears it was on bended knee—the senator from Arizona, the former navy aviator, the brave prisoner of war, the heroic American icon, bowed his head and said solemnly and so quietly that someone had to remind him that Rea Luft could barely hear: 'I have betrayed my family. I have betrayed my constituency. I am very sorry that I have hurt you and your families.'"[84]

CRIMINAL PROBES

National Thrift News made another significant contribution with Pizzo's reporting about criminal investigations of Keating. He reported on August 14, 1989, about a racketeering lawsuit being prepared against Keating.[85] *American Banker* carried a similar report on September 14, and the *Wall Street Journal* noted the lawsuit on September 18. The case in Pizzo's article was being brought by the Resolution Trust Corporation, a federal agency designed to clean up the failed thrifts. The *Wall Street Journal* later advanced the story, noting that Senator DeConcini had sponsored a bill to add a provision to the Racketeer Influenced Corrupt Organizations Act, usually referred to as RICO, that would have made retroactive changes to protect Keating and others from huge damage awards in lawsuits. DeConcini dropped the provision after the Keating exemption became public.[86] The *New York Times* wrote about the matter in an October 18 editorial.[87] Pizzo produced another important story on December 18 that described the emerging investigations by the House Banking Committee and

Justice Department into financier Michael Milken's Drexel Burnham Lambert, which helped finance Keating, David Paul, and other failed thrifts.[88]

Eventually, Keating went to prison for his role in the scandal. Keating was convicted of seventeen counts of securities fraud in Los Angeles County Superior Court, sentenced to ten years in prison, and fined $250,000.[89] Writing in another case, U.S. District Judge Stanley Sporkin offered this observation about American Continental: "It is abundantly clear that ACC's officials abused their positions with respect to Lincoln."[90] Keating served 4.5 years. Keating had appealed his convictions, which were overturned in 1996. As the legal drama continued, California prosecutors dropped their case. Keating was awaiting a federal retrial in 1999 but pleaded guilty to four counts of wire and bankruptcy fraud and was sentenced to time already served.[91] In August 1990, the Office of Thrift Supervision sued Keating, seeking millions that represented improper gains from Lincoln Savings. Regulators sought $130.5 million in restitution from Keating and five American Continental officers, as well as a ban on Keating and the officers from ever participating in the affairs of a federally insured financial institution. The Office of Thrift Supervision argued that "Mr. Keating and his associates profited from improper use of depositors' funds, and we want that money returned to Lincoln," said OTS director Timothy Ryan. "This is the largest amount of restitution we have ever sought in a thrift enforcement case."[92] The Office of Thrift Supervision later banned Keating from the industry and ordered him to repay $36 million.[93]

ACCOUNTING

To measure the watchdog function of business journalism, the content analysis examined how the newspapers reported on fundamental trends in the thrift industry, including accounting issues.[94] The review of coverage showed *National Thrift News* was among the first to report on the complicit role of accounting firms in the scandal. For example, an August 14, 1989, story was headlined "Accountant: Lincoln Profits Based on Gimmicks."[95] The *Wall Street Journal* also pursued accounting's role after the seizure of Lincoln Savings. In particular, the *Journal* emphasized the responsibility of Keating's outside accountants in the fraud. An August 7, 1989, article reported the federally appointed auditors found "accounting gimmickry" at Lincoln. It quoted an examination report comparing the thrift's books as trading of "two one-million-dollar cats for a two-million-dollar dog."[96] The *Journal* article delved into the company background and identified Keating's outside accounting firm, Arthur Young, even though Arthur Young was not specifically named in the regulatory report. It was an important piece of reporting that implicated the accounting firm responsible for assisting with the improper financial transactions. In a November 15, 1989, article, the *Journal* again took Lincoln's accounting firms to task, reporting that more than half of Lincoln's profits were the result of "sham" transactions "approved by the accounting firm of Arthur Young & Co."[97]

The *New York Times* explored Lincoln's "accounting quagmire" in a 3,684-word article on December 28, 1989, a hard-hitting report that accused Lincoln's accounting firms of failing to do their jobs.[98] The *Times* also delivered a major analytical article on July 9, 1989, spelling out Keating's influence and the Lincoln collapse.[99] *American Banker* lacked such biting coverage. It carried a lengthy interview with Keating on June 29, 1989, during which he defended his accounting policies.[100] Another article focused on the criticism of Arthur Young but noted the firm had not been sued or charged by regulators.

CONCLUSION

The mainstream news media coverage of the Keating Five case was a media failure. The *Wall Street Journal*, the *New York Times*, *American Banker*, and the Associated Press missed the significance of the Keating Five meeting in 1987, despite ample warning signs in the trade press, local news media—and even their own previous reporting. The delay in covering the Keating meeting and reporting on its consequences was a factor in allowing the fraud to continue for another two years, which expanded the cost of the taxpayer bailout, estimated at $3.4 billion. Some twenty-five thousand bond investors lost an estimated $250 million when American Continental bonds proved worthless after the bankruptcy. The scale and enormity of the media failure is seen in the large volume of coverage news organizations gave to the Keating scandal during the Gonzalez hearing. It was newsworthy, by any measure, and they missed it. This behavior aligns with Bennett's indexing theory, "which refers to the tendency of mainstream news organizations to index or adjust the range of viewpoints in a story to the dominant positions of those whom journalists perceive to have enough power to affect the outcome of a situation."[101] Bennett's work and similar academic studies on media framing finds journalists have been too reliant on government officials and elite sources in reporting and framing their stories.

The silence in mainstream media after the September 1986 Keating Five story left Strachan dejected. Strachan expressed frustration in an editorial he wrote during the Gonzalez hearings, "Better Late Than Never": "When this newspaper disclosed in September 1987 that five United States Senators had met with regulators from the Federal Home Loan Bank of San Francisco to discuss the examination of Lincoln Savings and Loan Association, Irvine, Calif., we expected a sharp reaction from the press, the political establishment and the public. Nothing happened."[102]

National Thrift News may have been ignored, but it can at least count itself in good company. Ben Bagdikian wrote that the U.S. news media has a long tradition of ignoring truth tellers such as I. F. Stone and George Seldes who challenge the establishment with independent journalism.[103] Other research shows major investigative journalism can meet with silence. David Protess's 1991 study of the impacts of investigative journalism found "inconsistencies in the impact of muckraking on the public's agenda of social ills."[104] These result from the "weak and unreliable" role of public opinion in the political and policymaking process. "Investigative reporters may miscalculate the boundaries of civic morality. Sometimes the public or policy makers respond with indifference to exposés of alleged wrongdoing."[105] Dyck and Zingales showed how difficult it was for news organizations to be out front on a story about corporate wrongdoing:

> It is more costly for a reporter to antagonize a company when he or she is the only one doing it, than when many others are doing so. Questioning the integrity of a company's numbers when the company is doing well is very dangerous. A single pundit or reporter can be easily harassed or even sued, since the company can hope, with this strategy, to prevent others from following the first's example. But when a company is openly questioned by multiple sources, the aggressive strategy becomes self defeating and each reporter runs little risk of being harassed or sued.[106]

The review of these five news organizations' coverage from 1986 to 1990 showed that although *National Thrift News* was far ahead of the competition on the Keating Five story, it was eclipsed by the other news organizations on other important developments. Its beat reporting was admirable but inconsistent. *National Thrift News* trailed the competition on significant stories such as the sale of Lincoln Savings and the settlement between Wall and Keating. It was also behind on some aspects of the Lincoln and regulatory relationship first reported in the *Mesa Tribune* and *Regardie's* magazine. In these ways, *National Thrift News* did not always provide comprehensive coverage of a dominant and controversial player in its industry.

Keating's reputation for litigation against his opponents weighed on the press coverage, but the extent was difficult to discern. The *New York Times* and the *Wall Street Journal* published strong and critical stories about Keating, yet most were after the April 13, 1989, bankruptcy and the seizure of Lincoln Savings.

Certainly, significant evidence was available in the public record to raise questions about Keating's background and behavior before the bankruptcy, such as the 1979 SEC fraud settlement and the significant reporting by Binstein in *Regardie's* magazine. With the benefit of hindsight, we see the importance of early press coverage of these regulatory stories, particularly in a deregulated environment when government agencies were not always doing their job.

After Lincoln failed, the *New York Times* and the *Wall Street Journal* provided some excellent and interesting reporting on the case, exploring the vulnerable elderly bondholders and the complicit accountants. They called politicians such as Senator Cranston to account. The *Wall Street Journal's* post–Lincoln Savings collapse coverage was solid and energetic and used a diversity of sources, such as the consumer group Common Cause. The editorial page wrote important pieces that contributed to the understanding of the crisis. The *New York Times* also had aggressive and extensive beat reporting on the case after regulators' seizure of Lincoln Savings. One would wish they had been on the story earlier, before widespread damage was done to the national economy and to elderly people who lost their savings.

These findings about the lack of diligence on the Keating Five story align with the conclusions of the National Commission on Financial Institution Reform, Recovery and Enforcement, which examined the causes of the savings-and-loan debacle:

> Reporters now readily admit that they missed one of the biggest stories of the century. The story was missed because the news media have grown accustomed to being spoon fed news. If the story is hard to understand, or does not have great pictures, it is often ignored. If it doesn't bleed, it doesn't lead.
>
> Evidence existed very early on to indicate that the S&L industry's house was in trouble. It simply would have required diligence and digging to bring the story to the attention of the public. After the damage was done, and the story became obvious, the news media jumped on the bandwagon. It is easy to show the crooks and the devastated investors and frantic depositors on the evening news. Until the collapse became the debacle, the media were not interested in the story because it was hard to understand and was not sexy.[107]

7

"THE CHARLES KEATING OF FLORIDA"

If Charles Keating had a doppelgänger in the savings-and-loan industry, it would be David L. Paul, chairman of CenTrust Savings and Loan in Miami. Once dubbed the "Charles Keating of Florida,"[1] Paul followed the same playbook, using his thrift to invest heavily in junk bonds, to buy influence with politicians, and to file lawsuits against regulators who were asking questions about Cen-Trust's operations. As the *Wall Street Journal* noted on October 23, 1990, "The similarities between the two thrifts are striking: a high-living chief executive, huge investments in risky real estate and in junk bonds underwritten by Drexel Burnham Lambert Inc., a combative and litigious attitude toward savings-and-loan regulators, and hobnobbing with politicians."[2]

Under Paul, CenTrust grew rapidly and became the largest thrift in the Southeast. He invested some $4.4 billion in junk bonds—Paul was a major customer of Milken's Drexel Burnham Lambert—and the CenTrust collapse cost taxpayers $1.7 billion. That represented the fourth-largest savings-and-loan failure in history.[3] Paul later was sentenced to eleven years in prison on bank-fraud charges, including his scheme to use bank funds to acquire $25 million in rare art, such as a Rubens painting. Media accounts painted Paul as an iconic figure of 1980s greed and excess. As the *St. Petersburg Times* reported when Paul was convicted of fraud in 1993, "Paul's lifestyle was seen as a symbol of the 1980s. He entertained Elizabeth Taylor on his yacht, gave to Democratic Party candidates and causes, jetted to Cannes to relax and surrounded himself with millions of dollars' worth of Old Masters paintings, Oriental rugs, and Baccarat crystal. His income tax forms for the last five years of the '80s listed $17 million in income, but he estimated his net worth last year at minus $1.7 million. Joking or not, Paul listed his occupation on his 1990 tax return as 'defendant.'"[4] Cheryl Bell, the financial crimes coordinator in the Miami U.S. attorney's office, called Paul "south Florida's most notorious white-collar criminal. . . . It's safe to say that there is no greater S&L crook on the East Coast than Paul. You have Keating on the West Coast and Paul on the East."[5]

This chapter examines how *National Thrift News* covered Paul and his troubled CenTrust as a study of autonomy and journalistic independence in the trade press. Unlike the Keating case, the case of Paul and CenTrust presented a particular dilemma for *National Thrift News*: Strachan had a personal relationship with Paul, right up to the point of his sentencing. It is an illustration of the web of personal and professional connections between trade journalists and industry officials. Here is the overriding question: Did Strachan's relationship with Paul influence the newspaper's coverage of CenTrust?

Strachan's former reporters said no. On the contrary, they said Strachan allowed his young reporters to pursue negative stories about his source, and the stories were printed in *National Thrift News*. Pizzo recalled his conversations with Strachan about how to cover Paul. "We started writing some very tough stuff on David Paul," Pizzo recalled. "He said boy you guys ought to be right. . . . It wasn't the David Paul that he thought he knew." Despite his doubts, Strachan allowed the critical stories to be published in the newspaper. "He never spiked a single story," Pizzo said.[6] Muolo wrote critical stories about Paul's art investments and junk-bond dealings with Drexel. "Stan never once called me off doing any kind of reporting on CenTrust. . . . That never happened," Muolo said.[7]

The Strachan and Paul relationship should be a classic case study to support the political economy theory in communications. Strachan was the publisher of a newspaper financially dependent on the savings-and-loan industry that was established to serve its industry. He had a social and professional relationship with a dynamic and politically active banker who advertised in the newspaper. Under the political economy theory, a trade publication such as *National Thrift News* would tread gently to avoid challenging or alienating a major corporate actor such as CenTrust. Yet that is not what happened. The analysis of CenTrust news coverage did not find evidence that *National Thrift News* gave favorable treatment to Paul and CenTrust. *National Thrift News*, in fact, printed some highly critical stories of Paul that were later cited by congressional investigators. The study finds *National Thrift News* reporting turned critical at about the same time as the other newspapers, except for the leader in the overall coverage, the *St. Petersburg Times*. *National Thrift News* made some significant contributions, for example, with investigative reporting into CenTrust's involvement in the international bank scandal of Bank of Credit and Commerce International. The resolute reporting is yet another example of how the political economy theory does not explain the coverage decisions of *National Thrift News*. As argued in the prior chapter, Strachan's professional values as a journalist and the newspaper's culture of accountability are possible explanations for the deviation.

I conducted a content analysis of CenTrust coverage by examining *National Thrift News*, the *Wall Street Journal*, the *New York Times*, *American Banker* and the *St. Petersburg Times*,[8] an influential regional newspaper that covered CenTrust closely. My CenTrust content analysis began on January 1, 1984, at a time when the savings-and-loan crisis was not on the national agenda, and concluded December 31, 1993, when the crisis had peaked and was beginning to fade from the public agenda. The analysis reviewed 516 articles between 1984 and 1993. The Keating and Lincoln Savings study, by contrast, looked at the 1986–90 time period, when the crisis built and became a national news story. The review of CenTrust served as a valuable case study of media coverage of the crisis in that it covered this broader time period.

As this chapter will discuss, the *St. Petersburg Times* excelled in coverage of the Paul fraud. It covered the bank closely and published a May 1988 profile of Paul that reported he had falsified his resumé,[9] a story that preceded much of the critical national news coverage of CenTrust. The *St. Petersburg Times* reporting helps illustrate a point about media ownership. Unlike the other four newspapers, the *St. Petersburg Times* was owned by a nonprofit organization, the Poynter Institute, which provides training for journalists and studies changes in the media industry. The strong accountability journalism by this major newspaper is another piece of evidence about how media ownership can affect news production positively.

The five newspapers' coverage of CenTrust and Paul showed how the journalists relied on the government to help set the agenda for news coverage. Scholars such as W. Lance Bennett, Robert Entman, and Stuart Hall describe how government officials legitimize certain news narratives.[10] By and large, bank regulators' criticism of CenTrust and Paul put the story in play. *National Thrift News* and the other newspapers did not write probing stories about Paul until regulators revealed in March 1989 he had used bank funds to acquire $25 million in art. Key trends in the Paul and CenTrust story, including the battles with regulators to his opulent spending and his risky investments in junk bonds, were broader themes in the savings-and-loan crisis as a whole.

PAUL AND KEATING

Unlike Keating, Paul and CenTrust were not well known. Major histories of the savings-and-loan crisis provide mostly a passing mention of Paul and CenTrust, unlike the detailed examinations of the Keating and Lincoln Savings saga.[11] The Lincoln Savings case drew more attention because of Keating's public battle with regulators and explicit influence peddling with congressmen. The Lincoln case also came before the CenTrust collapse and was featured in a major congressional hearing in October and November 1989.

Paul and Keating crossed paths in several instances. In a 1992 criminal indictment, Paul was charged with conspiring to structure stock transactions with Lincoln Savings so that both institutions could book illusory profits.[12] Paul and Keating were named as codefendants in a January 1991 fraud lawsuit against Drexel Burnham Lambert's Michael Milken. The lawsuit described the three as part of a conspiracy to use inflated junk bonds to further their illegal schemes at the respective thrifts.[13] U.S. House Banking Committee chairman Henry Gonzalez also paired CenTrust and Lincoln. He described how Paul, like Keating, met with the Federal Home Loan Bank Chairman M. Danny Wall several times while the regulator was considering new examinations of CenTrust. "CenTrust has the same sad-bottom line (as the Lincoln case)—Washington could not get up the courage to act forcefully and support its troops in the field," Gonzalez said."[14] This article also noted Paul's propensity for litigation, a trait similar to Keating's. The *New York Times* reported Paul paid $12 million in legal fees to his main outside law firm, Paul Weiss, between 1983 and 1990, using more than fifty-five of the firm's lawyers on various CenTrust-related litigation activities.[15]

ROGUE BANK

One key theme in the content analysis involves the portrayal and evolution of CenTrust as a rogue bank. In general terms, rogue banks tend to have nepotism in management, sell risky bonds to customers, and make campaign contributions in order to pressure politicians.[16] Pizzo, writing in *Inside Job*, said rogue bank owners typically use bank funds to finance a lavish personal lifestyle or attract outside investors with marginal reputations.[17] Rogue banks, among other things, will participate in land flips to fraudulently boost the price of real estate while using bank funds for speculative investments or land deals, according to Martin Mayer in *The Greatest Ever Bank Robbery*. Their marginal reputations cause rogue banks to have trouble attracting sufficient funds from local depositors, and so they resort to paying above-market rates to gather funds from the national brokered deposit market, a volatile and sometimes unpredictable funding source.

The rogue bank framework helps explore the question of how the *National Thrift News* reporting differed from that of mainstream and general-interest business publications. As the analysis in this chapter will show, *National Thrift News* did not lead on key developments in the CenTrust saga, in contrast with its leadership role in the Keating and Lincoln Savings stories. The *St. Petersburg Times* produced early reporting that raised questions about Paul's business activities and the *Wall Street Journal* described significant concerns about CenTrust. Still, *National Thrift News* did produce some significant and detailed reporting on CenTrust, which included its 1991 coverage of CenTrust and its ties with to the Pakistan-based Bank of Credit and Commerce International, which was involved in money laundering and financing other criminal activities.

For Paul and CenTrust, the rogue bank narrative began in March 1989 when the *St. Petersburg Times* and the *New York Times* reported that Paul used the bank's money to acquire $25 million of rare art. The *St. Petersburg Times* on March 8, 1989, first reported on regulators' objections to CenTrust buying *Portrait of a Man as the God Mars*, a painting by Flemish master Paul Peter Rubens.[18] The artwork was hanging in Paul's home instead of the CenTrust office. The *New York Times* followed up with a 1,760-word story that described how Paul overpaid for the Rubens painting, perhaps as much as $10 million.[19] The Rubens painting tale provided a vivid symbol of excess and opulence that served to define Paul in press coverage from this point on. References to Paul's "extravagant" or "opulent" lifestyle were images with considerable staying power: as recently as January 2000, the *Wall Street Journal* referred to Paul and art purchases.[20] The review of news articles captured in a 1984–93 search contained fifty-three references to "lavish" or its variations; thirty-six references to "extravagant," and fifteen to "opulent."

The art tale was entertaining, but it represented a deeper, ongoing battle between Paul and the regulators over management of CenTrust. Florida regulators, in ordering Paul to sell the art, released a letter that described fundamental problems with the bank. *National Thrift News* picked up on the theme, noting CenTrust's art investments totaled $25 million, or "3% of its regulatory net worth"; although the article did not fully explain the concept of regulatory net worth, it suggested the highly speculative nature of the thrift's basic financial cushion. The article contained an interview with Paul, who defended his decision to have the Rubens painting hang in his house: "The thrift's new office tower has yet to be completed and he fears that humidity in the 'uncompleted office space' could harm the paintings."[21]

Paul, when asked in a 2016 interview about media coverage of the art, said the $25 million art investment was never significant relative to the size of the bank, which had $5 billion in assets. "The art was insignificant. . . . The point is relative to our size, the art was an excuse" to embarrass the company and make the case against Paul, he said in an interview. "And by the way, the art ultimately sold more than what we paid for it. And I don't know a major bank in a country that doesn't have an art collection."[22]

The *Wall Street Journal* was late to report on the art controversy, with its first article published on April 12, 1989, and the article that did not provide new details.[23] The newspaper eventually published a detailed and highly critical story on October 18, 1989. Although it did not break new ground, the *Wall Street Journal*'s 3,313-word article was striking for its negative tone, which described Paul as a "flamboyant chairman" and cited shareholder lawsuits that "say the chairman and his collection epitomize the excesses of speculation that set off the national S&L crisis."[24]

STRACHAN AND COVERAGE OF PAUL

The issue about Strachan's relationship with Paul allows an exploration of independence and autonomy in the business press. Did this politically active banker's social and professional relationship with Strachan shape the coverage? Strachan was friendly with Paul, to the point of inviting him to his daughter's bat mitzvah at a time when Paul was awaiting sentencing in the early 1990s. Kleege recalled a scene from the event: "David Paul was there and the videographer came around and David lifted up his menu to cover his face, because he didn't want to be on video. And in fact, I think he was due to go to jail in a few days, partly as a result of what Stan and other journalists had dug up."[25] Accounts of the depth of that relationship vary. Strachan's reporters alternatively called Paul a friend or a source. Pizzo recalled Paul as "a close friend of Stan's."[26] Paul himself provided conflicting accounts. "I didn't know him that well," Paul said. Later, when pressed to elaborate, Paul said, "I would say we were friendly and I was a source for what was going on. He would call and we would talk, as I am doing with you now. I have nothing bad at all to say about him. He tried to collect information."[27]

A mutual friend was Lewis Ranieri. Like Strachan, Ranieri had a professional and personal relationship with Paul: Ranieri served on CenTrust's board for six months in 1987–88.[28] Ranieri said he and Strachan "both liked David Paul very much. . . . He was an amazing, charismatic guy. . . . Sometimes a charismatic nature can blind you to some things. . . . I have no better explanation. I honestly did not think that he (Paul) was a bad guy. I thought he was kind of on the edge but not a bad guy. And I would let him speak for himself but that is probably what Stanley would say."[29]

A second narrative arose after the story about the paintings, the tales about Paul's ninety-five-foot yacht, the *Grand Cru*, a French phrase for superior vineyards. The *St. Petersburg Times* said the $7 million ocean liner, with an interior "studded with 14-karat gold nails," set "the standard for nautical narcissism."[30] The yacht featured comforts such as $700 bedsheets and a skeet-launching device to allow guests shoot clay pigeons at sea. Tales of the yacht first arose in the *St. Petersburg Times* profile of Paul in May 1988.[31] The yacht then became the foundation for a political bribery story involving a mayor of Miami Beach.[32] Paul used the *Grand Cru* to throw political fundraisers and to entertain influential community figures, including journalists.

Strachan and Ranieri both took their families to Miami for a ride on the *Grand Cru*.[33] Photos of that trip are in Strachan's family albums. "I got to ride on the boat like Stanley did," Ranieri said, adding he thought the gold ceilings in the yacht's dining room were "kind of odd." Ranieri recalled Strachan was upset about Paul's poor judgment about buying the art with CenTrust's money. "That didn't go over very well with Stan," Ranieri said. "And I just thought it was crazy."[34]

Strachan's relationship with Paul, however, is perhaps not remarkable or unusual at all. "David was a source of Stan's. They traded information like any reporter-source does," Muolo recalled.[35] Pizzo, in a 1997 remembrance printed after the editor's death, recalled that Strachan "had the opportunity many times to 'play along' with the high-flyers. After all, Stan enjoyed the good life as much as anyone I've ever known, and he could have had plenty of it if he'd killed the right stories at the right time. But Stan never did that. Not once. He let his reporters call it the way they saw it, even when it hurt. That's what he meant when he said, 'this is a reporter's newspaper.'"[36] The one anomaly, and in contrast with the Keating Five coverage, was this: *National Thrift News* did not publish an editorial containing the terms "David Paul" and "CenTrust" during the time period examined. Neither did *American Banker* nor the *New York Times*, for that matter. The omissions are curious in light of the gravity of Paul's crimes and the size of the taxpayer bailout of CenTrust. The *St. Petersburg Times*, on the other hand, mentioned CenTrust and Paul in fifteen editorial or commentary pieces, primarily references to Paul's attempts to influence local and state political leaders. And the *Wall Street Journal* wrote six editorials or opinion columns on the CenTrust scandal.

NEGATIVE COVERAGE

After revelations about the Rubens painting in March 1989, the tone of the CenTrust media coverage shifted and became increasingly negative. Clearly, Paul would not have been happy with some of the critical coverage in *National Thrift News*. Some 29 percent of its stories after the revelations contained negative portrayals of Paul. A content analysis of *National Thrift News* coverage showed the newspaper, despite its smaller size, was competitive with the larger newspapers in its negative coverage.

The *St. Petersburg Times* carried the lowest percentage of negative articles, at 16 percent. This statistic should be considered in the context of its overall coverage: the *St. Petersburg Times* published the greatest number of negative articles, at thirty-six, which again was due partly to its comprehensive coverage of a major business figure in Florida. By contrast, the percentage of negative news coverage of Paul in the *New York Times* was 30 percent; in *National Thrift News*, 29 percent; in the *Wall Street Journal*, 27 percent; and in *American Banker*, 22 percent. As with the Keating analysis, articles were coded as negative on the basis of regulatory action, violation of banking industry norms, guilt by association, or descriptions of Paul as manipulating the political or regulatory process. Negative articles, therefore, would describe Paul as in regulatory trouble such as under criminal investigation; as violating banking industry norms by being "flamboyant" or "risky"; as seeking to sway politicians to intervene on his behalf through campaign donations.

One important element of critical business journalism involves the press identifying problems early on, hopefully in time to mitigate damage to society. The standard is high, and the review of all the news coverage showed there was room for improvement. Aside from a critical May 1988 *St. Petersburg Times* profile, none of the newspapers carried negative articles about Paul before regulators' March 1989 public enforcement action against Paul for the art purchases. The analysis did find some challenges to Paul's business plans before this time but no explicit negative coverage.

At the same time, *National Thrift News* did not break news early on major CenTrust developments, unlike its Keating Five coverage. Why? One possible explanation involved timing and availability of resources. Muolo, Pizzo, and Fricker also were working long hours in late 1988 to meet a publisher's deadline for *Inside Job*, their investigation of the savings-and-loan crisis.[37] CenTrust's collapse, beginning in the fall of 1989, came during a historic downturn and collapse of the savings-and-loan industry. Lincoln Savings became a dominant

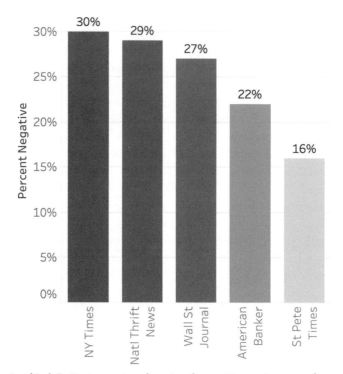

David Paul, CenTrust, percentage of negative references. News media coverage (516 articles), 1984–93.

story and the subject of major congressional hearings at that time. CenTrust was seized by regulators two weeks before the bankruptcy of one of the most influential financial firms in the 1980s, Drexel Burnham Lambert.

Although *National Thrift News* did not break the Rubens painting story, it advanced the Paul story with details about the thrift's shaky finances. It also provided considerable detail about the relationship between CenTrust and Bank of Credit and Commerce International, the Saudi-owned bank that laundered money for arms dealers and drug runners.[38] Global bank regulators seized BCCI in July 1991, and later New York prosecutors filed bribery and fraud charges. The Federal Reserve fined BCCI $200 million for illegally infiltrating the U.S. banking system. These stories were published before Paul's trial, which certainly could not have helped his defense.

Ghaith Pharaon, the Saudi investor who fronted for BCCI, acquired a 28 percent stake in CenTrust in 1988. Regulators were concerned that Pharaon had violated regulations with his purchase of CenTrust shares. Through Pharaon, Paul engaged in a sham transaction in which CenTrust deceived regulators about its financial health. The deception was arranged by temporarily "parking" a $150 million debt offering with BCCI; the phony debt sale was designed to deceive regulators by falsely showing CenTrust had increased its capital cushion against loan losses.[39] This illegal transaction allowed CenTrust to remain open for another two years and expanded the cost of the taxpayer bailout by $250 million. Paul and Pharaon knew each other well; both visited Keating's vacation home at Cat Cay in the Bahamas.[40]

All the newspapers except the *New York Times* reported on Pharaon's investment in CenTrust in 1987.[41] *American Banker's* coverage was particularly noteworthy and forward-looking. *American Banker* carried a rare interview with Pharaon on June 3, 1991, one of the major pieces exploring the Saudi investor's activities in the U.S. market.[42] *National Thrift News* published investigative stories about the BCCI and CenTrust relationship in 1991 that examined Pharaon's ownership in CenTrust and a California-based thrift, Viking Savings, his relationship with Paul, and other pro-Israel political fundraisers.[43] A second investigative report in September 1991 described how CenTrust was becoming

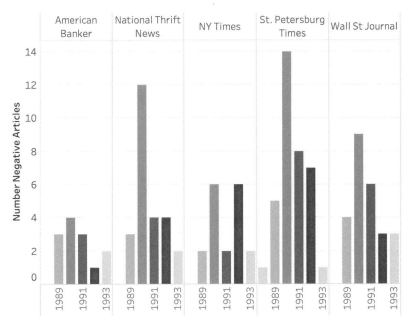

Negative news coverage of CenTrust-David Paul, 1987–93. After the March 1989 stories about Rubens painting, CenTrust coverage became negative.

"a banking surrogate" for BCCI in the United States, a significant advance in the understanding about the BCCI-CenTrust relationship.[44] Pizzo's story also defied trade press norms by covering politics and international affairs, something far beyond the normal scope of trade publications.[45] The *St. Petersburg Times* had a significant article about Pharaon's investment in CenTrust in August 1987, which emphasized the Saudi investor's connections to Bert Lance, the former aide to President Jimmy Carter. The *St. Petersburg Times* story cast a critical eye on the Saudi's investment history, noting he overpaid twice the market value for Lance's National Bank of Georgia and was facing financial trouble from falling oil prices.[46] It also carried a major story in June 1990 describing the BCCI relationship and the investigation of the illegal debt deal.[47]

ST. PETERSBURG TIMES

A content analysis showed the *St. Petersburg Times* was the clear leader on the CenTrust story among the five newspapers. It was first to publish a critical profile of Paul, on May 16, 1988, an extensive article by reporter Alecia Swasy that questioned Paul's business activities and highlighted his lavish lifestyle. The story came a full ten months before regulators began to act and before the news media narrative turned sharply critical against Paul and CenTrust. Swasy's *St. Petersburg Times* article was a rare instance of a significant story that was not pegged to an official announcement or regulatory action. Was Swasy's hard-hitting profile of Paul the equivalent of the *National Thrift News* exposé of the Keating Five meetings? The only similarity would be that Swasy's article described some aggressive business practices that would end up being at the heart of CenTrust's financial problems. Read in hindsight, the profile offered clear clues about Paul's extravagant lifestyle that turned into significant regulatory problems. And, like the Keating Five story, the rest of the news media essentially ignored Swasy's profile of Paul until state regulators announced their concerns about the art collection in March 1989—a development the *St. Petersburg Times* also was first to report. The *National Thrift News* report on the Keating Five clearly described influence peddling at a national level and involving five U.S. senators. This political narrative was dominant in the *St. Petersburg Times*, which regularly reported on Paul's influence on the Miami Beach mayor, state comptroller, candidates for governor, and the state's U.S. senators. The newspaper spelled out Paul's meetings with former president Jimmy Carter and his $100,000 donation to the Carter Center, which was funneled through the CenTrust Foundation. Carter met with Paul and Pharaon.[48] The *St. Petersburg Times* devoted numerous articles to comptroller Gerald Lewis, criticized for his relationship with Paul and his failure to shut down CenTrust quickly. Other articles described how Paul hired lobbyists to block legislation that would have affected his business; in one instance, Paul paid $100,00 to a lobbyist to block a bill backed by Lewis to expand thrift supervision.[49]

The relationship between Paul and Florida's Democratic U.S. Senator Bob Graham drew considerable attention. In a March 29, 1990, article, the *St. Petersburg Times* reported that Senator Graham and other Florida congressmen complained that the Federal Home Loan Bank in Atlanta was being too hard on Florida thrifts, echoing a complaint that Keating's allies had made about the San Francisco FHLB examinations.[50]

The *St. Petersburg Times* followed up with an editorial that took Graham to task: "At the very least, though, public officials should have distanced themselves and their staffs from Paul as soon as CenTrust's problems became known. No national politician—and certainly not Bob Graham—can be naive enough to fail to understand the ways in which the David Pauls and Charles Keatings of the world can manipulate the political system to insulate themselves from scrutiny."[51]

8

THE FUTURE OF BUSINESS JOURNALISM

A central argument of this book is that business journalism needs to evolve to serve a broader audience. This chapter explores the building blocks to make that evolution happen, such as using the tools and techniques of trade press reporters to examine businesses and hold them accountable while targeting a more general readership. We have seen elements of the evolution in the preceding chapters, such as the importance of newsroom culture, an enlightened ownership structure and business model, and a willingness to engage in investigative journalism to challenge economic power. These building blocks helped Strachan support his reporters to pursue in-depth projects, such as the book *Inside Job*, that provided a significant public service by describing the national scale of the savings-and-loan crisis. The *National Thrift News* case also suggests there is a market for accountability business journalism. My research showed important examples of media owners who valued the public-service mission of journalism were also able to make money. A number of trade-press journalists described how thorough coverage of businesses and industry can align with societal benefits. Profits and award-winning journalism are compatible, as the examined cases illustrate, when media owners put journalism first and don't demand hedge-fund-like returns from their media "properties."

I finish with recommendations for how business journalism can improve by orienting toward "early warning" reporting to detect crises at their embryonic stages. Other needed changes include collaborating with other news organizations on major projects in the public interest. In other words, the mainstream media organizations may have ignored *National Thrift News*, but they could have learned a lot from it.

JOURNALISTS AS THE OWNERS

This study has shown that three central factors helped support accountability journalism at the *National Thrift News* and at other trade publications: ownership of the media organization, a strong grounding in traditional journalistic values, and the willingness to assert journalistic autonomy from commercial influences. The following section will discuss the three factors, which are interwoven.

Strachan's role as owner, for example, allowed him to take significant editorial risks with the Keating Five coverage. Besides Strachan, another owner of the *National Thrift News* had some significant experience in journalism. Wesley Lindow had a distinguished career in banking and was a published author. He wrote *Inside the Money Market*, published by Random House in 1972, and also wrote a column called "Investors Corner" in *National Thrift News* in the 1980s.[1]

The academic literature on creation of corporate culture shows how owners can set priorities for their organizations in addition to making a profit and those priorities can embrace professional values such as autonomy. Rohlinger and Profitt studied how media ownership shaped news content and found "independently owned newspapers cover controversial ideas more often—even on the opinion pages."[2] Kurt and Gladys Lang also described how ownership can assist in publication of controversial material: "Some owners possessed of a social conscience are prepared to take on acceptable financial risks, while other media personnel have sometimes been able to use the leeway, autonomy, prestige, and authority they enjoy getting their version of a major news event out to the public, thereby pressuring political leaders to confront a problem they preferred to ignore."[3]

Stan Strachan's influence and support of his investors enabled him to define the *National Thrift News* as a reporter's paper, a clear example of how ownership directly shaped the reporting culture. Muolo recalled he and other reporters brought stories to the editors: "Stan and Mark (Fogarty) always gave us carte blanche to do what we wanted."[4] Strachan's newsroom was in sharp contrast to other newsrooms such as the *Wall Street Journal*, known for a top-down approach run by teams of editors.[5] The interviews with trade-press journalists yielded numerous examples of how editorial autonomy was exercised in the face of commercial pressures. One dramatic case involved former *PC World* editor Harry McCracken, who was ousted briefly in 2007 after proposing a story highly critical of Apple. He resigned when the story was blocked by the *PC World* CEO Colin Crawford. The magazine's owner and publisher, IDG's Pat McGovern, intervened and assured McCracken he would have full editorial autonomy. Crawford was reassigned and McCracken returned to *PC World*. McCracken said at the time: "I made a bigger statement by leaving than I thought I was making. And I'm now making an even bigger statement in coming back because I am 100 percent confident that *PC World* will continue to be a place where editors decide how to serve the people who use their content. I would never have come back unless I was completely confident of that."[6]

One of McCracken's first order of business: publishing a story called "10 Things We Hate about Apple." Reflecting on this experience later, McCracken said, "Having an editor as firewall is really important. That's what led me to decide to resign, because I felt my job wasn't to buckle at issues like that. . . . You did not want an associate editor working on a story that might be controversial even thinking about problems it might cause from a business standpoint."[7]

Rick Bush, editorial director of *Transmission and Distribution World*, said he has been able to assert a great degree of independent editorial decision making at his magazine, which serves the electric power industry. "I told our president that in certain areas, I could shape the direction of the industry. And he said no, the best you could do is be a champion," Bush recalled. "And I said, well, that's your opinion and your opinion doesn't count. I can do this and I'm doing it."[8] Bush said the Timothy White Award recognized editors who were "standing up to the advertisers and not kowtowing to the advertisers but also for not kowtowing to your own management."

Bush recalled an incident in which an advertiser, a president of a major contractor, proposed to write a column for *Transmission and Distribution World*. Bush viewed the offer as a test of his authority. "I said you can write it, but it will never run as long as I am the editor of T&D, which meant you're not telling me what to do," he said. Bush's boss was horrified at the remark, but the contractor wound up making a major advertising purchase just the same. "This guy was testing me to see if I was real or not," Bush said. "Once you stand up, they feel like you could be a formidable partner."[9]

The review of ownership aligns with a trend of innovation taking place in today's small digital newsrooms. These local reporting initiatives "are bubbling up to fill the gaps left by shrinking newsrooms," Victor Pickard and Josh Stearns wrote in their survey of new media projects.[10] The literature suggests innovation and autonomy are more likely in smaller newsrooms, an encouraging idea since many of the modern digital newsrooms are much smaller than their Industrial Era predecessors.[11] The *Voice of San Diego* and *MinnPost* are two of the more celebrated digital-first newsrooms devoted to accountability journalism. "Those projects share a public service mission, and many focus on sending reporters to cover beats that have been long forgotten or neglected, including coverage of city halls and statehouses," Pickard and Stearns wrote.[12] One promise of these new digital newsrooms involves the potential for greater autonomy, assuming they are able to secure steady funding. Researchers could examine the new digital publications within the Investigative News Network, a confederation of nonprofit news outlets with more than 150 members.[13] New research on nonprofit news funding is showing some early success for major players:

> These outlets have also diversified their revenue base by way of individual donors and in some cases have strongly benefited from the "Trump bump" in funding. For example, following the 2016 election, *ProPublica* more than tripled its combined revenue from foundations, large gifts, and individual donations. The five top state or local news organizations raised more than $20 million in grants over the same 6-year period and the Institute for Nonprofit News received approximately $5 million to build capacity across the sector. The *Texas Tribune, Voice of San Diego*, and *MinnPost* have similarly boosted their revenue by way of advertising, donors, events, and corporate sponsors.[14]

The case of the *St. Petersburg Times* and its reporting on the CenTrust Savings case again suggests the beneficial effects that enlightened media ownership can have on news production. Pickard and Stearns cited the nonprofit ownership of the *St. Petersburg Times* as an example of "alternative ownership structures that might allow news organizations to focus more on their public mission instead of just their returns to investors."[15] The Poynter Institute, which produces academic research on journalism and provides professional training, had a set of priorities significantly different from those of a company with an owner or a company owned by public shareholders. "One conclusion is incontrovertible: To support new forms of reporting and new methods of distribution, newspapers must think outside of the current media system," Pickard and Sterns wrote.[16]

THE MARKET FOR HARD NEWS

The preceding chapters described the peril of the trade-press business model, such as the degree to which the publications reported and relied economically on industries they covered and how that influenced news coverage. Although dependent on its industry for revenue, the *National Thrift News* envisioned an unfulfilled market for hard news valued by savings-and-loan executives. For example, the 1975 business proposal for *National Thrift News* said, "Developments now taking place within the industry demand a publication with greater news reporting, national coverage and frequency than now exist in this industry."[17]

"It was a trade paper. It was created because he saw an opportunity to make money," recalled Kleege. What made Strachan unusual was he pursued the news even if it made his advertisers uncomfortable. "He would have gravitated toward covering the difficult thing rather than trying to cover only good news and profitable things."[18]

What does this market for hard news look like today? People will pay for serious news: The *Financial Times* said its digital subscriptions grew 10 percent in 2017 to 714,000. "The demand for our quality, independent journalism has never been greater and this business performance underlines the dynamism of our global business and brand," John Ridding, chief executive of *Financial Times*, said.[19] In examining the future news landscape, Richard Tofel of *ProPublica* argues that consumers will continue to pay for certain types of hard news: "There is considerable evidence that hard news, much of which is of direct economic value to at least some readers, is among the forms of journalism least endangered by the business crisis of the press. That is, hard news, at least at the national level, seems likely to remain a profit-making business, and the measurement of its impact will likely be undertaken by market-driven forces, including those undergirding advertising and business-to-business sales of information."[20]

The Reuters Institute Digital News Report for 2017, which surveyed some seventy thousand people in thirty-six countries, asked consumers what type of news content they would purchase. Breaking news earned a 41 percent response rate as a priority for news consumers, followed by reporting on recent events at 38 percent. In-depth analysis was cited by one-third of consumers, at 34 percent. "People valued quality content, in particular good writers, exclusives, and behind- the-scenes access," the survey found. "Comparatively few people (23 percent) pay for access to entertaining or amusing news content." Publishers are getting the message that people will pay for original, quality stories. "Change is in the air with many media companies shifting models towards higher quality content and more emphasis on reader payment," the Reuters Institute survey found.[21]

The *National Thrift News* readers valued such hard-edged reporting because it would help them identify problems in their industry. One prominent banking industry economist, David Olson, wrote that Strachan and his newspaper clearly achieved the goal of identifying issues and suggesting improvements: "He was truly a power to be reckoned with and he used it to educate thousands in the industry and push for appropriate reforms."[22]

The overall business climate for online news remains challenging, of course. The Reuters Institute survey showed just 16 percent of those surveyed in the United States pay for online news subscriptions. The reason? About half of respondents said they can still get the news for free online.[23] Yet within this survey were some silver linings. The share of millennials paying for online news jumped from 4 percent in 2016 to 18 percent in 2017. The authors credited this trend to the "Trump Bump," or a surge in online subscriptions by primarily left-leaning readers who hope journalists will hold the new administration accountable. Here we see a key demographic group, millennials, showing a willingness to pay for news because they believe it will yield a personal benefit in their lives. This conclusion is in line with the broader argument of this book: people will pay for business journalism if it is crafted in a format that is readable and relevant.

Further, there is an established pattern in which consumers readily pay for other forms of digital media; in 2017, Reuters Institute found some 33 percent of those surveyed paid for online video services such as Netflix, 22 percent paid for audio such as Spotify, and 16 percent paid for news. The challenge for news managers is to combat the "culture of free" in the early history of online news consumption and re-educate consumers, selling them on the idea that news is worth paying for to receive a product that is valuable. Growth in Netflix and Spotify could spill over and alter habits, encouraging people to pay for news. "If these services and others like them become more popular, the 'culture of free' may begin to erode, particularly in the minds of those who have only ever experienced an internet where paying for digital media is normal," Richard Fletcher and Rasmus Nielsen wrote.[24]

Recent research on audience engagement describes the value of offering insightful, in-depth reporting that speaks to a community of readers. "To attract subscribers in a noisy news landscape, news organizations must excel at a few key coverage areas instead of trying to cling to the notion of being equally comprehensive about everything—a publication of record," notes Tran Ha in a 2017 report for the American Press Institute.[25] By providing readers with essential information to enable them to survive in the modern society, business journalism can make a compelling case for its relevance to the reader. Trade journalists covering industries as diverse as defense, technology, or food agreed that businesses will pay for critical yet constructive reporting on their respective industry. "It's very important that a business-to-business publication be willing to state these things because if they don't, they can't help their industries. They can't actually help their industries move forward and improve," said Jim Prevor, the food-industry journalist and owner of Phoenix Media Network. His stories about food safety and similar issues described the industry's role in the problems and suggested paths for the future. "We played an important role in getting the industry focused on not so much being defensive about these things but recognizing the problem," he added.[26] In fact, Prevor argues that trade publications have an incentive to publish critical reporting, since the go-with-the-flow attitude starts a downward spiral for them. "That leads to a certain type of short-term timidity. And in the long run, of course, that leads to weaker business-to-business publications, because they are not stating the truth," he said. "In the long run that leads to less important readers, less engaged readers and that ultimately leads to less advertising."

Fabey had a similar viewpoint on working for *Aviation Week*: "One of the reasons they would turn to *Aviation Week* was because they knew they would get unvarnished news. And because of that, they knew they could trust it."[27] Making the case for hard news to the industry "wasn't as a hard as a sell as you might necessarily think," he added. Maryfran Johnson, a former *Computerworld* editor, said the newsweekly was focused "on being the advocates for the computer users" and holding large technology vendors such as Oracle and IBM accountable for their market power.[28] For reporters, money and professional prestige are also at stake in this type of reporting. Dyck, Morris, and Zingales describe market incentives, such as book deals, better jobs, and professional acclaim, for journalists who uncover business wrongdoing. "Journalists who break a story about a company's fraud are more likely to find a better job than a comparable journalist writing for the same newspaper/magazine at the same time," they write.[29]

Some publications make the case for investigative journalism by focusing closely on providing "actionable material" that readers can use in their jobs. *Aquatics International*, which serves the swimming-pool industry, would incorporate reader surveys on topics related to investigative projects. For example, the 2010 exposé on sexual abuse by swimming coaches included a survey of 515 *Aquatics International* readers that revealed "32 percent of aquatics professionals say they are not confident they have adequate protocols in place when hiring a new staff member. . . . But only 9 percent plan to make any changes."[30] *Aquatics International* Kendra Free said such surveys allowed them to gather new information on an issue and advance reader engagement. Free also conducted an investigation of waterborne diseases at water parks. "With these investigative articles, and really all of our articles, we focused on making it as relevant as possible to our audience," Free said.[31]

Rob Blackwell, editor in chief of *American Banker*, recalled making the case for hard news when he spoke to a group of Oklahoma bankers in 2017: "The message I gave to them was this: I am not here, and *American Banker* is not here, to tell what you want to hear. That's not useful. You have the ABA (the trade group the American Bankers Association). You have community banking groups. You have lobbyists. Those people are there to tell you what you want to hear. I'm here to tell you what you need to hear."[32] He added, "We're not any good to anybody if we are just parroting the industry's lobbying notes."

TRADE PRESS CHALLENGES

Despite the industry's size and growing revenues, trade publications are not immune to the broader problems in journalism, problems caused by the onset of the internet and the resulting decline in traditional print advertising. Many journalists said these trends were forcing publications to cut staff and alter their production to more quick-hit web stories; a number had left their former employers and some were no longer in journalism. "We've had a lot of staff reductions and a huge amount of digital transformation and layoffs going on throughout the technology media companies," Johnson said of *Computerworld*. Whitney Sielaff of *National Jeweler* agreed. "Trade journalism really took a huge hit, as did all journalism with advent of Internet," he said. "Trade journalism was a very lucrative business for a long time."[33]

Some journalists fear these trends will reduce in-depth reporting at the trade press. "Ironically, as the trade press has gotten bigger and better resourced, its inclination to do longer, deeper enterprise journalism appears to be declining," John Heltman writes.[34] Julie Triedman said *American Lawyer* had difficulty adapting to the quick trigger of online news. Since 2008, "things got tougher and tougher for the company. The web-first, everything online right away that environment made it hard to leave the office," Triedman said. When she first started at *American Lawyer* in 1994, she was writing a lengthy story of at least four thousand words every three months, supplemented by a few brief five-hundred-word items and some editing duties. Toward the end of her tenure at *American Lawyer*, the workload grew significantly as the magazine had suffered repeated rounds of layoffs. "So the amount of content just grew inexorably and the amount of reporting on each thing declined a little bit at the end," Triedman said. "I just felt like it was going to be harder and harder to do that level of quality. . . . I worry about what is going on with trade journalism, or any journalism, now."[35] Triedman is now working at a law firm.

During Harry McCracken's stint at *PC World*, the magazine was making significant money and had a staff of forty-five people. They could afford to spend money on investigative projects. One example was a series on flawed computer repair at a major retailer, a reporting project that involved buying ten computers and flying reporters around the country to test repair services at various retail outlets. "Now, we're in this era where so many publications are feeding a website that wants short stories and fresh content on a moment-by-moment basis. It is harder to do that stuff," McCracken said. McCracken said the economic challenges in the trade press, or any genre of journalism, may result in editors weighing financial considerations in their editorial decisions. "I think especially as times have gotten tougher in the media business, there's more likelihood that editors may wonder if they should secretly do stuff based on financial issues rather than serving a reader," he said.[36]

Some research suggests the increase in workload in digital publications invites reporters to take shortcuts or rely more heavily on corporate public-relations materials to meet their story quotas. One journalist told researchers at Cardiff University that his workload of two stories a day has more than doubled. "Today it's not uncommon to be knocking out 5 or 6 in a day—and when you're doing that you rely more on the wires and on PR than you did before."[37] Interviews with business journalists about technology and news production in 2015 described a similar trend. One reporter said that with the current technology revolution, especially the "fire hose of information created by Twitter" caused her to feel anxious as "there are suddenly so many more things for me to keep an eye on."[38]

VandeHei, the former *Politico* editor and an innovator in digital newsrooms, argued news organizations are wedded to outdated formats that do not respond to readers' needs. Legacy journalism was writing too long. Modern audiences, especially the new corporate executive, demand brevity. "People don't want the pieces we're writing. . . . They're too damn long," he told Recode.[39] VandeHei believes his publications can still produce journalism in the public interest despite the deep corporate relationships: "That doesn't mean you're still not producing journalism of consequence for a huge audience. . . . It just gives you another way to fund it."[40] One such model involves producing narrowly tailed news for specialized audiences, so-called "paywall journalism," which resembles the traditional trade-press model of serving a discreet audience with in-depth information. Some journalists fear paywall journalism will have an adverse effect of creating publications that serve only elite audiences. "But the fact remains that on a day-to-day basis more and more information is flowing to Washington's elite while less trickles out to the American public,"[41] Heltman wrote.

Historically, trade publications have supplemented their income by sponsoring industry conferences to generate revenue. Industry conferences are significant money-makers; in 2017, the trade-press industry generated $13 billion from conferences and events.[42] *National Thrift News* and its parent company sponsored conferences and seminars for the thrift industry. One was a 1984 seminar on hedge trading strategies, sponsored by the Dorset Group, parent of the *National Thrift News*. Attendees were charged $375 for the program. Such events raise another set of conflicts as conferences represent another financial relationship between corporations and journalists. Consider the trade-offs for a journalist who is seeking to attract major industry speakers to one of its conferences. "If you hit too hard, you lose keynotes, ticket buyers, and support in the tech space," Jason Calacanis, founder of Weblogs, told *Vanity Fair*.[43] Journalist Nick Bilton raised similar concerns for hard-hitting technology trade publications: "The system here has been molded to effectively prevent reporters from asking tough questions. It's a game of access, and if you don't play it carefully, you may pay sorely. Outlets that write negatively about gadgets often don't get pre-release versions of the next gadget. Writers who ask probing questions may not get to interview the C.E.O. next time he or she is doing the rounds. If you comply with these rules, you're rewarded with page views and praise in the tech blogosphere."[44] There are ample challenges ahead with the restructuring of the news industry. "This type of journalism whether in the trades or anywhere else, is extremely important. And in danger of being extinct," said Fabey, former naval reporter for *Aviation Week*. The higher priced experienced reporters are being replaced by less expensive inexperienced writers, he noted. "It's a sign of the times. Investigative reporting it has just become tougher to afford."[45]

FURTHER RESEARCH

Further research is needed into other news organizations with business models similar to that of *National Thrift News*, to determine whether other publications enjoyed similar editorial autonomy. Some of the following questions will help guide journalism scholars and industry officials about factors that lead to accountability journalism in the trade press and journalism in general:

- Does the ownership protect and enforce editorial independence?
- Are there editors with a track record of producing watchdog accountability or investigative reporting?
- Are the editors producing significant hard news reporting?

- Do experienced beat reporters have the opportunity to pursue in-depth reporting?
- Does the publication produce reporting that leads to industry reforms that benefit society?
- Is the company's brand associated with accountability journalism?
- Does the trade journal envision an audience outside its core advertisers?

No single publication will fulfill each of the separate goals described in the sections that follow, but these goals would represent a starting point for identifying the trade publications with a more robust approach to reporting. Perhaps such publications should be categorized as watchdog trade press.

BUSINESS JOURNALISM AND THE FUTURE

As we consider the future of business journalism, the following recommendations describe how the field can reenvision its reporting mission and employ techniques to better connect with readers and viewers. This section is intended to add to an ongoing conversation about advancing the profession.

In face of the criticism of mainstream business journalists missing clues to financial scandals, researchers and journalists should consider the ideal of "early warning journalism" or "preventative journalism" that seeks to highlight financial abuses before they become systemic crises. This idea is championed by investigative business journalist and Pulitzer Prize–winner Michael Hudson, who worked on the *Panama Papers* investigation and was one of the first journalists to write about subprime lending abuses in the early 1990s.[46] Hudson's approach focuses on the internal watchdogs of the corporate world, such as the risk managers, quality-control staff, internal fraud investigators, loan underwriters, and real-estate appraisers. Hudson made a point of speaking to these internal corporate watchdogs and found a pattern: "They did their jobs, they found fraud, they red-flagged it. But instead of being rewarded and promoted . . . they were ignored, marginalized, harassed, demoted or fired, or some combination" thereof, he said.[47] For mainstream journalists, one way to find these story tips could involve a partnership with the trade press. Hudson said encouraging reporters to flag early warnings would provide an immense public service: "You may not always be able to completely stop bad practices or a meltdown from happening, but good, early, hard-hitting reporting can at least reduce the level of damage, popping the bubble early or forcing bad actors to rein in their worst practices."

Business journalists could adopt the format of popular fact-check columns, used primarily in political reporting, and apply them to corporate announcements.[48] Such columns can let journalists set the news agenda, tell readers what is important, and assess the level of misinformation coming from business leaders.[49] Pizzo has called his approach to reporting the connect-the-dots game. "If you don't connect the dots, you don't get the picture," Pizzo said.[50]

JOURNALISTIC ECOSYSTEM

In this era of limited budgets, business journalists can leverage their impact by collaborating with like-minded publications to conduct complex investigations. Collaboration goes against the existing practices, especially in daily print publications, historically loath to cooperate with competitors. Business journalists should use their strength in numbers to fortify the existing media ecosystem, as in the case of Strachan's *National Thrift News* and Pizzo's *Russian River News*. Hudson's involvement in the recent *Panama Papers* investigation of international tax shelters is another example. This collaboration of some three hundred reporters on six continents won the 2017 Pulitzer Prize and serves as a valuable template for journalists in many fields. The International Consortium of Investigative Journalists worked to uncover tax shelters of world leaders and celebrities in Russia, Iceland, Saudi Arabia, and China. The *New York Times* and *Bloomberg News* were not included in this project, yet both news organizations gave significant coverage to the consortium's findings after the initial release on April 4, 2016.[51] Other examples of collaboration include ProPublica's *Documenting Hate*, which involved teamwork of hyperlocal, regional, and national print and broadcast partners.[52]

"Collaboration remains an important trend in U.S. newsrooms, supported by a growing variety of conferences, funding sources, and collaborative reporting tools," the 2018 Reuters Institute survey found.[53] The watchdog function of the press works best when multiple media outlets recognize quality reporting and follow up with their own stories, helping raise visibility on an issue. In this vein, *National Thrift News* often cited the important stories of other mainstream publications such as the *Arizona Republic* and the *Orange County Register*, two hometown papers in the Keating business empire. Sharing the credit was less common at the *Wall Street Journal* or the *New York Times* during the savings-and-loan crisis period, although those publications have become more willing to acknowledge competing works since that time.

University of Michigan professor Gregory S. Miller described the value of rebroadcasting information in his study of media reporting on accounting frauds: "Even if the potential issue was identified by another public information intermediary, the press can still provide an important function by publishing an article that synthesizes this concern with other information regarding the firm."[54] The concept of collaboration among journalistic outlets fits within the communitarian ethical framework. "Thinking as a communitarian mutes the competition among journalistic organizations while amplifying the collective effect that journalists and their organizations have on society and culture," Patterson and Wilkins wrote.[55]

Mainstream news organizations should consider content-sharing arrangements with the trade press, as in the agreements between the investigative news website ProPublica and legacy media outlets such as the *New York Times,* the *Washington Post,* and others. *Bloomberg News* has such arrangements with regional newspapers across the country. Content-sharing arrangements would provide a broader audience for specialized journalism that has societal impact. What does the trade press need to do to better reach a broader audience? The modifications needed may not be that dramatic. *American Banker's* Rob Blackwell recalled one recent story with broad general interest, an exclusive story about a showdown between the Trump administration and the Consumer Financial Protection Board. He knew it would attract a broader audience, and so he made a few additional editing touches before posting it outside the newspaper's paywall. "It wasn't radically different what I would have given to a story," Blackwell said. Senator Elizabeth Warren of Massachusetts and an early leader of the consumer agency quickly retweeted the story. *American Banker* will post certain technology and political news outside its paywall "when we are competing on a broader environment. They might be able to get the same news elsewhere but not with the same analytical focus," Blackwell said.[56]

TRAINING

Journalists' illiteracy with numbers and market concepts are long-standing problems, dating back to the beginnings of modern business journalism.[57] As Diana Henriques wrote, "I submit that there is no form of ignorance more widely tolerated in the American newsroom than ignorance about business and finance."[58] Many commentators have called for journalists to improve their basic financial skills. To see what a difference financial skills can make, consider Pizzo's training and how it helped him write *Inside Job*. Pizzo's background as a real-estate agent allowed him to conduct property research and trace financial transactions, skills that allowed him to raise original questions about Centennial Savings and Loan well before other media caught on. Consider some of the warning signs about American Continental's financial condition, such as the Moody's and Standard and Poor's rating downgrades in early 1987. Downgrades are clear red flags that experienced financial journalists would identify as problems for the company.

The need for basic accounting skills is a common theme in business journalism curriculum and professional training sessions at groups such as the Society for Advancing Business Editing and Writing. Fluency with basic accounting concepts allowed reporters at the *Wall Street Journal* to describe the potential impact of new capital standards and warn readers about significant weaknesses in some eight hundred savings-and-loan associations.[59] Even a general orientation about the role and operations of accounting firms could have led to more aggressive reporting. For example, the *New York Times* reported in 1989 that Keating's company had hired Jack Atchison, formerly a lead accountant for Lincoln's outside auditors Arthur Young (now Ernst and Young), as a vice president of American Continental.[60] Such a hire suggested the outside auditing firm lacked the requisite independence from its client, which was a red flag that gained little attention until Atchison's conflict and advocacy for his client were described in the House Banking Committee hearings. In addition to accounting training, business journalists should improve skills in handling large datasets and producing data visualizations. Such approaches can help provide better context about issues and improve reader engagement.

After criticism of the media's failure to detect the Enron fraud, significant steps were made to improve business reporting training, such as establishment in 2003 of the Donald W. Reynolds National Center for Business Journalism. The Reynolds Center, which funded research into business journalism and funded academic fellowships, provided resources in addition to existing professional training offered by the Society of American Business Editors and Writers and the Investigative Reporters and Editors.[61] Business journalism education has expanded at universities, although more work needs to be done.[62]

OFFICIAL SOURCES

The review of the *National Thrift News* coverage of Keating yields a few reporting lessons, one on sourcing and the other on corporate culture. The content analysis showed most of the four newspapers' coverage was clustered around official events such as congressional hearings or pegged to an official source, such as a company announcement. Yet some of this coverage revealed a surprising disconnection. The newspapers had ample coverage of the 1988 deal between Keating and Wall, yet they neglected to write in detail about the Keating Five senators meeting, which was part of Keating's complaint against the agency. In this respect, *National Thrift News* performed a significant watchdog function by using sources to report on the Keating Five and the racketeering investigations. They did not wait for a regulator's press release. The newspaper advanced the cause of transparency and accountability in other ways: *National Thrift News* repeatedly identified the Keating Five senators by their individual names, even in routine background references in other stories. The *Wall Street Journal* and the *New York Times* only began doing so after the Gonzalez hearings. The pattern of the *New York Times* and the *Wall Street Journal* ignoring good trade-press coverage continued late into 1989. *American Banker* delivered important reporting about Keating's Kuwaiti investors in October 1989, which gained little attention in the large newspapers. In light of the *Wall Street Journal*'s late start on the Keating story, its November 20, 1989, headline during the Gonzalez hearings was quite ironic: "Sleeping Watchdog."

One reporting tip business journalists should explore is to examine the culture and sociology of a business, particularly a large bank or industrial enterprise, to understand that dysfunction within such organizations can result in public harm. Gillian Tett, now U.S. editor of the *Financial Times*, provided original and insightful reporting on how the infighting and lack of communication within large London banks contributed to broader lending problems, an issue in the 2008 financial crisis. Tett, who holds a doctoral degree in anthropology, saw the separate bond, stock, and commodities trading desks at banks as warring tribes. The conflict led to a breakdown in the bank's risk-management culture and was a cause of some of the major trading losses.[63] Donald MacKenzie made a similar observation, saying the media can play a useful outsider role in examining the organization and identifying problems that specialists do not see.[64] In the Enron and 2008 financial crises, journalist Bethany McLean found that stubbornness and excessive ambition were common traits of senior executives who led their organizations into disaster.[65] The study showed Keating's character traits, such as litigiousness and significant risk-taking, figured into later regulatory problems. The reputation of a firm is important and should be explored as a reporting construct.

COMBAT INSULARITY

Many successful journalists work diligently to expand their contacts and diversity of sources and to listen carefully to outside voices. A consistent criticism of business reporters is their overreliance on securities analysts, regulators, and business executives, which results in the journalists sharing their worldview, a type of intellectual capture.[66] This capture problem, of course, is not unique to business journalism; it is a source of criticism for political journalism and sports journalism.[67] The dilemma of capture is a longstanding issue in business journalism. It was cited as a flaw in coverage of the 1929 market crash, the savings-and-loan crisis, the Enron crisis, and the 2008 financial crisis. In 1938, for example, Carswell criticized business reporters for relying excessively on the New York Stock Exchange for news. Antonis Kalogeropoulos et al. wrote this critique about how narrow sourcing continues today: "In comparison to their political counterparts, financial journalists use fewer sources per item, are more reliant on PR and they take less initiatives in contacts with sources."[68] Going outside the official sourcing channels can allow reporters to break news about systemic problems in the markets. Hudson learned about the subprime loan problem in his community from legal-aid attorneys whose low-income clients were losing their homes to foreclosure.[69]

Bilton faults the technology trade press for taking an uncritical view of Theranos, the controversial blood-testing startup that attracted billions of dollars in startup funding and positive media coverage despite having an unproven medical technology. "They embraced Holmes and her start-up with a surprising paucity of questions about the technology she had supposedly developed. They praised her as 'the next Steve Jobs,' over and over (the black turtleneck didn't hurt), until it was no longer a question, but seemingly a fact."[70] It was *Wall Street Journal* investigative reporter John Carreyrou who exposed questions about Theranos's technology in a 2015 investigative story, which led to the company's demise. Carreyrou won a George Polk Award for his Theranos coverage.[71]

A 2016 American Press Institute study provided a good menu of character traits and habits of effective accountability journalists, a list that can serve as a benchmark for business reporters seeking to combat insularity. The API study of local and national accountability journalists found that they generally share the following traits: broad curiosity; adaptability to new technologies and platforms; ability to address multiple audiences; capacity for hard work to create context for their audiences; a balance between their time on story choices and audience interactions; investment of considerable time building relationships with sources, readers; connections and teamwork within their own newsrooms; and ability to find their own way and direct their own work.[72]

END THE BACKWATER MINDSET

One major problem for the journalism profession is the insistence of pigeonholing business journalism as a backwater assignment, a prisoner of the old industrial-era paradigm of print journalism. The legacy of placing business journalism in a separate category is out of step with theories of history and the centrality of capitalism in the U.S. political and cultural experience. "In a market economy, money is both the means and ends of life," Randy Martin observed.[73] Karl Marx's influential historical theories noted how the disciplines of politics and economics were intertwined.[74] On this point, Angus Burgin wrote that "For better or for worse, we now live in an era in which economists have become our most influential philosophers, and when decisions made or advised by economistic technocrats have broad and palpable influence on the practice of our everyday lives."[75] The economy and history are two sides of the same coin. Our journalism should reflect that reality rather than pushing business news into an obscure corner of the website or back pages of a publication.

If business journalism is to evolve and serve the broader society as its primary audience, it needs to shed the legacy of the newsroom backwater and adopt the language and identity of watchdog and accountability journalism. Johnson of *Computerworld* summarized the worldview that's necessary for this evolution: "I very much always saw myself as a crusading reporter," Johnson said.[76] Business journalism perhaps should be viewed as a mindset that allows it to work fluidly with the evolving nature of news and establishes a path forward for it to evolve into a genre to better serve the general readership.[77] One benefit of business journalism that serves a broader society is that it will integrate the skills and insight of business journalism fully into the regular news production. Such an approach would be useful as modern newsrooms emphasize team reporting across beats and specialties. In this way, business journalism would reflect the commercial and economic mindset of our society.

WARY OPTIMISM

The steps presented in this chapter may help business journalism evolve and assert itself as a force for the public good. The enhanced ownership role of journalists and greater focus on collaboration and orientation toward warning the public about systemic problems should help reporters better connect the dots and better see through the complex financial murk. A more vibrant, assertive journalism will engage the audience, who may very well be inspired to pay for something that is relevant to and valuable for their immediate lives and future dreams. New generation of news organizations likely will be digital first and have smaller newsrooms, led by industry veterans and powered by younger talent. *National Thrift News*, while not perfect, should serve as a useful model for that next generation. In the words of the George Polk Award judges, it set a standard for the rest of the industry when its reporting "alerted those closest to the crisis of its immense implications in an impartial, credible and thorough manner."[78]

This project approaches the changes to business journalism with a wary sense of optimism. Ben Bagdikian offered a hopeful note: "Each generation has to establish its own priorities and re-invigorate the best principles for the society."[79] To this end, he noted the rise of media reform organizations—more than one hundred operating by 2003—as evidence of energy to force change in the industry. One such project is Report for America, an effort to pair nonprofit and legacy newsrooms to cover local news in underserved and low-income communities, such as Appalachia. Charles Sennott, a former *Boston Globe* foreign correspondent and a founder of Report for America, approaches potential funders and media partners with this pitch: "The idea that the crisis in journalism is a crisis for democracy is a very powerful idea."[80] Sennott's vision presents an opportunity for the trade press to challenge that dominance. There is an opportunity to evolve and improve.

"If you look at some of the trade publication you will find some really good journalism," Fabey said. "Because of the nature of the beast you are not going to find poetry and prose. In a good publication what you will find is really good clear, coherent sentences and analysis."[81]

"In some ways, the trade press is one of the last bastions of really good day in and day out journalism."

APPENDIX
METHODOLOGY

KEATING FIVE COVERAGE

A content analysis was performed on major news coverage of Charles Keating and Lincoln Savings story. It explored coverage by the *Wall Street Journal*, the *New York Times, American Banker*, the Associated Press, and *National Thrift News*. The analysis of 460 articles from 1986 to 1990, involving a database search for articles containing the terms "Keating" and "Lincoln Savings," measured how *National Thrift News* reporting differed from that of mainstream business publications.[1] Each article was read several times and evaluated on the basis of a codebook I developed to measure narrative characteristics, sourcing, and negative portrayal. The Keating study was divided into two time periods: before and after the April 13, 1989, bankruptcy of Lincoln's parent company and subsequent seizure by regulators.

CENTRUST COVERAGE

I conducted a content analysis of CenTrust coverage by examining *National Thrift News*, the *Wall Street Journal*, the *New York Times, American Banker*, and the *St. Petersburg Times*,[2] an influential regional newspaper that covered Cen-Trust closely. The CenTrust content analysis began on January 1, 1984, at a time when the savings-and-loan crisis was not on the national agenda, and concluded December 31, 1993, when the crisis had peaked and was beginning to fade from the public agenda. The analysis reviewed 516 articles from 1984 to 1993. The Keating and Lincoln Savings study, by contrast, had looked at the 1986–90 time period, when the crisis built and became a national news story. As a result, the review of CenTrust served as a valuable case study of media coverage of the crisis in that it covered this broader time period.

ANALYSIS AND CODING STRUCTURE AND STRATEGY

The coding and analysis was conducted using the MaxQDA content-analysis software, and Excel and Tableau were used for additional data analysis. Further insights were gained by employing the method of triangulation—analyzing the interviews against the articles, archival documents and historical record to place events in proper context. The coding and analysis also examined how the *National Thrift News* trade publication status helped or hurt its reporting.

To measure how Keating was portrayed in a positive, negative, or neutral fashion in the news articles, I conducted a textual and rhetorical analysis of how Keating was described in each article. Articles were read in their entirety three times and were given only one portrayal code, positive, negative, or neutral, even if there were multiple positive or negative references. Articles with mixed portrayals were rare, and they were not coded.

Adjectives, adverbs, and other descriptors were examined using a keyword search for "Keating." The portrayals were reviewed for the immediate context in the paragraph containing "Keating" and in the immediately preceding or following paragraphs. This approach is in keeping with Neuendorf's and Berelson's emphases on maximizing reliability and replicability by clearly defining the unit of analysis, which in this case would be the immediate or companion paragraphs.[3] Berelson, one of the giants of this field, described content analysis as an "objective, systematic and quantitative description of the manifest content of communication." It is useful for business journalism to analyze issues such as sourcing and story selection, inquiries that would help illuminate the complex relationship between business journalists and the businesses and the markets they cover. In reviewing the manifest content, this project also employed the historical method of mass communications research and a focus on evidence, interpretation, and narrative.[4]

Negative Portrayal

My typology of negative portrayal was influenced by the work of Erica Scharrer and her analysis of news coverage of Hillary Clinton's U.S. Senate campaign,[5] Jamieson, Waldman, and Sherr's content analysis of negative political advertising[6] and Margaret Cissel and her analysis of the Occupy Wall Street news coverage.[7] In my analysis, I coded an article with a negative portrayal if it described behavior that deviated from the norms of the banking industry.[8] Examples would include Keating as the subject of regulatory action or his being described as manipulating the regulatory process. A final frame involved whether Keating's reputation amounted to guilt by association.

Any ambiguity or uncertainty about a negative portrayal was coded as neutral.

Regulatory Action. Events coded under the regulatory action frame would include Keating or Paul facing regulatory enforcement actions, being under criminal investigation, references to fraud allegations against them (such as allegations of fraud, seizure of his thrift, or a freeze of his bank accounts), or descriptions of Paul in jail or going to jail, or references to a bankruptcy filing. For example, references to Keating's involvement in an expensive thrift bailout, typically described as the largest savings-and-loan rescue ever, were coded as negative. Keating's decision to file for bankruptcy in April 1989 and the regulatory seizure of Lincoln Savings were coded as negative. Other events analyzed as negative were Paul's inability to pay bills arising from legal obligations imposed by regulators. References to Paul's involvement in an expensive thrift bailout were also coded as negative.

Banking Normative Behavior Frame. Examples of negative portrayal involved descriptions of Keating, Paul, or their activities as "aggressive," "risky," "controversial," "unsafe and unsound," or "flamboyant," which would violate the normative values of bankers.[9] To establish normative behavior in the banking system, I consulted academic literature on business ethics and practices in the banking system. An analysis by Valentina Fetiniuc emphasized an industry normative value of "fostering collaboration, avoidance and resolution of external conflicts of banks," norms that Keating and CenTrust's David Paul violated with their constant litigation against regulators and industry actors.[10] Fetiniuc cited several principles of banking ethics such as the "principle of business compromise and business tolerance" so as "to harmonize conflicting interests of participants in the business process." Material describing Keating's contentious relationship with bank regulators, which said he was "clashing" or "fighting" with the Federal Home Loan Bank Board, were coded as negative. A more neutral description of Keating as "an outspoken critic" was not coded as negative. The Federal Reserve Board's *Commercial Bank Examination Manual* addressed normative behavior in a discussion of reputational risk, which "is the potential that negative publicity regarding an institution's business practices, whether true or not, will cause a decline in the customer base, costly litigation, or revenue reductions."[11] Keating's explicit attempts to manipulate the regulatory system through campaign contributions posed risks to the institutions' reputation, for example.

Because conflict resolution and avoidance were banking industry norms, instances of Paul's contentious relationship with bank regulators were coded as negative. Paul's decision to buy expensive artwork with CenTrust funds was another sort of event coded as negative. Events related to Paul's pushing the rapid growth of CenTrust were also coded as negative: to federal regulators, fast growth at a bank has "long been viewed as a potential precursor to credit quality problems."[12]

Manipulation. Examples of attempting to manipulate the political and regulatory process were coded as negative. Simple references to Keating's or Paul's political contributions were not coded as negative unless the immediate context described a manipulation of the regulatory process or showed that the contributions were excessive or somehow violated industry norms. The manipulation frame included descriptions of manipulating or attempting to manipulate the political and regulatory process. Full-text searches were conducted for the following descriptors of Keating's or Paul's activities: manipulate, control, influence, exploit, maneuver, engineer, steer, direct, rig, distort, alter, or change. One example included references to Keating offering employment to Ed Gray in order to remove the regulator from his job; the event was coded as negative because it represented Keating's attempt to manipulate the regulatory process and was a form of bribery. A simple description of Keating or Paul as "a major contributor to candidates" was not coded as negative unless the reference showed an attempt to benefit his company.

Guilt by Association. Events under the guilt-by-association frame that would prompt negative coding were portrayals containing suggestions of notoriety, such as references of someone's association to Keating or Paul as if the mere existence of a relationship was newsworthy. Such events were coded as guilt by association. For example, an article was coded as a negative portrayal when Senator Riegle returned Keating's campaign contributions or Senator Graham's returning of Paul's campaign contributions; in these case, Keating's or Paul's reputation was so negative that a politician felt compelled to return his money. Similarly, Senator William Proxmire's opposition to Federal Home Loan Bank Board Commission nominee Lee Henkel because of Henkel's association with Keating was coded as negative. The event suggests Keating was somehow politically or ethically toxic. Further, references to someone associating with Paul was coded as negative when the article described Paul's reputation running a failed thrift.

Positive Portrayal

Examples of the positive portrayal category were reporting that elevated Paul's stature and emphasized his narrative without any rebuttal or element of skepticism. Put another way, it would involve a simple summarizing of a Paul press release or statement that spoke about growth of the business without evidence of any additional outside reporting to verify whether the statement was accurate. One example was Keating's claims that his purchase of Lincoln Savings rescued the bank; there was no attempt to verify such a claim, and the article thus was coded as a positive portrayal. Another example was coverage of Keating's business plan without any mention of risks. Coverage of Paul's civic engagement, kindness, generosity, or philanthropy fell under this category as well.

Neutral Portrayal

Examples of neutral portrayal included references to Paul that did not contain value judgments about his activities or in which no such judgment was implied or suggested. His characterization as a "free-market thrift executive" was one example. Further, any event involving Keating or Paul that was not coded as either positive or negative was coded as neutral.

Story Narratives

The following seven narrative categories emerged from the study of the savings-and-loan crisis history and news coverage of the Paul episodes. Coding articles with these narratives allowed for an in-depth comparison among the four newspapers and their coverage priorities and emphasis. A single article generally was coded with one narrative, although some articles had multiple narrative codes.

Accounting. The article was coded as an accounting event if the article primarily dealt with accounting issues in the thrift industry. Accounting coverage was significant in that many of the savings-and-loan frauds were matters of illegal inflation of property values and capital reserves and similar measures. Subsequent analysis showed that inflated property values resulted in loans at far less than prevailing market rates.[13] An accounting code could overlap with a regulation code; an article coded with "accounting" primarily focused on issues such as asset valuation, whereas a regulation code could involve accounting and other issues.

Congressional oversight. An article received the congressional oversight code if the article primarily involved a congressional hearing or legislative action involving the savings-and-loan industry.

Regulation. An article received the regulation code if the article primarily described a dispute between a savings-and-loan executive and the regulator over rules to restrict investment options or demonstrated how regulatory actions had devalued loan portfolios. Regulation matters were key issues in Paul's disputes with regulators. The regulation code also captured a discussion of deregulation, a priority for the Reagan administration. The Reagan administration discussions constituted a complex narrative filled with attempts by some regulators to crack down on thrifts' egregious investments and behavior.

Thrift failure. The thrift failure code was applied to coverage of savings-and-loan failures other than Lincoln or CenTrust. The code was useful in analyzing whether a newspaper was looking at broader industry issues.

S&L industry trend. The S&L industry trend code was used for articles that primarily reported on general trends in the S&L industry; Keating or Paul were not the focus of the lead paragraphs or the story but were mentioned in the material elsewhere.

Politics. The politics code was used for articles that primarily focused on political campaigns or political issues, such as Keating or Paul's contributions to candidates.

Other. The other code was used for articles that did not fit into any of the other coding categories.

CENTRUST-SPECIFIC ISSUES

As with Keating, text and rhetoric were analyzed to measure whether CenTrust's Paul was portrayed in a positive, negative, or neutral fashion in the news coverage.[14] Negative portrayals were grouped in the same four frames as the Keating case study. The following paragraphs describe several elaborations and modifications specific to the Paul case.

BCCI. The BCCI code was applied to events of CenTrust's involvement in the international bank scandal of Bank of Credit and Commerce International, a significant investor in CenTrust.

CenTrust expansion. The CenTrust expansion code was applied to articles that emphasized CenTrust's rapid expansion, including merger announcements, new executives, and the new headquarters.

CenTrust decline. The CenTrust decline code was applied to articles that focused on the thrift's demise up to the February 3, 1990, when regulators seized it. The code would also apply to regulatory actions such as orders to suspend dividend payments, cease and desist orders, or earnings reports that emphasized losses.

Faked biography. The faked biography code was applied to articles that described Paul's faked biography.

Junk bonds. The junk bonds code was applied to articles that described risky debt financing at CenTrust.

Opulence. The opulence code was applied to articles that contained descriptions of a lavish lifestyle, including expensive art, yachts, or expensive meals.

NOTES

Introduction

1. *Savings and Loan Situation* (Washington, DC: C-SPAN, May 9, 1990), https://www
.c-span.org/video/?12225–1/savings-loan-situation&start=3369.

2. Jill Abramson and Paul Duke Jr., "The Keating Five: Senators Who Helped Lincoln
S&L Now Face Threat to Their Careers—Coming Ethics Panel Probe Holds the Greatest
Danger for Cranston, DeConcini—Grist for Comedians' Routines," *Wall Street Journal*,
December 13, 1989.

3. Nathaniel Nash and Philip Shenon, "A Man of Influence: Political Cash and Regulation—A Special Report; In Savings Debacle, Many Fingers Point Here," *New York Times*,
November 9, 1989.

4. *Lincoln Savings and Loan Assn. v. Wall*, nos. 89–1318, 89–1323 (D.D.C. August 22, 1990).

5. Dave Skidmore, "FDIC Investigating Contributions to Five Senators," Associated
Press, October 18, 1989.

6. Keating net worth: Doug Sword, "Charles Keating Aims to Take Phoenix Firm Private, Broker Says," *Cincinnati Business Courier*, January 26, 1987. $5.5 billion is the value of
Lincoln Savings assets as of December 31, 1988 (Office of Thrift Supervision, "Supervi-
sory Chronology of Lincoln Savings and Loan Association: Press Advisory," OTS 89–38
(1989), October 25, 1989, WestLaw).

7. Howard Kurtz, *Media Circus* (New York: Times Books, 1993), 56. Hunt's comments
were reflected by reviews of the media scholars. Bartholomew H. Sparrow wrote, "Most
prominent political journalists and news organizations never pulled the story together
or paid sustained attention to the deregulation and the abuse of the thrifts that was hap-

pening across the whole country" *Uncertain Guardians* (Baltimore, MD: Johns Hopkins University Press, 1999), 154.

8. Alexander Dyck and Luigi Zingales, *The Corporate Governance Role of the Media*, NBER Working Paper No. 9309 (Washington, DC: National Bureau of Economic Research, 2002), 121.

9. Dyck and Zingales, *Corporate Governance Role*, 121.

10. Kurtz, *Media Circus*, 62.

11. Kandel was unable to locate the nomination letter to the Pulitzer Prize board and there is no record of Strachan being a Pulitzer finalist. Myron Kandel, telephone interview with the author, July 13, 2015.

12. C. Ann Hollifield, "The Specialized Business Press and Industry-Related Political Communication: A Comparative Study," *Journalism and Mass Communication Quarterly* 74, no. 4 (1997): 757–72.

13. Matt Kinsman, "B2B Media & Information Industry Up 2.7% to $28.35 Billion in 2015," July 18, 2016 (Washington, DC: Software and Information Industry Association), http://www.siia.net/blog/index/Post/67710/B2B-Media-Information-Industry-Up -2-7-to-28-35-Billion-in-2015.

14. Pew Research Center, "State of the News Media, 2017," August 7, 2017,

15. Kathleen Endres, "Research Review: The Specialized Business Press" *Electronic Journal of Communication* 4, nos. 2–4 (1994), http://www.cios.org/EJCPUBLIC/ 004/2/004211.html.

16. Mike Fabey (former *Aviation Week* reporter), telephone interview with the author, January 31, 2018.

17. Fabey interview. Fabey, "Ship Shape: Investigation Finds Major Flaws in New Navy Ships," *IRE Journal*, fall 2013, 12–16.

18. Fabey interview.

19. Timothy White Award, https://www.siia.net/neals/Leadership-Awards/Tim-White -Award.

20. Maryfran Johnson, telephone interview with the author, February 5, 2018.

21. Paul Starr, *The Creation of the Media: Political Origins of Modern Communications* (New York: Perseus, 2004).

22. National Commission on Financial Institution Reform, Recovery and Enforcement, *Origins and Causes of the S&L Debacle: A Blueprint for Reform* (Washington, DC: National Commission on Financial Institution Reform, 1993), 10.

23. Howard Carswell, "Business News Coverage," *Public Opinion Quarterly* 2, no. 4 (1938): 613–21.

24. Financial Crisis Inquiry Commission, *The Financial Crisis Inquiry Report, Authorized Edition: Final Report of the National Commission on the Causes of the Financial and Economic Crisis in the United States* (New York: PublicAffairs, 2011).

25. Carswell, "Business News Coverage"; Gillian Doyle, "Financial News Journalism A Post-Enron Analysis of Approaches towards Economic and Financial News Production in the UK," *Journalism* 7, no. 4 (November 1, 2006): 433–52; Robert McChesney, "The Prob-

lem of Journalism: A Political Economic Contribution to an Explanation of the Crisis in Contemporary US Journalism," *Journalism Studies* 4, no. 3 (2003): 299–329; Dean Starkman, *The Watchdog That Didn't Bark: The Financial Crisis and the Disappearance of Investigative Journalism* (New York: Columbia Journalism Review Books, 2014); Francis X. Dealy, *The Power and the Money: Inside the "Wall Street Journal"* (Secaucus, NJ: Carol, 1993).

26. Justin Lewis and Andrew Williams. "A Compromised Fourth Estate? UK News Journalism, Public Relations and News Sources," *Journalism Studies* 9, no. 1 (2008), 17.

27. Lewis and Williams, "Compromised Fourth Estate?" 17.

28. Keith J. Butterick, *Complacency and Collusion: A Critical Introduction to Business and Financial Journalism* (London: Pluto, 2015), 126.

29. Geneva Overholser, "Journalists and the Corporate Scandals: What Happened to the Watchdog?" in *Restoring Trust in American Business*, ed. Jay W. Lorsch, Leslie Berlowitz, and Andy Zelleke (Cambridge, MA: MIT Press, 2004), 145–55; Nikki Usher, *Making News at the "New York Times"* (Ann Arbor: University of Michigan Press, 2014).

30. Julien Elfenbein, *Business Journalism* (New York: Greenwood, 1969); John Quirt, *The Press and the World of Money: How the News Media Cover Business and Finance, Panic and Prosperity, and the Pursuit of the American Dream* (Byron, CA: Anton/California-Courier, 1993).

31. Michael Palmer, Oliver Boyd-Barrett, and Terhi Rantanen, "Global Financial News," in *The Globalization of News*, ed. Oliver Boyd-Barrett and Terhi Rantanen (London: Sage, 1998), 61.

32. Wayne Parsons, *The Power of the Financial Press* (New Brunswick, NJ: Rutgers University Press, 1990), 1.

33. Gerald F. Davis, *Managed by the Markets: How Finance Reshaped America* (New York: Oxford University Press, 2009).

34. Hyman P. Minsky, "The Financial Instability Hypothesis: A Restatement," in *Can "It" Happen Again?* (New York: M. E. Sharpe, 1982).

35. Gregory Miller, "The Press as a Watchdog for Accounting Fraud," *Journal of Accounting Research* 44, no. 5 (December 1, 2006): 1001–33.

36. Diana Henriques, "What Journalists Should Be Doing about Business Coverage—but Aren't," *Harvard International Journal of Press/Politics* 5, no. 2 (Spring 2000): 119.

37. Matt Murray, "Tweet by @murraymatt," *Twitter*, June 15, 2018, https://twitter.com/murraymatt/status/1007800503693135872.

38. Stephen Kleege, telephone interview with the author, June 15, 2015.

39. Eugene Carlson, "An Industry Remembers Stan Strachan," *National Mortgage News*, January 20, 1997, 3.

40. Randy Martin, *Financialization of Daily Life* (Philadelphia: Temple University Press, 2002), 12.

41. The term *spike* is a journalistic term for killing a story. Stephen P. Pizzo, telephone interview with the author, December 8, 2014.

42. Kathleen Endres, "Ownership and Employment in the Specialized Business Press," *Journalism Quarterly* 65 (Winter 1988): 997.

43. Damian Tambini, *What Is Financial Journalism For? Ethics and Responsibility in a Time of Crisis and Change* (London: Polis Media, 2008), 24.

44. Judith Stein's *Pivotal Decade* and Henry Kaufman's *On Money and Markets* were especially influential in elucidating the context for the upheaval in the U.S. economy and the growth of the U.S. bond and financial markets from the 1970s on. See Judith Stein, *Pivotal Decade: How the United States Traded Factories for Finance in the 1970s* (New Haven, CT: Yale University Press, 2010); Henry Kaufman, *On Money and Markets: A Wall Street Memoir* (New York: McGraw-Hill, 2000).

45. Douglas Galbi, "U.S. Advertising Expenditure Data," *Purple Motes*, September 14, 2008, http://www.purplemotes.net/2008/09/14/us-advertising-expenditure-data/.

46. Daniel Boorstin, *The Americans: The National Experience*, 2nd ed. (Scranton, PA: Random House, 1966), 296.

47. Donald J. Trump with Tony Schwartz, *Trump: The Art of the Deal* (New York: Random House, 1987).

48. Society of Professional Journalists, *SPJ Code of Ethics* (Indianapolis, IN: Society of Professional Journalists), revised September 6, 2014, http://www.spj.org/ethicscode.asp.

49. Aristotle, *Rhetoric*, ed. W. Rhys Roberts (New York: Modern Library, 1984), 165.

50. W. Lance Bennett, *News: The Politics of Illusion*, 10th ed. (Chicago: University of Chicago Press, 2015), 15.

51. W. Lance Bennett, "Toward a Theory of Press-State Relations in the United States," *Journal of Communication* 40, no. 2 (June 1990): 116, https://doi.org/10.1111/j.1460-2466.1990.tb02265.x.

52. Bennett, *News*, 17.

53. Bennett, *News*, 15.

54. Dave Skidmore, "Hearings 'Just the Beginning' of S&L Probe," Associated Press, December 6, 1989.

55. "Investigation of Lincoln Savings & Loan Association Hearing Transcript," Pub. L. No. 101–59, Part 2, Hearing before the H. Select Committee on Banking, Finance, and Urban Affairs, 101st Cong. 101–59 (1989), https://hdl.handle.net/2027/pur1.32754074124128.1134–44.

56. Stephen Kleege, "Keating Next House Witness: Wall 'Caved In' on Lincoln Action," *National Mortgage News*, November 6, 1989, 1.

57. Jim Upchurch, "Confidential Memorandum to Charles Keating Re Prudential Capital Markets Amcor Loan Denial," January 27, 1988, box XB-627, FHLBB Litigation, American Continental Corporation Records circa 1971–1993 (hereafter, ACC records), Greater Arizona Collection, Arizona State University Library, Tempe, Arizona; Judy J. Wischer, "American Continental Corp Memo on First Interstate, FHLB Exam to Keating and Kielty," April 25, 1988, box XB-627, FHLBB Litigation, ACC records.

58. *Lincoln v. Wall*, 25.

59. Gail Tabor, "No Man Is an Island, Even in Lovely Hawaii," *Arizona Republic*, September 17, 1986.

60. MWL to Robert Kielty, March 20, 1980, ACC records.

61. "Trump Clock.com," revised October 1, 2018, http://www.trump-clock.com/.

62. Charles J. Harder to Michael Wolff, January 4, 2018, https://apps.washingtonpost .com/g/documents/politics/read-trump-lawyers-letter-to-michael-wolff-and-steve -rubin/2695/.

63. Jake Flanagin, "Donald Trump's Support of Hillary in 2008 Reflects His History of Changing Parties," *Quartz*, March 3, 2016, https://qz.com/631148/donald-trumps -support-of-hillary-in-2008-reflects-his-erratic-politics/.

64. Charles H. Keating Jr., "Statement by Charles H. Keating Jr.," April 17, 1989, Series V: Other Corporate Records (accession #1994–01435C), Sub-series A: General, ACC records.

65. Maha Rafi Atal, "The Cultural and Economic Power of Advertisers in the Business Press," *Journalism* 19, no. 8 (September 13, 2017): 1079–95, https://doi.org/10.1177/ 1464884917725162.

66. James T. Hamilton, *Democracy's Detectives: The Economics of Investigative Journalism* (Cambridge, MA: Harvard University Press, 2016), 9.

67. Steven Waldman, and Charles Sennott, "The 'New Business Model': Non-profit Journalism," *Report for America*, May 7, 2018, https://www.reportforamerica.org/ blog/2018/5/7/the-new-business-model-non-profit-journalism.

68. David Protess, *The Journalism of Outrage: Investigative Reporting and Agenda Building in America* (New York: Guilford, 1991), 4.

69. Michael Hudson, email correspondence with the author, August 2012.

70. Fabey interview.

Chapter 1. The Reporter and His Industry

1. Hillary Wilson, telephone interview with the author, June 23, 2015.

2. Certified copy of an Entry of Birth, Stanley Kenneth Strachan, 20 August 1938 (General Register Office of England, January 20, 1992), in possession of the author.

3. Wilson expressed skepticism about the story but said her aunt claimed it was true.

4. *Where Was the Press during the S&L Crisis?* (Washington, DC: C-SPAN, May 1, 1989), http://www.c-span.org/video/?7307–1/press-sl-crisis, video, 121 min.

5. Wilson interview.

6. Mark Fogarty, telephone interview with the author, October 24, 2014.

7. Paul Muolo, telephone interview with the author, December 8, 2014.

8. Paul Muolo, telephone interview with the author, October 19, 2014.

9. Brad Henderson, "A Newspaper Changing Along with the Industry," in *The American Banker: 150th Anniversary* (New York: American Banker, 1986), 8.

10. Phil Roosevelt, "Letter to Tobyann and Hillary Strachan," January 13, 1997, in possession of the author.

11. Al Daly, "Remembering Stan Strachan," speech given at the New York Financial Writers' Association Annual Awards Dinner, May 6, 1997, New York, N.Y.

12. Strachan developed a strong dislike for the *American Banker* and considered it an archrival for much of the rest of his career, according to Muolo and others (Muolo, October 19 interview).

13. Poem in personal records of Hillary Strachan, Virginia Beach, Va.

14. "Proposed New Publication for the Savings and Loan Industry," April 1975, Exhibit 6–2, *Rollo v. Glynn* (N.Y. Sup. Ct., #20079/82).

15. "Proposed New Publication."

16. Glynn, Lindow, and Strachan *affs.*, August 11, 1982, in *Rollo v. Glynn*, 12.

17. Mark Fogarty, "Keeping a Careful Eye on the Mortgage Industry," *National Mortgage News*, December 20, 1999.

18. The first edition of *National Thrift News* apparently is lost. The October 14, 1976, issue is the first issue on file in the SourceMedia offices.

19. Rollo lost a federal lawsuit in 1982 and a related state case in New York State Supreme Court in June 1990: *Rollo v. Glynn et al.*, 79 Civ. 2596 (WK) (D.D.N.Y. 1982), Lexis 17724; Fed. Sec. L. Rep. (CCH) P98,650. A decision was issued March 30, 1982. State case: *Rollo v. Glynn*, 162 A.D.2d 145 (N.Y.A.D. 1 Dept., June 7, 1990).

20. Robert Gehlmeyer, "Memo to John Glynn," December 13, 1978, exhibit in *Rollo v. Glynn*.

21. Muolo, October 19 interview.

22. *Rollo v. Glynn*.

23. Lewis Ranieri, telephone interview with the author, August 12, 2015.

24. Stephen Kleege, telephone interview with the author, June 15, 2015.

25. David Mason, "Savings and Loan Industry (U.S.)," *EH.Net Encyclopedia*, ed. Robert Whaples (University of Wisconsin—La Crosse, Department of Economics, Economic History Association, 2003), http://eh.net/encyclopedia/savings-and-loan-industry-u-s/.

26. National Commission on Financial Institution Reform, Recovery, and Enforcement, *Origins and Causes of the S&L Debacle: A Blueprint for Reform*, report to the President and Congress of the United States (Washington, DC: National Commission on Financial Institution Reform, Recovery, and Enforcement, July 1993), 1.

27. National Commission, *Origins and Causes*, 20.

28. Timothy Curry and Lynn Shibut, "The Cost of the Savings and Loan Crisis: Truth and Consequences," *FDIC Banking Review* 13, no. 2 (2000): 26–36.

29. David Hollanders, "The Reception of the Financial Crisis in Hollywood Movies," in *Moneylab: Overcoming the Hype*, 115–20 (Amsterdam: Institute of Network Cultures, 2018).

30. Kenneth J. Robinson, "Savings and Loan Crisis: 1980–1989" (Federal Reserve History, November 22, 2013), http://www.federalreservehistory.org/Events/DetailView/42).

31. National Commission, *Origins and Causes*, 7.

32. Clyde Farnsworth, "Aid Studied for Savings Industry," *New York Times*, March 6, 1981; Larry Martz, "S&Ls: Blaming the Media," *Newsweek*, June 25, 1990, 42.

33. William Black, *The Best Way to Rob a Bank Is to Own One* (Austin: University of Texas Press, 2005), 19.

34. Hyman P. Minsky, "'The Financial Instability Hypothesis: A Restatement,'" in *Can "It" Happen Again?*, 59–70 (New York: M. E. Sharpe, 1982); John Cassidy, *How Markets Fail: The Logic of Economic Calamities* (New York: Macmillan, 2009).

35. National Commission, *Origins and Causes*; Financial Crisis Inquiry Commission, *Final Report of the National Commission on the Causes of the Financial and Economic Crisis in the United States* (New York: PublicAffairs, 2011).

36. John Liscio, "Anatomy of a Mess—the True Villains behind the S&L Crisis," *Barron's*, February 27, 1989, 14.

37. This is the total amount of debt owed by households, government agencies, nonprofit organizations, or any company not in the financial sector.

38. Henry Kaufman, *On Money and Markets: A Wall Street Memoir* (New York: McGraw-Hill, 2000).

39. The 1987 stock-market crash did not result in a recession. A recession began in July 1990 and ended in March 1991 (Business Cycle Dating Committee, National Bureau of Economic Research, "US Business Cycle Expansions and Contractions," *US Business Cycle Expansions and Contractions* [Cambridge, MA: National Bureau of Economic Research, September 20, 2010], https://www.nber.org/cycles/sept2010.pdf). See also Charles R. Geisst, *Wall Street: A History* (Oxford: Oxford University Press, 2012), 332.

40. George Anders, *Merchants of Debt : KKR and the Mortgaging of American Business* (New York: BasicBooks, 1992), xiv.

41. One of Strachan's closest friends and sources was Lewis Ranieri, a former vice chairman of Salomon Brothers, who is credited with inventing the mortgage-backed bond (Michael McKee, "Lewis S. Ranieri: Your Mortgage Was His Bond," *BusinessWeek*, November 28, 2004).

42. Brian Mooney and Barry Simpson, *Breaking News: How the Wheels Came off at Reuters* (London: Capstone, 2003), 10.

43. Peter Kjaer and Tore Slaatta, *Mediating Business: The Expansion of Business Journalism* (Copenhagen: Copenhagen Business School Press, 2007), 20.

44. Mooney and Simpson, *Breaking News*, 13.

45. Wayne Parsons, *The Power of the Financial Press* (New Brunswick, NJ: Rutgers University Press, 1990), 204.

46. Robinson, "Savings and Loan Crisis."

47. Paul Muolo, "'S&L Hell' an '80s Low-Water Mark," *National Mortgage News*, December 20, 1999.

48. Bartlett Naylor, "Gray Says S&L Tried to Hire Him Away; Institution Often at Odds with Regulator Made Offer," *American Banker*, October 7, 1986. The regulators' failure to review Keating's background emerged in the November 1989 congressional hearings. A Federal Home Loan Bank Board official, Alvin Smuzynski, who handled Keating's application to buy Lincoln Savings, said he didn't know about the SEC's case against Keating. Brooks Jackson, "Sleeping Watchdog: How Regulatory Error Led to the Disaster at Lincoln Savings—Charles Keating Had History of Alleged Abuse but Still Was Allowed to Run S&L—Five Senators in His Camp," *Wall Street Journal*, November 20, 1989.

49. Stephen Pizzo, Mary Fricker, and Paul Muolo, *Inside Job: The Looting of America's Savings and Loans* (New York: McGraw-Hill, 1989).

50. By 1980, there were more savings and loans than banks (Federal Deposit Insurance Corporation, "Bank Data & Statistics," accessed April 27, 2016, https://www.fdic.gov/bank/statistical/).

51. James O'Shea, *Daisy Chain—The Tale of Big Bad Don Dixon and the Looting of a Texas S&L* (New York: Pocket Books, 1991).

52. National Commission, *Origins and Causes*, 7.

53. John Cassidy, *How Markets Fail: The Logic of Economic Calamities* (New York: Macmillan, 2009).

54. Curry and Shibut, "Cost of the Savings and Loan Crisis," 2000.

55. John J. McCusker, "The Demise of Distance: The Business Press and the Origins of the Information Revolution in the Early Modern Atlantic World," *American Historical Review* 110, no. 2 (April 1, 2005): 295–321. McCusker's assertion about the origins of business journalism is disputed. I chose McCusker's version because it contained the most thorough research and clear documentation. The competing versions include Jesse Neal, a leading trade press editor, who argued that Adam Smith's *Wealth of Nations* in 1776 "was the real beginning of business press history" (Jesse H. Neal, "A Review of Business Paper History," *N. W. Ayer and Son Annual and Directory* [Philadelphia: N. W. Ayer and Son, 1922]). Mitchell Stephens wrote that business journalism can trace its origins back to 1568 and the House of Fugger, led by German financier Philip Eduard Fugger, who produced a series of newsletters involving business and economic matters. Mitchell Stephens, *A History of News*, 3rd ed. (New York: Oxford University Press, 2006), 66.

56. David P. Forsyth, *The Business Press in America* (Philadelphia: Chilton, 1964), 20.

57. Dean Starkman, *The Watchdog That Didn't Bark: The Financial Crisis and the Disappearance of Investigative Journalism* (New York: Columbia Journalism Review Books, 2014).

58. McCusker, "Demise of Distance," 303.

59. Michael Palmer, Oliver Boyd-Barrett, and Terhi Rantanen, "Global Financial News," in *The Globalization of News*, ed. Oliver Boyd-Barrett and Terhi Rantanen (London: Sage, 1998), 61.

60. Parsons, *Power of the Financial Press*, 41.

61. Daniel Boorstin, *The Americans: The National Experience*, 2nd ed. (Scranton, PA: Random House, 1966), 125.

62. The managerial capitalism phase is a break from a financial capitalism model that dominates the later nineteenth century, one that put banks and financial intermediaries in the center of the economy. Financial capitalism focused on financial returns for shareholders and corporate investment performance (Gerald F. Davis, *Managed by the Markets: How Finance Reshaped America* [New York: Oxford University Press, 2009]).

63. *Rollo v. Glynn* (D.D.N.Y., May 16, 1980) (Deposition of Wesley Lindow), 5.

64. Kathleen Day, *S & L Hell: The People and the Politics behind the $1 Trillion Savings and Loan Scandal* (New York: W. W. Norton, 1993), 278.

65. Ranieri interview.

66. Stephen P. Pizzo, telephone interview with the author, December 8, 2014.

67. Lew Sichelman, telephone interview with the author, June 15, 2015.

68. "Hip Hip Hoorah," *National Thrift News*, January 3, 1980.

69. May Belle Flynn, "The Development of Business Papers in the United States," PhD diss., Graduate School of Business Administration, New York University, 1944.

70. Janet Laib, "The Trade Press," *Public Opinion Quarterly* 19, no. 1 (1955): 31–44. Poor's name lives on as one-half of Standard and Poor's Corporation. Poor's work also presaged the data-gathering operations of the trade press and business information companies, such as Standard & Poor's and Bloomberg. "Poor compiled running histories of no fewer than 120 different railroad companies—plus a great mass of statistical and organizational data on other firms" (Thomas K. McCraw, "The Challenge of Alfred D. Chandler, Jr.: Retrospect and Prospect," *Reviews in American History* 15 [March 1987]: 160–78). See also Alfred D. Chandler, *Henry Varnum Poor* (Cambridge, MA: Harvard University Press, 1956); Chris Roush, *Profits and Losses: Business Journalism and Its Role in Society* (Portland, OR: Marion Street, 2006).

71. McCraw, " Challenge of Alfred D. Chandler."

72. Roland B. Smith, "The Genesis of the Business Press in the United States," *Journal of Marketing* 19 (October 1954): 146–51.

73. Julien Elfenbein, *Business Journalism* (New York: Greenwood, 1969); Laib, "Trade Press"; Kathleen Endres, "Ownership and Employment in the Specialized Business Press," *Journalism Quarterly* 65 (Winter 1988): 996–98.

74. Roush, *Profits and Losses*.

75. Don Gussow, *The New Business Journalism: An Insider's Look at the Workings of America's Business Press* (San Diego, CA: Harcourt Brace Jovanovich, 1984).

76. Jesse H. Neal, "A Review of Business Paper History," *N. W. Ayer and Son's American Newspaper Annual and Directory* (Philadephia: N. W. Ayer and Son, 1922), 1: 1245.

77. Jack Lule, *Daily News, Eternal Stories: The Mythological Role of Journalism* (New York: Guilford, 2001).

78. Parsons, *Power of the Financial Press*, 40.

79. Peter Kjaer and Tore Slaatta, *Mediating Business: The Expansion of Business Journalism* (Copenhagen: Copenhagen Business School Press DK, 2007), 160.

80. "The First Reporter: 'Dear Friends, I Have a Wonderful Story to Tell You . . . '" *NOVA Science Programming on Air and Online*, PBS, September 2003, http://www.pbs.org/wgbh/nova/wright/reporter.html. Thanks to Doug Cumming, Washington and Lee University, for this tip.

81. Parsons, *Power of the Financial Press*; James Ross, "When Trades Lead the Pack," *Columbia Journalism Review*, November 1990, 18.

82. Ben H. Bagdikian, *The New Media*, rev. ed. (Boston: Beacon, 2004), 160.

83. John Quirt, *The Press and the World of Money: How the News Media Cover Business and Finance, Panic and Prosperity, and the Pursuit of the American Dream* (Byron, CA: Anton/California-Courier, 1993), 40.

84. Tracy L. Lucht, "Sylvia Porter: Gender, Ambition, and Personal Finance Journalism, 1935–1975," PhD diss., University of Maryland, 2007, 1.

85. Quirt, *Press and the World of Money*.

86. Bagdikian, *New Media*, 107.

87. "Causes That Produced the Crisis of 1857 Considered," *Hunt's Merchant's Magazine and Commercial Review* 40, no. 1 (January 1859): 19–38.

88. Roush, *Profits and Losses*, 65.

89. "Code of Conduct" (New York: Dow Jones and Company), accessed January 30, 2019, https://www.dowjones.com/code-conduct/; "SABEW's Code of Ethics," *Society of American Business Editors and Writers*.

90. Quirt, *Press and the World of Money*, 39.

91. John Kenneth Galbraith, *The Great Crash, 1929* (Boston: Houghton Mifflin, 1972), 73.

92. *Stock Exchange Practices*, Hearings on S. Res. 84 before the S. Select Comm. on Banking and Currency, 72nd Cong., 1st Sess. (1932), 603–4, https://fraser.stlouisfed.org/scribd/?item_id=33978&filepath=/docs/publications/sensep/sensep_1_pt02.pdf#scribd-open.

93. Maury Klein, *Rainbow's End : The Crash of 1929* (Oxford: Oxford University Press, 2001), 151.

94. Quirt, *Press and the World of Money*, 39.

95. Timothy W. Hubbard, "The Explosive Demand for Business News," *Journalism Quarterly* 43, no. 4 (Winter 1966), 706, https://doi.org/10.1177/107769906604300410.

96. Ernest C. Hynds, "Business Coverage Is Getting Better," *Journalism Quarterly* 57, no. 2 (Summer 1980): 297–368.

97. S. Prakash Sethi, "The Schism between Business and American News Media," *Journalism Quarterly* 54, no. 2 (1977): 247.

98. Peter Drier, "The Corporate Complaint against the Media," in *American Media and Mass Culture, Left Perspectives*, ed. Donald Lazere (Berkeley: University of California Press, 1987), 65.

99. "Where Was the Press?"

100. Quirt, *Press and the World of Money*, 151.

101. Mark Fogarty, "Stan Strachan, a Poet of the Deadline," *National Mortgage News*, January 9, 1997, 1.

102. Debra Cope, telephone interview with the author, October 17, 2014.

103. *Rollo v. Glynn* (D.D.N.Y., May 16, 1980) (Deposition of Irwin Huebsch).

104. Fogarty interview.

105. James L. Aucoin, *The Evolution of American Investigative Journalism* (Columbia: University of Missouri Press, 2005), 206.

106. Fogarty interview.

107. Sichelman interview.

108. Geisst, *Wall Street*, 345.

109. A recession began in July 1990 and ended in March 1991 (National Bureau of Economic Research, "US Business Cycle"). See also Geisst, *Wall Street*, 332.

110. Kleege interview.

111. Muolo, October 19 interview.

112. Fogarty, "Careful Eye," 3.

113. Flynn, "Development of Business Papers," 170.

114. Fogarty, "Careful Eye," 3.

115. Muolo, December 8 interview.

116. Ross, "When Trades Lead"; Martz, "S&Ls"; Kathleen Quinn, "As S&Ls Sink, a Trade Weekly Is Soaring," *New York Times*, August 27, 1990.

117. Text of Polk Award program, in possession of the author. Document is undated, believed to be 1989.

118. American History of Business Journalism, Loeb Award Winners 1958–1996, accessed February 24, 2013, https://ahbj.sabew.org/awards/03302013loeb-award-winners-1958–1971/.

119. The trade publications that won Polk Awards prior to the *National Thrift News* award were *Sponsor Magazine*, 1951; *New England Journal of Medicine*, 1977; *Chronicle of Higher Education*, 1978; *American Banker*, 1982; *Chemical and Engineering News*, 1984; *Science News*, 1987. Brookville, New York: Long Island University, George Polk Awards, accessed January 30, 2019, http://liu.edu/George-Polk-Awards/Past-Winners.

120. The Stan Strachan Scholarship dates to at least 1997, when it was mentioned in an NYFWA awards program. "New York Financial Writers' Association Inc. Annual Awards Dinner," May 6, 1997, New York City (Britt Tunick, executive manager, New York Financial Writers' Association, email to the author, April 20, 2016).

121. Quinn, "As S&Ls Sink," D8.

122. Martin E. Lowy, *High Rollers: Inside the Savings and Loan Debacle* (New York: Praeger, 1991), 207.

123. Stanley Strachan, "Looking Back over 20 Years," *National Mortgage News*, October 7, 1996, 33.

124. Kandel was unable to locate the nomination letter to the Pulitzer Prize board and there is no record of Strachan being a Pulitzer finalist (Myron Kandel, telephone interview with the author, July 13, 2015).

125. The Faulkner and Gray transaction put *National Mortgage News* under the same corporate umbrella as its longtime rival, the *American Banker* newspaper; terms of the sale were not released. Thomson later was sold in 2000 to Investcorp and renamed Source-Media. The publication, now online only, has seen steady declines in staffing and circulation. In the 1985, circulation was 15,863; by 2014, circulation had fallen to eight thousand, according to Standard Rate and Data Service (Standard Rate and Data Service, "SRDS Business Publication Advertising Source," 1995. Subscription data from Standard Rate and Data Service directories, 1976–1998, bound volumes in the Library of Congress, https://lccn.loc.gov/sv93024949).

126. Aleksanders Rozens, "Letter to Tobyann and Hillary Strachan," 1997, in possession of the author.

127. David Maxwell, "Letter to Tobyann and Hillary Strachan," January 14, 1997, in possession of the author.

Chapter 2. The Enforcers

1. Stephen Kleege, telephone interview with the author, July 12, 2018.

2. Kleege interview.

3. Ida M. Tarbell, "The History of The Standard Oil Company," *McClure's Magazine*, November 1902; Bethany McLean, *The Smartest Guys in the Room: The Amazing Rise and Scandalous Fall of Enron [. . .]* (New York: Penguin, 2004); Gillian Tett, *Fool's Gold : How the Bold Dream of a Small Tribe at J. P. Morgan Was Corrupted by Wall Street Greed and Unleashed a Catastrophe* (New York: Free Press, 2009).

4. Paul Muolo, email to the author, December 8, 2014.

5. C. W. Anderson, Leonard Downie Jr., and Michael Schudson, *The News Media: What Everyone Needs to Know* (New York: Oxford University Press, 2016).

6. Stephen J. A. Ward, "Journalism Ethics," in *The Handbook of Journalism Studies*, ed. Karin Wahl-Jorgensen and Thomas Hanitzsch (New York: Routledge, 2009), 297.

7. See Immanuel Kant, "Perpetual Peace," in *Kant: Political Writings*, ed. Hans S. Reiss, trans. H. B. Nisbet, 93–130 (Cambridge: Cambridge University Press, 2010); Jeremy Bentham, *The Works of Jeremy Bentham*, ed. John Bowring (Edinburgh: W. Tait, 2007), 279. See also Cynthia Mitchell, "Checking Financial Power: Newspaper Coverage of the New York Stock Exchange's Bid to Control the Ticker, June 1889," *American Journalism* 27, no. 1 (2010): 37–65.

8. Slavko Splichal, *Public Opinion* (Lanham, MD: Rowman and Littlefield, 1999), 21.

9. See James Madison, *The Writings of James Madison*, ed. Gaillard Hunt (Chicago: University of Chicago Press, 1900); Burke reference is in Thomas Carlyle, "Lecture V: The Hero as a Man of Letters. Johnson, Rousseau, Burns," in *Sartor Resartus, and On Heroes, Hero-Worship, and the Heroic in History* (New York: E. P. Dutton, 1908), 392.

10. Colleges and universities advanced the notion of the professional journalist by offering journalism courses, beginning in 1878 at the University of Missouri. Washington and Lee University in Lexington, Virginia, began offering printing courses, which encompassed journalism, in the late 1860s. These courses were not continually offered, unlike those at the University of Missouri, which has had a continuous journalism program since 1878.

11. Fred Seaton Siebert, *Four Theories of the Press: The Authoritarian, Libertarian, Social Responsibility, and Soviet Communist Concepts of What the Press Should Be and Do* (Champaign: University of Illinois Press, 1956), 74.

12. The professionalism movement continued in 1923. The American Society of Newspaper Editors, founded in 1923, drafted a code of ethics called the "canons of journalism." Journalism colleges and press clubs were founded to reinforce a professional identity (Daniel Hallin, "Field Theory, Differentiation Theory and Comparative Media Research," in *Bourdieu and the Journalistic Field*, ed. Rodney Benson, 224–43 [Cambridge, UK: Polity, 2005]).

13. Julien Elfenbein, *Business Paper Publishing Practice* (New York: Harper and Brothers, 1952).

14. U.S. Postal Rate Commission, "Report of the Postal Commission: Authorized by Congress to Make Inquiry Regarding Second-Class Mail Matter," 59th Cong., 2nd Sess., H.R. Doc. No. 608 (Washington, DC: U.S. Government Printing Office, 1907).

15. Much of the SABEW Code of Ethics warns against advertising and investment conflicts of interest, such as "Regardless of news platform, there should be a clear delineation between advertising and editorial content" and "Promising a story in exchange for advertising or other considerations is unethical."

16. Sack is a former chief accountant in the Enforcement Division. The study found about half the leads come from reviews of financial statements and about one-third from the financial press (Ehsan H. Feroz, Kyungjoo Park, and Victor S. Pastena, "The Financial and Market Effects of the SEC's Accounting and Auditing Enforcement Releases," *Journal of Accounting Research* 29 [1991]: 111).

17. Alexander Dyck and Luigi Zingales, *The Corporate Governance Role of the Media*, NBER Working Paper 9309 (Washington, DC: National Bureau of Economic Research, 2002), 6.

18. Craig Carroll, *Corporate Reputation and the News Media: Agenda-Setting within Business News Coverage in Developed, Emerging, and Frontier Markets* (New York: Routledge, 2010).

19. Mike Fabey, telephone interview with the author, January 31, 2018.

20. Fabey interview.

21. James T. Hamilton, *Democracy's Detectives: The Economics of Investigative Journalism* (Cambridge, MA: Harvard University Press, 2016), 10.

22. Hamilton, *Democracy's Detectives*, 10.

23. Barack Obama, *The Audacity of Hope* (New York: Random House, 2006), 14.

24. Philip Patterson and Lee Wilkins, "An Introduction to Ethical Decision Making," in *Media Ethics*, 6th ed., 1–18 (New York: McGraw-Hill, 2008).

25. Fred Miller, "Aristotle's Political Theory," *Stanford Encyclopedia of Philosophy*, ed. Edward N. Zalta (Palo Alto, CA: Stanford University, 2017), https://plato.stanford.edu/archives/win2017/entries/aristotle-politics/.

26. Stephen J. A. Ward, "Journalism Ethics," in *The Handbook of Journalism Studies*, ed. Karin Wahl-Jorgensen and Thomas Hanitzsch, 295–313 (New York: Routledge, 2009).

27. Patterson and Wilkins, "Introduction to Ethical Decision Making," 16.

28. Clifford Christians, John Ferre, and Mark Fackler, *Good News: Social Ethics and the Press* (New York: Oxford University Press, 1993), as cited by Patterson and Wilkins, "Ethical Decision Making," 188.

29. Amitai Etzioni, "Communitarianism," in *Encyclopedia of Political Science*, ed. Bertrand Badie, Dirk Berg-Schlosser, and Leonardo Morlino (Thousand Oaks, CA: Sage, 2011), 326.

30. Etzioni, "Communitarianism," 327.

31. James L. Aucoin, *The Evolution of American Investigative Journalism* (Columbia: University of Missouri Press, 2005).

32. David Protess, *The Journalism of Outrage: Investigative Reporting and Agenda Building in America* (New York: Guilford, 1991), 36.

33. George P. Baker, and George David Smith, *The New Financial Capitalists: Kohlberg Kravis Roberts and the Creation of Corporate Value* (New York: Cambridge University Press, 1998).

34. Chris Roush, *Profits and Losses: Business Journalism and Its Role in Society* (Portland, OR: Marion Street, 2006), 40.

35. Ida M. Tarbell, *The History of the Standard Oil Company* (Gloucester, MA: Smith, 1963).

36. Morton Keller, "The Pluralist State: American Economic Regulation in Comparative Perspective, 1900–1930," in *Regulation in Perspective*, ed. Thomas K. McCraw (Cambridge, MA: Harvard University Press, 1981), 65.

37. David Protess, *Journalism of Outrage*, 15.

38. Ron Chernow, *The House of Morgan : An American Banking Dynasty and the Rise of Modern Finance* (New York: Atlantic Monthly Press, 1990), 151. As early as 1887, General Electric and Westinghouse hired publicity agents to promote their businesses, according to Roush, *Profits and Losses*, 43.

39. Michael Schudson, *The Sociology of News* (New York: W. W. Norton, 2011), 134.

40. Protess, *Journalism of Outrage*, 43.

41. W. Lance Bennett, "Toward a Theory of Press-State Relations in the United States," *Journal of Communication* 40, no. 2 (June 1990): 103–27, https://doi.org/10.1111/j.1460-2466.1990.tb02265.x.

42. Mark Feldstein, "A Muckraking Model: Investigative Reporting Cycles in American History," *Press/Politics* 11, no. 2 (2006): 1–16.

43. Aucoin, *Evolution*, 18.

44. David H. Weaver and LeAnne Daniels. "Public Opinion on Investigative Reporting in the 1980s," *Journalism Quarterly* 69, no. 1 (1992): 150.

45. Roger Burlingame, *Endless Frontiers: The Story of McGraw-Hill* (New York: McGraw-Hill, 1959), 129.

46. Aucoin, *Evolution*.

47. Gerry Lanosga, "New Views of Investigative Reporting in the Twentieth Century," *American Journalism* 31, no. 4 (2014): 490–506.

48. Marc Poitras and Daniel Sutter, "Advertiser Pressure and Control of the News: The Decline of Muckraking Revisited," *Journal of Economic Behavior and Organization* 72, no. 3 (December 2009): 945.

49. Keith J. Butterick, *Complacency and Collusion: A Critical Introduction to Business and Financial Journalism* (London: Pluto, 2015), xii.

50. Elfenbein, *Business Paper*, 326.

51. Dyck and Zingales, *Corporate Governance Role*, 4.

52. Bill Dedman, "The Color of Money," *Atlanta Journal-Constitution*, May 1, 1988. The article received a Pulitzer Prize in 1989: https://www.pulitzer.org/prize-winners-by-year/1989.

53. Lexis-Nexis search of Strachan broadcast transcripts, April 2015 and December 2017. Search terms: "Stan Strachan," Source: Transcripts. Accessed December 29, 2017.

Examples include *Face the Nation* (CBS News, September 23, 1990), "BankAmerica and Security Pacific Propose a Merger," *CBS Evening News* (CBS News, August 12, 1991); "Experts Offer Advice on Mortgage, Refinancing Decisions," *Your Money* CNN, September 16, 1995.

54. Kendra Free, telephone interview with the author, January 31, 2018.

55. ALM Media, "ALM's Julie Triedman Named Winner of Timothy White Award for Editorial Integrity for Her Coverage of Dewey & LeBoeuf," press release, March 6, 2013.

56. Gregory Miller, "The Press as a Watchdog for Accounting Fraud," *Journal of Accounting Research* 44, no. 5 (December 1, 2006): 1001–33.

57. Kriston Capps, "The Hidden Costs of Losing Your City's Newspaper," *Citylab*, May 30, 2018, https://www.citylab.com/equity/2018/05/study-when-local-newspaper-close-city-bond-finances-suffer/561422/?utm_source=twb.

58. Jim Prevor, telephone interview with the author, February 23, 2018.

59. Association of Business and Information and Media Companies (ABM), "The 61st Annual Jesse H. Neal Awards" (2015 winners), 2016, accessed January 25, 2019, https://www.siia.net/archive/neals/2015/gallery.asp.

60. Robert Freedman and Steven Roll, *Journalism That Matters: How Business-to-Business Editors Change the Industries They Cover* (Oak Park, IL: Marion Street, 2006), 16.

61. Freedman and Roll, *Journalism That Matters*, 88.

62. Chris Welles, "The Bleak Wasteland of Financial Journalism," *Columbia Journalism Review* 12, no. 2 (August 1973): 40–49.

63. Kathleen Endres, ed., *The Trade, Industrial and Professional Periodicals of the United States* (Westport, CT: Greenwood, 1994).

64. ABM, " 61st Annual Neal Awards."

65. ABM, "Tim White Award," *Jesse H. Neal Awards*, 2017, accessed January 25, 2019, https://www.siia.net/neals/Leadership-Awards/Tim-White-Award.

66. Jon Pareles, "An Unabashed Booster," *Rockcritics.Com*, June 2002, http://rockcritics archives.com/features/timothywhite/timothywhite.html.

67. Chuck Philips, "Timothy White, 50; Editor Revolutionized *Billboard Magazine*," *Los Angeles Times*, June 28, 2002 (obituary).

68. Richard Korman, telephone interview with the author, January 4, 2018.

69. Pizzo was a *National Thrift News* correspondent, Muolo was a senior reporter for *National Thrift News*, and Fricker was a business reporter for the *Santa Rosa Press-Democrat* (Stephen Pizzo, Mary Fricker, and Paul Muolo, *Inside Job: The Looting of America's Savings and Loans* [New York: McGraw-Hill, 1989]).

70. Pizzo et al., *Inside Job*, 303.

71. Paul Muolo, telephone interview with the author, December 8, 2014.

72. Dennis Cauchon, and Julie Morris, "Part 2: Salvaging the S&Ls; a Few Lived the High Life; 'They Spent Like There Was No Tomorrow'; Fraud Blamed in 80% of Sunken S&Ls," *USA Today*, February 14, 1989.

73. Francis X. Dealy, *The Power and the Money: Inside the "Wall Street Journal"* (Secaucus, NJ: Carol, 1993), 299.

74. Stephen Kleege, telephone interview with the author, June 15, 2015.

75. Dealy, *Power and the Money*, 299.

76. Pizzo appeared on the June 1990 edition of the Phil Donohue Show (Marcy Gordon, "Talk Show Host Whips Up Frenzy over Thrifts," Associated Press, June 2, 1990). Paul Muolo's résumé lists appearances on McLaughlin Report, CNN, CNBC, and FNN beginning in June 1989 (in possession of the author).

Chapter 3. The Developer

1. Charles H. Keating Jr., "Statement by Charles H. Keating Jr.," April 17, 1989, Series V: Other Corporate Records (Accession #1994–01435C), Sub-series A: General, American Continental Corporation Records circa 1971–1993 (hereafter, ACC records), Greater Arizona Collection, Arizona State University Library, Tempe, Arizona.

2. "Savings and Loan Situation" (Washington, DC: C-SPAN, May 9, 1990), https://www.c-span.org/video/?12225–1/savings-loan-situation&start=3369.

3. Nathaniel Nash and Philip Shenon, "A Man of Influence: Political Cash and Regulation—a Special Report; in Savings Debacle, Many Fingers Point Here," *New York Times*, November 9, 1989.

4. Tom Furlong, "Developer with a Cause Battles on Many Fronts," *Los Angeles Times*, March 13, 1988.

5. Marie J. Macnee, *Outlaws, Mobsters and Crooks* (New York: Gale, 2002).

6. Craig Harris, "Charles H Keating Jr. Dies at Age 90." *Arizona Republic*, April 1, 2014, https://www.cincinnati.com/story/news/history/lives-remembered/2014/04/01/keating-dies-ohio-arizona/7184557/.

7. Michael Binstein and Charles Bowden, *Trust Me: Charles Keating and the Missing Billions* (New York: Random House, 1993), 76.

8. Binstein and Bowden, *Trust Me*, 77.

9. "American Financial Corporation Reports Seven Years of Growth and Progress," *New York Times*, May 8, 1966, F9.

10. "In the Matter of Keating, Muething & Klekamo" (Securities and Exchange Commission, July 2, 1979), Release No. 15982, S.E.C. Release No. 34–15982, 1979 WL 186370 (WestLaw), quote in sec. 4, "Conclusions."

11. Financial capitalism displaced managerial capitalism, which gave managers greater discretion to invest and expand, sometimes without the approval of shareholders (George David Smith and Richard Eugene Sylla, *The Transformation of Financial Capitalism: An Essay on the History of American Capital Markets* [Cambridge, MA: Blackwell, 1993]).

12. George P. Baker and George David Smith, *The New Financial Capitalists: Kohlberg Kravis Roberts and the Creation of Corporate Value* (New York: Cambridge University Press, 1998).

13. "Carl H. Lindner, Jr.—Cincinnati Business Titan Passes Away at Age 92," *Business Wire*, October 18, 2011.

14. Binstein and Bowden, *Trust Me*, 96.

15. George Anders, *Merchants of Debt: KKR and the Mortgaging of American Business* (New York: Basic, 1992), xvi.

16. Judith Stein, *Pivotal Decade: How the United States Traded Factories for Finance in the 1970s* (New Haven, CT: Yale University Press, 2010).

17. Baker and Smith, *New Financial Capitalists*, 42.

18. Litigation Release No. 8806, 17 S.E.C. Docket 1219, 1979 WL 174206, *Securities and Exchange Commission v. American Financial Corp.*, July 2, 1979 (WestLaw).

19. Judith Miller, "S.E.C. Charges American Financial," *New York Times*, July 3, 1979.

20. Special to the *New York Times*, "Excerpts from Statement to the Panel by DeConcini," *New York Times*, November 20, 1990, B8.

21. John Trotto, "Desert Fox," *Cincinnati Magazine*, August 1989, 56–61.

22. Stephen Pizzo, "Keating's Troubles with the Government Began Back in '50s," *National Mortgage News*, November 18, 1991.

23. "Lincoln Savings Scandal Examined in Hearings," *CQ Almanac* 45 (1990): 133–39.

24. Carolyn Skorneck, "Drexel's Milken Subpoenaed in Congressional Probe," Associated Press, April 21, 1988.

25. "Chronology of the Lincoln Case," *National Mortgage News*, November 27, 1989.

26. James Stewart, *Den of Thieves* (New York: Simon and Schuster, 1991), 195.

27. "Events Chronology: American Continental Corporation," ACC records.

28. "Legislative Update & Campaign Contribution Ruling & Charles Keating," Arizona PBS, April 3, 2014. https://www.youtube.com/watch?v=r2Dq2S5nYk4.

29. *Lincoln Savings and Loan Assn. v. Wall*, Nos. 89–1318, 89–1323 (D.D.C. August 22, 1990), 8.

30. *Lincoln v. Wall*; Binstein and Bowden, *Trust Me*, 197–98.

31. "Gray: Senators Tried to Convince Me to 'Go Easy' on Lincoln Savings," *National Mortgage News*, November 27, 1989, 15.

32. Nathaniel Nash and Philip Shenon, "A Man of Influence: Political Cash and Regulation—a Special Report," *New York Times*, November 8, 1989.

33. Daniel C. Hallin, *The Uncensored War: The Media and Vietnam* (Berkeley: University of California Press, 1989).

34. Henry Kaufman, *On Money and Markets: A Wall Street Memoir* (New York: McGraw-Hill, 2001), 179.

35. Leonard Solomon Silk and David Vogel, *Ethics and Profits: The Crisis of Confidence in American Business* (New York: Simon and Schuster, 1976).

36. David Vogel, *Kindred Strangers: The Uneasy Relationship between Politics and Business in America* (Princeton, NJ: Princeton University Press, 1996), 144.

37. Wayne Parsons, *The Power of the Financial Press* (New Brunswick, NJ: Rutgers University Press, 1990), 204.

38. Timothy W. Hubbard, "The Explosive Demand for Business News," *Journalism Quarterly* 43 (Winter 1966): 703–8.

39. Don Gussow, *The New Business Journalism: An Insider's Look at the Workings of America's Business Press* (San Diego: Harcourt Brace Jovanovich, 1984), 62.

40. Business sections reaped revenues from required advertisements from various businesses. Tombstone advertisements are paid announcements, generally of stock placements or debt offerings. "Tombstone ads" have a barebones design that resemble a gravestone, usually a simple box with a heavy black border and centered print.

41. Damian Tambini, *What Is Financial Journalism For? Ethics and Responsibility in a Time of Crisis and Change* (London: Polis Media, 2008), 24.

42. George Anders, *Merchants of Debt: KKR and the Mortgaging of American Business* (New York: Basic, 1992), xiv.

43. *Wall Street: Money Never Sleeps*, directed by Oliver Stone (Los Angeles: Twentieth Century Fox, 1987).

44. Furlong, "Developer."

45. "Charles Keating—Obituary," *Telegraph*, April 2, 2014.

46. Ed Severson, "Master of the Game Keating's Fraud Served Up with Bowden's Touch," *Arizona Daily Star*, July 25, 1993.

47. "Other People's Money," *PBS Frontline*, May 1, 1990.

48. Binstein and Bowden, *Trust Me*, 143.

49. Furlong, "Developer."

50. Binstein and Bowden, *Trust Me*.

51. *Lincoln Savings and Loan Association v. Federal Home Loan Bank*, No. CIV 87–1985 (D.D.C. July 20, 1987), 57.

52. Doug Sword, "Charles Keating Aims to Take Phoenix Firm Private, Broker Says," *Cincinnati Business Courier*, January 26, 1987.

53. Brian Lamb, "Viewer Call-In: Interview with Charles H. Keating Jr." (C-SPAN, May 8, 1990), https://www.c-span.org/video/?12176-1/savings-loan-industry&start=11.

54. Binstein and Bowden, *Trust Me*, 167.

55. Lamb, "Viewer Call-In."

56. Jim Showalter, "'We'd Have to Be Idiots': Keating Blames Press, Goddard for Decision to Withdraw from State," *Greater Phoenix Business Journal*, February 2, 1987.

57. "Carl H. Lindner, Jr."

58. "Plans Set to Rehabilitate Cincinnati's Avondale Area," *Chicago Defender*, November 25, 1967.

59. "American Financial Group, Inc. Announces Carl H. Lindner Jr.—a Celebration Tour," *Business Wire*, October 20, 2011.

60. Michael Burns, "Cincinnati: Anti-porn Capital; Rest of Nation Catching Up with Cincinnati," *United Press International*, October 19, 1986.

61. Robert McFadden, "Charles Keating, 90, Key Figure in '80s Savings and Loan Crisis, Dies," *New York Times*, April 2, 2014.

62. *Perversion for Profit* (Cincinnati, OH: Citizens for Decent Literature, 1965), https://www.youtube.com/watch?v=om4kMTw-R6o.

63. Larry Flynt, *An Unseemly Man* (Los Angeles: Dove, 1996), 123. Redactions mine.

64. "Paralyzed Porn Purveyor Focus of New Stone Movie," Associated Press, August 15, 1995.

65. Lynn Borushko to Brad Boland, June 23, 1986, box XB-184, 0971, ACC records.

66. Mark Voigt, "Memo on Conversation with *Phoenix Business Journal* Reporter Chris Aaron," September 16, 1986, box XB-184, ACC records.

67. "FG 95 (Commission on Obscenity and Pornography)," *Richard Nixon Presidential Library and Museum*, January 9, 2007, https://www.nixonlibrary.gov/index.php/finding-aids/fg-95-commission-obscenity-and-pornography-white-house-central-files-subject-files.

68. *The Resolution Trust Corporation v. Michael R. Gardner*, No. 91–2226 (CRR) (D.D.C. July 30, 1992).

69. Lamb, "Viewer Call-In."

70. William Black, *The Best Way to Rob a Bank Is to Own One* (Austin: University of Texas Press, 2005), 63.

71. Megan Twohey, Russ Buettner, and Steve Eder, "Inside the Trump Organization, the Company That Has Run Trump's Big World," *New York Times*, December 25, 2016.

72. Simon Johnson, "Eric Trump: Nepotism Is a 'Beautiful Thing' as He Says US President's Children Are More Likely to Speak Truth to Power," *Telegraph*, April 10, 2017.

73. Severson, "Master of the Game."

74. "Other People's Money."

75. Lamb, "Viewer Call-In."

76. Lamb, "Viewer Call-In."

77. Binstein and Bowden, *Trust Me*, 175.

78. "Compustat Annual Updates," Wharton Research Data Services, May 27, 2018, wrds.wharton.upenn.edu.

79. Danielle Kurtzleben, "Most of Donald Trump's Political Money Went to Democrats—until 5 Years Ago," *It's All Politics* (Washington, DC: National Public Radio, July 28, 2015), https://www.npr.org/sections/itsallpolitics/2015/07/28/426888268/donald-trumps-flipping-political-donations.

80. David Cay Johnston, *The Making of Donald Trump* (Hoboken, NJ: Melville House, 2016), Kindle edition, 1307–8.

81. Lamb, "Viewer Call-In."

82. Stephen V. Ward, *Selling Places: The Marketing and Promotion of Towns and Cities 1850–2000* (London: Routledge, 1998), 3.

83. George Dangerfield, "The Way West," review of *The Americans: The National Experience*, by Daniel Boorstin, *New York Times*, October 31, 1965.

84. Daniel Boorstin, *The Americans: The National Experience*, 2nd ed. (New York: Random House, 1966), 296.

85. Gwilym Pryce and Sarah Oates, "Rhetoric in the Language of Real Estate Marketing," *Housing Studies* 23, no. 2 (2008): 319–48.

86. Society of Professional Journalists, "SPJ Code of Ethics," accessed September 24, 2014, http://www.spj.org/ethicscode.asp.

87. Aristotle, *Rhetoric*, ed. W. Rhys Roberts (New York: Modern Library, 1984), 25.

88. Aristotle, *Rhetoric*, 208–9.

89. Donald Trump and Tony Schwartz, *Trump: The Art of the Deal* (New York: Ballantine, 1987), 58.

90. Jon Hesk, "Trumpist Hyperbole and Its Classical-Rhetorical Critique," *Ancient and Modern Rhetoric* (St. Andrews, Scotland: University of St. Andrews, January 23, 2017), https://arts.st-andrews.ac.uk/rhetoric/trumpist-hyperbole-and-its-classical-rhetorical-critique/.

91. Lamb, "Viewer Call-In."

92. Mark Fogarty, "Remembering Charles Keating, Peddler of Junk Bonds and Influence," *National Mortgage News*, April 2, 2014.

93. *Hearing before a Subcommittee of the Select Committee on Government Operations*, 99th Cong., 1st Sess. (1985) (statement of Charles Keating Jr.), 210.

94. "Savings and Loan Situation" (Washington, DC: C-SPAN, May 9, 1990), https://www.c-span.org/video/?12225–1/savings-loan-situation&start=3369.

95. Petition for the Recusal or Disqualification of Edwin J. Gray, Examination Docket No. 3805 (Federal Home Loan Bank Board, March 20, 1987).

96. *American Continental Corp. v. Federal Home Loan Bank Board* (D. Ariz.), No. CIV-89–0691 (deposition of Charles H. Keating Jr., February 23, 1990), 108.

97. Charles Keating, "Keating Memo—Transcription 12/24/86 FHLB Leaks of Confidential Information," December 24, 1986, box XB-627, ACC records.

98. Keating deposition.

99. Francie Noyes, "American Continental Aims to Push Financial Services," *Arizona Republic*, March 26, 1987.

100. "Lincoln Savings Is Different from Their Prior Experience," Jack D. Atchison, a managing partner with Arthur Young, wrote to Senator McCain in 1987. McCain had sought to learn why the federal audit of Lincoln was going on for so long (Jack Atchison to John McCain, March 17, 1987, box XB-601, ACC records.

101. Stephen W. Andrews, "Confidential Investigation Report—Subject: George E. Shiffer," 1987, box XB-613, ACC records.

102. American Continental corporate files, box XB-613, ACC records.

103. Bartholomew H. Sparrow, *Uncertain Guardians* (Baltimore, MD: Johns Hopkins University Press, 1999), 156.

104. This agency was later abolished in the 2010 Dodd-Frank Wall Street Reform and Consumer Protection Act (U.S.C. Pub. L. 111–203, 124 Stat. 1376–2223), and its responsibilities were taken over by the Office of the Comptroller of the Currency.

105. John McCain to Edwin J. Gray, July 21, 1986, box XB-627, ACC records.

106. Charles Pashayan et al. to Edwin J. Gray, August 14, 1986, box XB-627, ACC records.

107. Howard Kurtz, "Asleep at the Wheel," *Washington Post*, November 29, 1992.

108. Binstein and Bowden, *Trust Me*.

109. Bill Roberts, "The Keating Connection," *Mesa Tribune*, December 28, 1986.

110. California Republican Party to Charles H. Keating Jr. (mailgram), October 21, 1988, box XB-601, ACC records.

111. Alan Greenspan to Thomas Sharkey, February 13, 1985, box XB-439, ACC records.

112. *Sarah B. Shields et al. v. Charles H. Keating Jr., Arthur Young & Co. et al.* (D. Ariz. 1991), 6.

113. "Former SEC Official Sought Confidential Data," *National Mortgage News*, November 27, 1989.

114. *Shields v. Keating et al.*, 7.

115. William B. O'Connell to Sen. Jake Garn, July 2, 1986, box RB-457, ACC records.

116. "Credit Ratings," *Wall Street Journal*, January 14, 1987; "Credit Ratings," *Wall Street Journal*, July 20, 1987.

117. Jim Upchurch to Charles Keating, January 27, 1988, box XB-627, ACC records.

118. Judy J. Wischer, "American Continental Corp Memo on First Interstate, FHLB Exam to Keating and Kielty," April 25, 1988, box XB-627, ACC records.

Chapter 4. Advertising and Controversy

1. Gerald J. Baldasty, *The Commercialization of News in the Nineteenth Century* (Madison: University of Wisconsin Press, 1992).

2. Denise E. Delorme and Fred Fedler, "An Historical Analysis of Journalists' Attitudes toward Advertisers and Advertising's Influence," *American Journalism* 22, no. 2 (April 1, 2005): 17.

3. Delorme and Fedler, "Historical Analysis."

4. Edwin Emery and Michael Emery, *The Press and America—an Interpretive History of the Mass Media*, 5th ed. (Englewood Cliffs, NJ: Prentice-Hall, 1984), 143.

5. Daniel Hallin, "Field Theory, Differentiation Theory and Comparative Media Research," in *Bourdieu and the Journalistic Field*, ed. Rodney Benson, 224–43 (Malden, MA: Polity, 2005), 234.

6. Michael Schudson, *Discovering the News: A Social History of Newspapers* (New York: BasicBooks, 1978); Emery and Emery, *Press and America*.

7. Frank Luther Mott, *A History of American Magazines*, vol. 4, *1885–1905* (Cambridge, MA: Belknap, 1957), 20.

8. Delorme and Fedler, "Historical Analysis."

9. Baldasty, *Commercialization*, 81.

10. Baldasty, *Commercialization*, 58.

11. Silvio Waisbord, *Reinventing Professionalism* (Malden, MA: Polity, 2013).

12. Vincent Mosco, *The Political Economy of Communication*, 2nd ed. (Thousand Oaks, CA: Sage, 2009), 2, 4.

13. Robert McChesney, "The Problem of Journalism: A Political Economic Contribution to an Explanation of the Crisis in Contemporary US Journalism," *Journalism Studies* 4, no. 3 (2003): 299–329; Edward S. Herman and Noam Chomsky, *Manufacturing Consent: The Political Economy of the Mass Media* (New York: Pantheon, 1988); Dallas W. Smythe, "On the Audience Commodity and Its Work," in *Dependency Road: Communications, Capitalism, Consciousness, and Canada* (Norwood, NJ: Ablex, 1981).

14. Karl Marx and Friedrich Engels, *The German Ideology* (New York: International, 1970), 64.

15. Mosco, *Political Economy*, 16.

16. Dallas W. Smythe, "On the Audience Commodity and Its Work."

17. Baldasty, *Commercialization*, 79.

18. Herman and Chomsky, *Manufacturing Consent*.

19. Bartholomew H. Sparrow, "A Research Agenda for an Institutional Media," *Political Communication* 23, no. 2 (2006): 145–57.

20. McChesney, "The Problem of Journalism"; Herman and Chomsky, *Manufacturing Consent*; Ben H. Bagdikian, *The New Media Monopoly*, rev. ed. (Boston: Beacon, 2004); Greg Philo, *Seeing and Believing: The Influence of Television* (London: Routledge, 1990).

21. Michael Schudson, *The Sociology of News* (New York: W. W. Norton, 2011); Daniel C. Hallin, "Commercialism and Professionalism in the American News Media," in *Mass Media and Society*, 3rd ed., ed. James Curran and Michael Gurevitch, 218–37 (London: Arnold, 2000).

22. Paul Starr, *The Creation of the Media: Political Origins of Modern Communications* (New York: Perseus, 2004), 394.

23. Hallin, "Commercialism and Professionalism," 226.

24. Richard D. Altick and J. F. C. Harrison. *The English Common Reader: A Social History of the Mass Reading Public, 1800–1900* (Chicago: University of Chicago Press, 1957).

25. Fred Seaton Siebert, *Four Theories of the Press: The Authoritarian, Libertarian, Social Responsibility, and Soviet Communist Concepts of What the Press Should Be and Do* (Champaign: University of Illinois Press, 1956).

26. Starr, *Creation of the Media*, 386.

27. Robert Freedman and Steven Roll, *Journalism That Matters: How Business-to-Business Editors Change the Industries They Cover* (Oak Park, IL: Marion Street, 2006).

28. Edward Jay Epstein, *News from Nowhere* (New York: Random House, 1973).

29. "SPJ Code of Ethics," Society of Professional Journalists, accessed September 24, 2014, http://www.spj.org/ethicscode.asp.

30. Lewis Ranieri, telephone interview with the author, August 12, 2015.

31. Hillary Wilson, telephone interview with the author, June 23, 2015.

32. Ranieri interview.

33. Boat trip photographs contained in Strachan family album, described in Wilson interview; Ranieri interview; Muolo, telephone interview with the author, June 15, 2015. Bat mitzvah scene described in Stephen Kleege, telephone interview with the author, June 15, 2015.

34. Paul Muolo, telephone interview with the author, December 8, 2014.

35. Kleege interview.

36. Mark Fogarty, telephone interview with the author, October 24, 2014.

37. Eugene Carlson, "An Industry Remembers Stan Strachan," *National Mortgage News*, January 20, 1997.

38. Schudson, *Discovering the News*; Daniel C. Hallin, *The Uncensored War: The Media and Vietnam* (Berkeley: University of California Press, 1989).

39. Starr, *Creation of the Media*.

40. Inflation calculator, http://www.westegg.com/inflation/.

41. Starr, *Creation of the Media*, 262.

42. Rodney Benson, "Rethinking the Sociology of Media Ownership," in *Routledge Handbook of Cultural Sociology*, 2nd ed., ed. Laura Grindstaff (New York: Routledge, 2018), 387–96.

43. Rodney Benson, Timothy Neff, and Mattias Hessérus, "Media Ownership and Public Service News: How Strong Are Institutional Logics?" *International Journal of Press/Politics* 23, no. 3 (July 1, 2018): 275–98, citing Susan Tifft and Alex Jones, *The Trust: The Private and Powerful Family behind the "New York Times"* (Boston: Back Bay, 2000), 6.

44. Jay Black and Jennings Bryant, *Introduction to Mass Communication*, 3rd ed. (Dubuque, IA: Brown, 1992), 585. Larry Powell and William R. Self, "Government Sources Dominate Business Crisis Reporting," *Newspaper Research Journal* 24, no. 2 (2003): 97–106.

45. Richard J. Tofel, *Restless Genius: Barney Kilgore, the "Wall Street Journal," and the Invention of Modern Journalism* (New York: St. Martin's, 2009), 78.

46. Chris Welles, "The Bleak Wasteland of Financial Journalism," *Columbia Journalism Review* 12, no. 2 (August 1973): 40–49.

47. Timothy W. Hubbard, "The Explosive Demand for Business News," *Journalism Quarterly* 43, no. 4 (December 1966): 703–8.

48. Lawrence Soley and Robert L. Craig, "Advertising Pressures on Newspapers—a Survey," *Journal of Advertising* 21 (December 1992): 1–10.

49. Andrea Blasco and Francesco Sobbrio, "Competition and Commercial Media Bias," *Telecommunications Policy*, 36, no. 5 (2012): 436.

50. Matthew Ellman and Fabrizio Germano, "What Do the Papers Sell? A Model of Advertising and Media Bias," *Economic Journal* 119, no. 537 (April 2009): 682, https://doi.org/10.1111/j.1468–0297.2009.02218.x; Ben H. Bagdikian, *The New Media Monopoly*, rev. ed. (Boston: Beacon, 2004), 167–68; Hewitt's account summarized in Kinney Littlefield, "How CBS, 60 Minutes Ethics' Went Up in Smoke," *Orange County Register*, November 2, 1999, https://www.sun-sentinel.com/news/fl-xpm-1999–11–02–9911010352-story.html.

51. Ellman and Germano, "What Do the Papers Sell?"

52. Blasco and Sobbrio, "Competition and Commercial Media," 436.

53. Soontae An and Lori Bergen, "Advertiser Pressure on Daily Newspapers: A Survey of Advertising Sales Executives," *Journal of Advertising* 36, no. 2 (June 1, 2007): 111–21.

54. Jonathan Reuter and Eric Zitzewitz, "Do Ads Influence Editors? Advertising and Bias in the Financial Media," *Quarterly Journal of Economics* 121, no. 1 (2006): 198.

55. An and Bergen, "Advertiser Pressure," 118.

56. Maha Rafi Atal, "The Cultural and Economic Power of Advertisers in the Business Press," *Journalism* 19, no. 8 (September 13, 2017): 1078–95.

57. Richard J. Tofel, "Non-profit Journalism Issues around Impact," White Paper (New York: ProPublica, 2014).

58. Paul Muolo, telephone interview with the author, October 19, 2014.

59. Denver Post Editorial Board, "Editorial: As Vultures Circle, the Denver Post Must Be Saved," *Denver Post*, April 16, 2018, https://www.denverpost.com/2018/04/06/as-vultures-circle-the-denver-post-must-be-saved/; Amanda Darrach, "McClatchy Upgrades CEO's Housing Stipend to $35K a Month amid Buyouts," *Columbia Journalism Review*, February 5, 2019, https://www.cjr.org/business_of_news/mcclatchy-upgrades-ceo-forman-housing-stipend-35k-month-buyouts.php.

60. Robert Maynard Hutchins, *A Free and Responsible Press: A General Report on Mass Communication: Newspapers, Radio, Motion Pictures, Magazines and Books* (Chicago: University of Chicago Press, 1947).

61. Victor Pickard and Josh Stearns, "New Models Emerge for Community Press," *Newspaper Research Journal* 32, no. 1 (2011): 47.

62. Charles Lewis, *935 Lies: The Future of Truth and the Decline in America's Moral Integrity* (New York: PublicAffairs, 2014), 131.

63. Pickard and Stearns, "New Models," 47.

64. Herman and Chomsky, *Manufacturing Consent*; Bagdikian, *New Media*; Bartholomew H. Sparrow, *Uncertain Guardians* (Baltimore, MD: Johns Hopkins University Press, 1999).

65. Mike Fabey, telephone interview with the author, January 31, 2018.

66. Maryfran Johnson, telephone interview with the author, February 5, 2018.

67. Don Tennant, telephone interview with the author, February 10, 2018.

68. Alan R. Earls, "IDG Chairman Patrick McGovern: Content for Readers Is Top Priority," *Newsletter Articles* (Wheaton, IL: ASBPE, 2004), http://www.asbpe.org/docs/archives_members_only/2004/07082004mcgovern.htm.

69. Shelby D. Hunt, Van R. Wood, and Lawrence B. Chonko, "Corporate Ethical Values and Organizational Commitment in Marketing," *Journal of Marketing* 53, no. 3 (1989): 80.

70. Epstein, *News from Nowhere*, 201.

71. Michael A. Hilltzik and Sallie Hofmeister, "Times Publisher Apologizes for Staples Center Deal," *Los Angeles Times*, October 28, 1999.

72. David Shaw, "Crossing the Line," *Los Angeles Times*, December 20, 1999.

73. Denver Post Editorial Board, "Editorial: As Vultures Circle."

74. Lloyd Grove and Maxwell Tani, "WSJ Editor-in-Chief Leaves to Host Show on Pro-Trump Fox Business Network," *Daily Beast*, June 5, 2018.

75. Hallin, "Commercialism and Professionalism."

76. Mark Fogarty, "Requiem for a Reporter," *National Mortgage News*, January 13, 1997.

77. David Olson and Christine Clifford, "An Industry Remembers Stan Strachan," *National Mortgage News*, Letters to the Editor, January 20, 1997.

78. Julie Triedman, telephone interview with the author, January 8, 2018.

79. Rob Blackwell, telephone interview with the author, January 8, 2018.

80. Kendra Free, telephone interview with the author, January 31, 2018.

81. Johnson interview.

82. Richard Korman, *Engineering News-Record* reporter, telephone interview with the author, January 4, 2018.

83. Free interview.

84. Whitney Sielaff, telephone interview with the author, February 5, 2018.

85. Muolo, October 19, 2014, interview; Fogarty interview.

86. Ranieri interview; Kleege interview.

87. Kathleen Day, *S & L Hell: The People and the Politics behind the $1 Trillion Savings and Loan Scandal* (New York: W. W. Norton, 1993), 277–78.

88. Fogarty interview.

89. Delorme and Fedler, "Historical Analysis."

90. Tofel, *Restless Genius.*

91. Johnson interview; Tennant interview.

92. Hubbard, "Explosive Demand."

93. Liam Stack, "BuzzFeed Says Posts Were Deleted Because of Advertising Pressure," *New York Times*, April 19, 2015.

94. Kleege interview.

95. Christi Harlan, telephone interview with the author, August 21, 2015.

96. Stanley Strachan, "Looking Back over 20 Years," *National Mortgage News*, October 7, 1996, 33.

97. Stephen P. Pizzo, email correspondence with the author, September 12, 2014.

98. Janet Laib, "The Trade Press," *Public Opinion Quarterly* 19, no. 1 (1955): 31–44.

99. Timothy W. Martin, "McGraw Hill Financial to Buy SNL Financial for $2.2 Billion," *Wall Street Journal*, July 27, 2015.

100. Matt Kinsman, "Revenue Flat for the B2B Media & Information Industry in 2016," SIAA, accessed July 25, 2018, http://www.siia.net/blog/index/Post/71911/Revenue-Flat-for-the-B2B-Media-Information-Industry-in-2016.

101. Max Willens, "A Return to Focus: Publishers Are Going High with Subscription Prices," *Digiday*, December 6, 2016, https://digiday.com/media/flight-focus-publishers-going-high-subscription-prices/.

102. David Cay Johnston, *Free Lunch: How the Wealthiest Americans Enrich Themselves at Government Expense* (and Stick You with the Bill) (New York: Penguin, 2007), Kindle edition, 108.

103. John Heltman, "Confessions of a Paywall Journalist," *Washington Monthly*, December 2015, https://washingtonmonthly.com/magazine/novdec-2015/confessions-of-a-paywall-journalist/.

104. Their mail survey of 190 farm journalists reveal that about two-thirds of the journalists say advertisers have threatened their journals on occasion, and about one-half say that advertising has actually been withdrawn (Robert G. Hays and Anne E. Reisner, "Feeling the Heat from Advertisers: Farm Magazine Writers and Ethical Pressures," *Journalism and Mass Communication Quarterly* 67, no. 4 [January 1990]: 936–42).

105. Hays and Reisner, "Feeling the Heat," 939.

106. Hays and Reisner, "Feeling the Heat," 941.

107. Sielaff interview.

108. "Capitalize on Your Business Press Editors," *Folio*, January 15, 1994, 10.

109. James Ross, "When Trades Lead the Pack," *Columbia Journalism Review*, November 1990, 18.

110. Don Gussow, *The New Business Journalism: An Insider's Look at the Workings of America's Business Press* (San Diego, CA: Harcourt Brace Jovanovich, 1984), 4.

111. C. Ann Hollifield, "The Specialized Business Press and Industry-Related Political Communication: A Comparative Study," *Journalism and Mass Communication Quarterly* 74, no. 4 (1997): 757–72.

112. Blackwell interview.

113. Sielaff interview.

114. Alexander Dyck and Luigi Zingales, "The Bubble and the Media," in *Corporate Governance and Capital Flows in a Global Economy*, ed. Peter K. Cornelius and Bruce Kogut, 83–103 (New York: Oxford University Press, 2003).

115. Tennant interview.

116. Paul Miller, telephone interview with the author, February 16, 2018.

117. Gillian Doyle, "Financial News Journalism: A Post-Enron Analysis of Approaches towards Economic and Financial News Production in the UK," *Journalism* 7, no. 4 (November 1, 2006): 411.

118. Aeron Davis, "Public Relations, Business News and the Reproduction of Corporate Elite Power," *Journalism* 1, no. 3 (December 1, 2000): 282.

119. Fogarty interview.

120. Triedman interview.

121. Kleege interview.

122. Jim Prevor, Phoenix Media Group publisher, telephone interview with the author, February 23, 2018.

123. Piet Verhoeven, "The Co-production of Business News and Its Effects: The Corporate Framing Mediated-Moderation Model," *Public Relations Review* 42 (2016): 514.

124. Harry McCracken, telephone interview with the author, March 7, 2018.

125. Free interview.

126. Triedman interview; Johnson interview.

127. Fabey interview.

Chapter 5. Keating's War with the Press

1. Jim Showalter, "'We'd Have to Be Idiots': Keating Blames Press, Goddard for Decision to Withdraw from State," *Greater Phoenix Business Journal*, February 2, 1987.

2. David J. Jefferson, "Keating of American Continental Corp. Comes Out Fighting—Chairman Blames Regulators for Plight of Concern and Lincoln S&L Unit," *Wall Street Journal*, April 18, 1989.

3. Teresa Carson, "Keating, Owner of Seized Thrift, Is in Eye of Storm," *American Banker*, May 1, 1989.

4. David Vogel, *Kindred Strangers: The Uneasy Relationship between Politics and Business in America* (Princeton, NJ: Princeton University Press, 1996), 144.

5. Peter Drier, "The Corporate Complaint against the Media," in *American Media and Mass Culture, Left Perspectives*, ed. Donald Lazere, 63–79 (Berkeley: University of California Press, 1987).

6. Trade Secrets Act, 18 US Code § 1905 (1948), https://www.law.cornell.edu/uscode/text/18/1905.

7. Louis Banks, "Media Responsibility for Economic Literacy," *Neiman Reports* 29, nos. 3–4 (Autumn–Winter 1975): 56; cited in S. Prakash Sethi, "The Schism between Business and American News Media," *Journalism Quarterly* 54, no. 2 (1977): 240–47.

8. Joseph R. Dominick, "Business Coverage in Network Newscasts," *Journalism Quarterly* 58, no. 2 (1981): 179–85.

9. Sethi, "Schism," 240.

10. Joe Bob Hester and Rhonda Gibson, "The Economy and Second-Level Agenda Setting: A Time-Series Analysis of Economic News and Public Opinion about the Economy," *Journalism and Mass Communication Quarterly* 80, no. 1 (2003): 73–90.

11. Howard Simons and Joseph A. Califano, eds. *The Media and Business* (New York: Vintage, 1979), ix.

12. National News Council, *In the Public Interest: A Report by the National News Council Inc.* (New York: National News Council, 1975), 2.

13. Thomas Suddes, "The National News Council, 1973–1984: A History" (Ph.D. diss., Ohio University, 2009), 38.

14. National News Council, *In the Public Interest*, 1.

15. Author's analysis of data in L. Paul Husselbee, "A Question of Accountability: An Analysis of Grievances Files with the National News Council, 1973–84" (Ph.D. diss., Ohio University, 1999), 106.

16. Damian Tambini, *"What Is Financial Journalism For? Ethics and Responsibility in a Time of Crisis and Change"* (London: Polis Media, 2008).

17. Robert McChesney, "The Problem of Journalism: A Political Economic Contribution to an Explanation of the Crisis in Contemporary US Journalism," *Journalism Studies* 4, no. 3 (2003): 299–329; Dean Starkman, *The Watchdog That Didn't Bark: The Financial Crisis and the Disappearance of Investigative Journalism* (New York: Columbia Journalism Review Books, 2014).

18. "U.S. League Supports DI Reg. Extension, National Council Opposes," *National Thrift News*, February 9, 1987.

19. William Black, *The Best Way to Rob a Bank Is to Own One* (Austin: University of Texas Press, 2005), 270.

20. Stan Strachan, "Direct Investment Vote Dec. 1," *National Thrift News*, November 24, 1986.

21. David B. Hilder and John E. Yang, "Bank Board Appointee Has Close Ties to Thrift with Controversial Investment," *Wall Street Journal*, December 18, 1986; John E Yang, "Bank

Board's Henkel Proposed a Rule That Would Have Aided S&L Tied to Him," *Wall Street Journal*, December 24, 1986.

22. "Financial Brief: Regulator Banned from Industry," *Wall Street Journal*, November 20, 1992.

23. *Lincoln Savings and Loan Association v. Federal Home Loan Bank*, No. CIV 87–1985 (D.D.C. July 20, 1987), 15.

24. Charles Keating, "Keating Memo—Transcription 12/24/86 FHLB Leaks of Confidential Information," December 24, 1986, box XB-627, American Continental Corporation Records circa 1971–1993 (hereafter, ACC records), Greater Arizona Collection, Arizona State University Library, Tempe, Arizona.

25. Bill Roberts, "The Keating Connection," *Mesa Tribune*, December 28, 1986. This was the lead of eight stories about Keating, his business, and his political activities that were featured in the newspaper's Perspectives section of that date. Other articles: Andrew Mollison, "Bank Board Appointee's Proposal Would Have Helped His Friend's Firm"; Ben Winton, "Attorney General, County Attorney Reap Big Donations from Keating"; Max Jennings, "Keating Questions. Stories' Troubling Issues Unanswered"; Ben Winton, "Development Help Coincides with Campaign Help"; "Goddard: Big Contributions Spur Questions"; W. Terry Smith, "Congressmen Say Keating's Aid Doesn't Influence Them"; W. Terry Smith, "Campaign Coffers in Chandler Found Friend in Keating."

26. "Trump Clock.com," accessed July 23, 2017, http://www.trump-clock.com/.

27. Donald J. Trump, "Remarks by President Donald Trump, Vice President Mike Pence, Senate Majority Leader Mitch McConnell, and House Speaker Paul Ryan after Congressional Republican Leadership Retreat, Camp David, Maryland," news release, White House Office of the Press Secretary, January 6, 2018.

28. David Cay Johnston, *The Making of Donald Trump* (Hoboken, NJ: Melville House, 2016), Kindle edition, 898–900.

29. *Donald Trump v. Timothy L. O'Brien*, Docket No. A-6141–08T3 (N.J. Sup. Ct. App. Div., September 7, 2011).

30. Ian Tuttle, "The Litigious—and Bullying—Mr. Trump," *National Review*, February 19, 2016.

31. Paul Farhi, "What Really Gets under Trump's Skin? A Reporter Questioning His Net Worth," *Washington Post*, March 8, 2016.

32. "Possible Libel Claims," 1987, box RB-35, ACC records.

33. "Investigation of Lincoln Savings & Loan Association Hearing Transcript," Pub. L. No. 101–59, Part 2, Hearing before the H. Select Committee on Banking, Finance, and Urban Affairs, 101st Cong. 101–59 (1989), https://hdl.handle.net/2027/pur1.32754074124128; Brooks Jackson, "Sleeping Watchdog: How Regulatory Error Led to the Disaster at Lincoln Savings—Charles Keating Had History of Alleged Abuse but Still Was Allowed to Run S&L—Five Senators in His Camp," *Wall Street Journal*, November 20, 1989.

34. *AMCOR Investment Corp. v. Cox Arizona Publications Inc.*, No. CV 87–05127 (Ariz. Sup. Ct., Maricopa County, February 24, 1987).

35. "Gray: Senators Tried to Convince Me to 'Go Easy' on Lincoln Savings," *National Mortgage News*, November 27, 1989.

36. Jim McTague, "Keating Bids to Remove Judge Who Was with SEC from Case," *American Banker*, August 18, 1989.

37. Stephen Pizzo, Mary Fricker, and Paul Muolo, *Inside Job: The Looting of America's Savings and Loans* (New York: McGraw-Hill, 1989).

38. Jill Dutt, "Media, S&Ls Square Off over Coverage of Crisis," *Newsday*, April 23, 1989.

39. Chris Roush, *Profits and Losses: Business Journalism and Its Role in Society* (Portland, OR: Marion Street, 2006), 51.

40. "Obituaries: William Tavoulareas; Mobil Executive, Libel Suit Figure," Associated Press; *Los Angeles Times*, January 17, 1996; Rodney A. Smolla, "Mobil Oil Meets the *Washington Post*: Can Investigative Journalism Ever Be Objective?" in *Suing the Press: Libel and the Media*, 182–96 (Oxford: Oxford University Press, 1986).

41. Rob Blackwell, telephone interview with the author, January 8, 2018.

42. American Continental to R. Lanning at the Phoenix Gazette, 1980, box WBO2139, ACC records.

43. MWL to Robert Kielty, March 20, 1980, box WBO2139, ACC records.

44. Virginia Novak to Robert J. Kielty, December 17, 1986, box RB-35, ACC records.

45. The February 26, 1988, memo described a call from Roger Martin at Detroit Newspaper Agency to Bill Keating alerting him to a forthcoming story about Charles Keating's connections to Don Riegle. "Memo on Detroit News Story and Bill Keating Phone Call," February 1989, box XB-627, ACC records.

46. "Memo on Detroit News Story."

47. Gail Tabor, "No Man Is an Island, Even in Lovely Hawaii," *Arizona Republic*, September 17, 1986.

48. "Worst Number-One Priority: Charles H. Keating Jr. and the Arizona House of Representatives," *New Times*, December 31, 1986.

49. "Builders Ignore Conservation," *Arizona Republic*, September 4, 1986, in Series I: Relevant Files (Accession #1994–01435A), box XB-184, ACC records.

50. Philip T. Goldstein to Phoenix Newspapers Inc., September 19, 1986, box XB-184, ACC records.

51. A. Melvin McDonald to Dennis G. Kimberlin, September 19, 1986, box XB-184, ACC records.

52. "Correction," *Arizona Republic*, October 10, 1986.

53. Michael Lacey, "Don't Go Away Mad, Charles Keating," *Phoenix New Times*, March 1987.

54. Vin Suprynowicz (*West Valley View* editor) to Philip Goldstein, November 26, 1986, box XB-184, ACC records.

55. Draft Complaint: *Keating v. Whitson*, Unfiled, Maricopa Cnty., Ariz., Sup. Ct., May 1989, box XB-613, ACC records.

56. Rudolph J. Gerber, Decision Granting Defendants Motion to Dismiss, *Amcor Investment v. Cox Arizona Publications*, No. CV 87–05127, Maricopa Cnty., Ariz., Sup. Ct., June 8, 1987.

57. Bill Roberts, "The Keating Connection," *Mesa Tribune*, December 28, 1986.

58. Virginia Novak to Robert J. Kielty, December 17, 1986, box RB-35, ACC records.

59. Philip T. Goldstein to *Mesa Tribune*, December 15, 1986, box XB-184, ACC records.

60. "Possible Legal Claims," American Continental Corporation, 1987, box RB-35, ACC records.

61. Rex Lee to William Weld, Assistant Attorney General, U.S. Department of Justice, January 20, 1987, box RB-457, ACC records.

62. William Weld to Rex Lee, February 13, 1987, box RB-457, ACC records.

63. "Summary of Interviews, Federal Bureau of Investigation, FOIA Response to Rob Wells; Subject: Federal Home Loan Bank Board" (Federal Bureau of Investigation, 1987), May 15, 2018, correspondence between author and David M Hardy, section chief, Record/Information Dissemination Section, Records Management Division, FBI Investigation of FHLB Media Leaks, 1987, Documents Obtained through FOIA Request #1391945–000.

64. Hardy, "Federal Bureau of Investigation FOIA Response."

65. Showalter, "We'd Have to Be Idiots."

66. Showalter, "We'd Have to Be Idiots."

67. Charles Keating, "Stands on Quality," *Greater Phoenix Business Journal*, January 5, 1987.

68. Martha Reinke, "Developers Are Amazed at Keating's Departure," *Greater Phoenix Business Journal*, February 2, 1987.

69. Doug Sword, "Charles Keating Aims to Take Phoenix Firm Private, Broker Says," *Cincinnati Business Courier*, January 26, 1987.

70. Paul E. Danitz to Charles Keating Jr., February 5, 1987, box RB-35, ACC records.

71. Brian Richards to *Greater Phoenix Business Journal*, February 6, 1987, box RB-35, ACC records.

72. Joseph A. Adams to Charles Keating Jr., January 14, 1987, box RB-35, ACC records.

73. Ronald H. Warner to Charles Keating, February 5, 1987, box RB-35, ACC records.

74. Joseph Schaffer, "Contributions to the Community Unpublicized," *Arizona Republic*, January 17, 1984.

75. Reinke, "Developers Are Amazed."

76. Francie Noyes, "The Keating Way of Doing Business," *Arizona Republic*, April 13, 1987.

77. Francie Noyes, "Keating's Firm Won't Build in a 'No Growth' Phoenix," *Arizona Republic*, March 20, 1987.

78. Judy Schriener, "Charles Keating: Ogre or Mr. Nice Guy?" *Arizona Business Gazette*, May 11, 1987.

79. "American Continental Files Suit against Regulators," Associated Press, April 18, 1989.

80. "Savings and Loan Situation" (Washington, DC: C-SPAN, May 9, 1990).

81. Video showed a packed room of journalists; "Savings and Loan Situation."

82. "Savings and Loan Situation."

83. "Interview with Charles H. Keating Jr." (C-SPAN, May 8, 1990), https://www.c-span.org/video/?12176–1/savings-loan-industry&start=11.

84. "Savings and Loan Situation."

85. "Savings and Loan Situation."

86. Michael Binstein, "Renegade vs. Regulator," *Regardie's*, July 1987.

87. Binstein, "Renegade vs. Regulator," *Regardie's*, 47.

88. Michael Binstein, "Renegade vs. Regulator," *Arizona Trend*, September 1987.

89. *American Continental Corp. v. Federal Home Loan Bank Board* (D. Ariz. CIV-89–0691), February 23, 1990 (Deposition of Charles H. Keating Jr.), 44.

90. Draft Complaint: *Lincoln Savings and Loan Association v. Michael Binstein*, 1987, box XB-627, ACC records.

91. Howard Kurtz, *Media Circus* (New York: Times Books, 1993).

92. Howard Kurtz, "Asleep at the Wheel," *Washington Post*, November 29, 1992.

93. Kurtz, "Asleep at the Wheel."

94. Stephen Kleege, "Lincoln Suit Hits 'Leaks,'" *National Thrift News*, July 27, 1987.

95. "Calif. S&L Withdraws Suit against FHLBB," *National Mortgage News*, August 24, 1987.

96. "Settlement Agreement," October 1988, box RB-457, ACC records.

97. "Settlement Agreement," ACC records.

98. Kurtz, *Media Circus*, 60.

99. Michael Binstein and Charles Bowden, *Trust Me: Charles Keating and the Missing Billions* (New York: Random House, 1993), 309.

100. Binstein and Bowden, *Trust Me*, 257.

101. Kurtz, *Media Circus*, 60.

Chapter 6. Media and the Keating Five

1. Paul Muolo, telephone interview with the author, June 26, 2018.

2. Stephen P. Pizzo, telephone interview with the author, December 8, 2014.

3. Richard Berke, "Ethics Committee Asking 5 Senators about Savings Tie," *New York Times*, November 4, 1989. See also "Where Was the Press during the S&L Crisis?" (Washington, DC: C-SPAN, May 1, 1989), http://www.c-span.org/video/?7307–1/press-sl-crisis; Stephen Pizzo, Mary Fricker, and Paul Muolo, *Inside Job: The Looting of America's Savings and Loans* (New York: McGraw-Hill, 1989).

4. Berke, "Ethics Committee."

5. Gary Gordon, "UPI Investigative Report: Arizona Firm Spreads $150,000 to Friends in Congress," United Press International, November 1, 1986.

6. Stephen Kleege, telephone interview with the author, June 15, 2015.

7. Keating in September 1987 filed a $35 million libel lawsuit against Binstein over coverage published in *Regardie's*. The case was later dropped.

8. Stephen Kleege and Stan Strachan, "Five Senators Met with District Bank on Disputed Appraisals at Lincoln," *National Thrift News*, September 28, 1987.

9. Kleege interview.

10. Kleege and Strachan, "Five Senators."

11. "Money & Politics," *National Mortgage News*, September 28, 1987.

12. Kleege interview.

13. Mark Fogarty, email message to the author, June 23, 2018.

14. "Events Chronology: American Continental Corporation," American Continental Corporation Records circa 1971–1993 (hereafter, ACC records), Greater Arizona Collection, Arizona State University Library, Tempe, Arizona.

15. Jill Abramson and Paul Duke Jr, "The Keating Five: Senators Who Helped Lincoln S&L Now Face Threat to Their Careers—Coming Ethics Panel Probe Holds the Greatest Danger for Cranston, DeConcini—Grist for Comedians' Routines," *Wall Street Journal*, December 13, 1989.

16. James S. Granelli, "Senators Met to Intercede for Lincoln S&L," *Los Angeles Times*, September 29, 1987.

17. Dave Skidmore, "Feds Seize Solvent Thrift, Say Its Practices Unsafe, Unsound," Associated Press, April 14, 1989.

18. David J. Jefferson and Pauline Yoshihashi, "American Continental Seeks Chapter 11 as Talks with U.S. Fail on Sale of S&L," *Wall Street Journal*, April 14, 1989.

19. Ronald G. Shafer, "A Special Weekly Report from the Wall Street Journal's Capital Bureau," Washington Wire, *Wall Street Journal*, May 26, 1989.

20. James Ross, "When Trades Lead the Pack," *Columbia Journalism Review*, November 1990.

21. Nathaniel Nash, "Showdown Time for Danny Wall," *New York Times*, July 9, 1989.

22. "World's Greatest: Senatorial Shills," *Wall Street Journal*, June 13, 1989.

23. John Fund, "The S&L Looters' Water-Boy," *Wall Street Journal*, August 28, 1989.

24. Jim McTague, "Bank Board Liberates Lincoln Savings from San Francisco Exam," *American Banker*, May 24, 1988.

25. "FHLBB Probes Big CPA," *National Thrift News*, October 12, 1987.

26. Kleege and Strachan, "Five Senators."

27. Timothy Curry and Lynn Shibut, "The Cost of the Savings and Loan Crisis: Truth and Consequences," *FDIC Banking Review*, January 2000.

28. Kleege and Strachan, "Five Senators."

29. Jack Atchison to John McCain, March 17, 1987, box XB-601, ACC records.

30. Stephen Kleege, "Lincoln Funds Returned," *National Mortgage News*, March 21, 1988.

31. Mary Fricker, telephone interview with the author, October 10, 2014.

32. "Where Was the Press?"

33. Stan Strachan, speech at a National Press Club forum, May 1, 1989.

34. *American Continental Corp v. Federal Home Loan Bank Board* (D. Ariz. CIV 89–0691), February 15, 1990 (Deposition of Karl Hoyle), 60–61.

35. "Where Was the Press?"

36. For the period January 1, 1986, to April 12, 1989, $n = 33$ for *National Thrift News*, or 36 percent of the total, and $n = 31$ for *American Banker*, or 34 percent.

37. For the period of April 13, 1989, to January 1, 1990, $n = 61$ for *National Thrift News*, $n = 61$ for *American Banker*, $n = 58$ for the *Wall Street Journal*, and $n = 65$ for the *New York Times*.

38. Hollifield has written that the trade press is less likely than the mainstream media to write about the big picture, "to cover the social implications of industry policy proposals" (C. Ann Hollifield, "The Specialized Business Press and Industry-Related Political Communication: A Comparative Study," *Journalism and Mass Communication Quarterly* 74, no. 4 [1997]: 757–72).

39. Jill Dutt, "Media, S&Ls Square Off over Coverage of Crisis," *Newsday*, April 23, 1989.

40. Dave Skidmore, "Regulators Say Lincoln Owner Used Political Influence," Associated Press, October 27, 1989.

41. Dave Skidmore, "Seidman Says Lincoln Warranted Action Three Years before Takeover," Associated Press, October 17, 1989.

42. Dave Skidmore, "SEC Chairman Says Federal Regulators Undermined Lincoln Probe," Associated Press, November 14, 1989.

43. McTague, "Bank Board Liberates Lincoln."

44. David B. Hilder, "American Continental's Lincoln S&L Settles Long Dispute with Regulators," *Wall Street Journal*, May 23, 1988.

45. "Savings Unit Review Ends," *New York Times*, May 23, 1988.

46. Paul Muolo, "Wall: California Officials Consulted on Lincoln," *National Mortgage News*, June 27, 1988.

47. "Keating Regrets Acquisition of Lincoln Savings," *American Banker*, July 3, 1987.

48. David J. Jefferson, "American Continental's Lincoln Thrift Is Being Investigated by U.S. for Fraud," *Wall Street Journal*, March 2, 1989.

49. Jefferson, "American Continental's Lincoln Thrift."

50. W. Lance Bennett, "Toward a Theory of Press-State Relations in the United States," *Journal of Communication* 40, no. 2 (June 1990): 103–27, https://doi.org/10.1111/j.1460-2466.1990.tb02265.x.

51. In the January 1, 1986, to April 13, 1989, period, *National Thrift News* had n = 33 articles and the *Wall Street Journal* carried n = 15.

52. See the Methodology appendix for a detailed discussion of the portrayal criteria.

53. In the 1979 SEC settlement, Keating is portrayed as violating bank industry norms of ethics and accountability. Similar behavior is seen in his dealings with federal regulators during the savings-and-loan crisis (Bartlett Naylor, "Gray Says S&L Tried to Hire Him Away; Institution Often at Odds with Regulator Made Offer," *American Banker*, October 7, 1986).

54. Richard W. Stevenson, "California's Daring Thrift Unit," *New York Times*, May 25, 1987.

55. Richard W. Stevenson, "Plan Collapses to Sell California Savings Unit," *New York Times*, March 2, 1989.

56. Richard W. Stevenson, "Developer Agrees to Sell California Savings Unit," *New York Times*, December 21, 1988.

57. Richard W. Stevenson, "Regulators Express Doubts on California Savings Deal," *New York Times*, February 25, 1989.

58. For these percentages, articles categorized with negative references, *New York Times*, n = 53; *Wall Street Journal*, n = 33; *American Banker*, n = 42; Associated Press, n = 75; *National*

Thrift News, n = 33. Totals do not match overall article count of the search because some Keating references were too brief for categorization. Looking broadly at the articles, *National Thrift News* carried negative portrayals, including references to the failed business—the term *conservatorship* was used 74 times, *bankruptcy* 47 times, *receivership* 33 times, *failure* 31 times, and *insolvent* 21 times in the articles. The term *criminal* arose 23 times; *unsafe* 20 times; *unsound* 17 times; *racketeering* 15 times; *fraud* 14 times; *scandal* 10 times.

59. David J. Jefferson, "Keating of American Continental Corp. Comes Out Fighting—Chairman Blames Regulators for Plight of Concern and Lincoln S&L Unit," *Wall Street Journal*, April 18, 1989.

60. Paulette Thomas, "House Committee Votes to Subpoena Thrift Executive," *Wall Street Journal*, October 13, 1989.

61. Charles Keating, "Letters to the Editor: S&L Was Seized Following . . .," *Wall Street Journal*, June 22, 1989.

62. The hearings were held on October 17, October 26, November 7, and November 21, 1989.

63. "Lincoln Inquiry Reopening Due," *New York Times*, August 30, 1989.

64. "The Keating Five," *Wall Street Journal*, October 16, 1989.

65. A *Times* editorial on October 23, 1989, used the term "the Senate Five."

66. "Lincoln Savings Scandal Examined in Hearings," *CQ Almanac* 45 (1990): 133–39.

67. *National Thrift News, American Banker* circulation per Standard Rate and Data Service, "SRDS Business Publication Advertising Source," 1995; *New York Times, Wall Street Journal* subscription from *Editor and Publisher International YearBook, 1989* (New York: Editor and Publisher, 1989).

68. Brooks Jackson, "Thrift Examiners Say They Saw Signs of Criminal Wrongdoing at Lincoln," *Wall Street Journal*, November 1, 1989.

69. Paulette Thomas, "Comments by Bush Suggest Danny Wall Lacks President's Support in S&L Post," *Wall Street Journal*, November 14, 1989. The *New York Times* matched this story on November 18, 1989.

70. John Fund, "The S&L Looters' Water-Boy," *Wall Street Journal*, 1989.

71. See "Lincoln Bonds Unlikely to Get US Insurance," *American Banker*, April 18, 1989; "Criminal Probe Begun into Sale of Bonds by Lincoln Savings," *Wall Street Journal*, November 24, 1989.

72. Martin Mayer, *The Greatest Ever Bank Robbery* (New York: Charles Scribner and Sons, 1990), 168.

73. Paul Muolo, "Lincoln Challenges Takeover; Sub Debt in Danger," *National Thrift News*, April 24, 1989.

74. Paul Muolo, "ACC Charged with 'Bait and Switch' on Sub Debt," *National Thrift News*, May 8, 1989.

75. Muolo, "ACC Charged."

76. "Cranston Proposes Payoff on Sub Debt," *National Thrift News*, July 24, 1989.

77. Stephen Pizzo, "Attorneys Submit $250MM Claim in ACC Suit," *National Mortgage News*, July 24, 1989.

78. "Too Late, Sen. Cranston?" *National Mortgage News*, August 14, 1989.

79. Muolo, "Lincoln Challenges Takeover."

80. David J. Jefferson and Paulette Thomas, "American Continental Chapter 11 Filing," *Wall Street Journal*, April 17, 1989.

81. "World's Greatest: Senatorial Shills," *Wall Street Journal*, June 13, 1989.

82. Nathaniel Nash, "Washington Talk: Once Again, Cranston Takes Center Stage on Bailout Issue," *New York Times*, August 1, 1989.

83. "Criminal Probe Begun into Sale of Bonds by Lincoln Savings," *Wall Street Journal*, November 24, 1989.

84. Patrick Dillon and Carl M. Cannon, *Circle of Greed* (New York: Broadway, 2010).

85. Stephen P. Pizzo, "FDIC Will Sue Lincoln, Parent," *National Mortgage News*, August 14, 1989.

86. Jill Abramson and Christi Harlan, "Supporters of RICO-Reform Bill to Scrap Retroactivity Provision," *Wall Street Journal*, September 28, 1989.

87. "A 'Reform' That RICO Doesn't Need," *New York Times*, October 18, 1989.

88. Stephen P. Pizzo, "Congress to Investigate 'Daisy Chain' of Thrifts," *National Mortgage News*, December 18, 1989.

89. "Events Chronology: American Continental Corporation."

90. *Lincoln Savings and Loan Assn. v. Wall*, Nos. 89–1318, 89–1323 (D.D.C., August 22, 1990).

91. Robert McFadden, "Charles Keating, 90, Key Figure in '80s Savings and Loan Crisis, Dies," *New York Times*, April 2, 2014.

92. Office of Thrift Supervision, U.S. Department of the Treasury, "OTS Seeks $40.9 Million Restitution from Keating and Five ACC Directors," press release, September 9, 1990. The amount of restitution was later raised to $130.5 million (Office of Thrift Supervision, U.S. Department of the Treasury, "Four Keating Associates Consent to $75 Million Restitution, Banning," press release, August 25, 1992).

93. Office of Thrift Supervision, U.S. Department of the Treasury, "Keating Banned by OTS Order; Ruling Caps Three-Year Action," press release, October 26, 1993.

94. A search of "Keating" and "Lincoln Savings" captured just a subset of the newspapers' coverage of thrift failures, which escalated dramatically during this period and was a key historical narrative. The FDIC reported 48 failed in 1987, 185 in 1988, and 327 in 1989.

95. "Accountant: Lincoln Profits Based on Gimmicks," *National Mortgage News*, August 14, 1989.

96. Roy Harris Jr., "The Thrift Rescue: Report Criticizes Accounting Practices of American Continental Thrift Unit," *Wall Street Journal*, August 7, 1989.

97. Paulette Thomas, "Auditors Say Lincoln S&L 'Sham' Deals Were Approved by Arthur Young & Co," *Wall Street Journal*, November 15, 1989.

98. Eric N. Berg, "Losing $2 Billion—an Accounting Quagmire; the Lapses by Lincoln's Auditors," *New York Times*, December 28, 1989.

99. Nathaniel Nash, "Showdown Time for Danny Wall," *New York Times*, July 9, 1989.

100. Jim McTague, "Banking Mavericks Refuse to Give Up; Keating Summons All His Firepower to Fight Regulators," *American Banker*, June 29, 1989.

101. W. Lance Bennett, *News: The Politics of Illusion*, 10th ed. (Chicago: University of Chicago Press, 2015), 15.

102. Stan Strachan, "Better Late Than Never," *National Thrift News*, November 13, 1989.

103. Ben H. Bagdikian, *The New Media Monopoly*, rev. ed. (Boston: Beacon, 2004), 95.

104. David Protess, *The Journalism of Outrage: Investigative Reporting and Agenda Building in America* (New York: Guilford, 1991), 19.

105. Protess, *Journalism of Outrage*, 11.

106. Alexander Dyck and Luigi Zingales, "The Bubble and the Media," in *Corporate Governance and Capital Flows in a Global Economy*, ed. Peter K. Cornelius and Bruce Kogut (New York: Oxford University Press, 2003), 99.

107. National Commission on Financial Institution Reform, Recovery and Enforcement, *Origins and Causes of the S&L Debacle: A Blueprint for Reform* (Washington, DC: U.S. National Commission on Financial Institution Reform, Recovery and Enforcement, 1993).

Chapter 7. "The Charles Keating of Florida"

1. "Review & Outlook: The People's Business," *Wall Street Journal*, October 25, 1990.

2. Paulette Thomas, "CenTrust Donated Political Funds, House Data Show," *Wall Street Journal*, March 27, 1990.

3. "CenTrust Chairman Sentenced to 11 Years," *Los Angeles Times*, December 2, 1994.

4. "Former CenTrust Chief Paul Convicted," *St. Petersburg Times*, November 25, 1993.

5. Christopher Rhoads, "Prosecutions of '80s S&L Figures Winding Down," *American Banker*, January 10, 1995.

6. Stephen P. Pizzo, telephone interview with the author, December 8, 2014. *Spiking* is a journalistic term for killing a story.

7. Paul Muolo, telephone interview with the author, December 8, 2014.

8. It is now known as the *Tampa Bay Times*.

9. Alecia Swasy, "On Top and in Command: David Paul Is on a Mission to Build His CenTrust Kingdom," *St. Petersburg Times*, May 16, 1988.

10. Robert Entman describes how government officials, from the president on down, can spread news frames to reporters and the public. See Robert M. Entman, "Cascading Activation: Contesting the White House's Frame after 9/11," *Political Communication* 20 (2003): 415–32; W. Lance Bennett, "Toward a Theory of Press-State Relations in the United States," *Journal of Communication* 40, no. 2 (June 1990): 103–27, https://doi.org/10.1111/j.1460-2466.1990.tb02265.x; Stuart Hall, Chas Critcher, Tony Jefferson, John Clarke, and Brian Roberts, *Policing the Crisis: Mugging, the State, and Law and Order* (New York: Macmillan, 1978), 53–60.

11. Martin Mayer, *The Greatest Ever Bank Robbery* (New York: Charles Scribner and Sons, 1990). CenTrust is mentioned in detail on two pages. Keating and Lincoln Savings are featured in two chapters.

12. Stephen Pizzo, "CenTrust's Paul and Associate Indicted on 100 Charges," *National Mortgage News*, May 18, 1992.

13. "FDIC, RTC Suing Milken on S&L Junk Losses," *National Mortgage News,* January 28, 1991.

14. Brian Collins, "CenTrust Loss Is 'Near $ 2B,'" *National Mortgage News,* April 2, 1990.

15. Stephen Pizzo, "CenTrust's Paul and Associate Indicted on 100 Charges," *National Mortgage News,* May 18, 1992.

16. Mayer, *Greatest Ever Bank Robbery,* 36, 54, 166, 168.

17. Stephen Pizzo, Mary Fricker, and Paul Muolo, *Inside Job: The Looting of America's Savings and Loans* (New York: McGraw-Hill, 1989), 5.

18. "CenTrust Ordered to Sell Pricey Painting," *St. Petersburg Times,* March 8, 1989.

19. The story was reported by the *New York Times* art critic, not a member of the business reporting staff. See Grace Glueck, "Florida Bank Ordered to Sell Part of $28 Million Art Holdings," *New York Times,* March 15, 1989.

20. Ken Bensinger, "Relic of S&L Scandal Rubens Painting Has Deflated Auction Prospects—Portrait Now a Familiar Face at Sotheby's Played a Role In," *Wall Street Journal,* January 20, 2000.

21. Paul Muolo, "CenTrust Told to Sell Rubens," *National Mortgage News,* March 20, 1989.

22. David L. Paul, telephone interview with the author, April 17, 2016.

23. José de Cordoba, "Art before Profit May Be Noble, but for a Savings Bank?—Florida Tells Shaky CenTrust to Unload Its Collection, Which Features a Rubens," *Wall Street Journal,* April 12, 1989.

24. Martha Brannigan, "Musty Masters S&L's Art Collection Ordered to Be Sold Faces Skeptical Market," *Wall Street Journal,* October 18, 1989.

25. Stephen Kleege, telephone interview with the author, June 15, 2015; Hillary Wilson, interview with the author, Virginia Beach, Virginia, June 23, 2015.

26. Pizzo interview.

27. Paul interview.

28. Charles McCoy, Richard B. Schmitt, and Jeff Bailey, "Behind the S&L Debacle—Hall of Shame: Besides S&L Owners, Host of Professionals Paved Way for Crisis—Auditors, Advisers, Officials," *Wall Street Journal,* November 2, 1990, A1.

29. Lewis Ranieri, telephone interview with the author, August 12, 2015.

30. James Greiff, "Burning a Hole in the Bank," *St. Petersburg Times,* January 22, 1990.

31. Swasy, "On Top."

32. Paul's house on Miami Beach's La Gorce Island had a dock that required an extension to accommodate a ninety-five-foot yacht. He sought a variance from the Miami Beach city council and was accused of bribing the Miami Beach mayor, Alex Daoud, $35,000 to vote for the dock extension. Daoud was convicted of bribery in 1992 related to the dock vote ("Former Mayor Guilty of Bribery," *St. Petersburg Times,* September 26, 1992).

33. The issue of other savings-and-loan executives splurging on expensive yachts was described in earlier *National Thrift News* coverage. See "Use of Vernon Yacht Will Cost Democrats," *National Thrift News,* July 13, 1987. The Vernon yacht article describes the controversy of U.S. Representative Tony Coelho, a Democrat from California, using a

yacht owned by Vernon Savings and Loan chief Don Dixon. Coelho used Dixon's yacht for campaign fundraising and did not reimburse the thrift executive.

34. Ranieri interview.

35. Muolo, December 8, 2014, interview.

36. Stephen P. Pizzo, "A Friend and Colleague Remembers Stan Strachan," *National Mortgage News*, January 13, 1997.

37. Fricker recalled that she went on part-time status at the *Santa Rosa Press-Democrat* to meet a critical deadline of November 1, 1988, for the manuscript submission for *Inside Job*. Muolo and Pizzo had Strachan's support to juggle their reporting and book-writing duties. "Even with these accommodations, we were working nights (sometimes all night) and weekends. . . . Looking back now, the years 1987–1989 are a blur," Fricker wrote (Mary Fricker, "The Inside Story," *IRE Journal*, Spring 1990, 36–37).

38. John J. Fialka and Peter Truell, "Rogue Bank: BCCI Took Deposits from Drugs, Noriega, and Now Is in the Red—Offshore Operator Cultivated Powerful U.S. Friends and Hired Clark Clifford—Sting at the Mazur 'Wedding,'" *Wall Street Journal*, May 3, 1990; Rob Wells, "Unusual Cash Flows at Houston Bank Once Owned by BCCI Operatives," *AP News Archive*, August 8, 1991.

39. "CenTrust's Paul Sent to Jail for Contempt," *National Mortgage News*, March 2, 1992.

40. Stephen P. Pizzo, "Special Report: CenTrust's Deep Entanglement with BCCI," *National Mortgage News*, September 23, 1991.

41. The *New York Times* did not address Pharaon and Paul's relationship until March 25, 1989.

42. CenTrust plays a secondary role in this extensive article about Pharaon's U.S. activities. Kenneth Cline, "Mystery of Ghaith Pharaon: Front Man or Real Investor?" *American Banker*, June 3, 1991.

43. Stephen P. Pizzo, "BCCI Figure Has S&L Ties," *National Mortgage News*, April 1, 1991.

44. Pizzo, "Special Report" 1991.

45. As Janet Laib wrote in her 1956 study of the trade press, "If they dilute the subject matter with political coverage and other supported irrelevancies, they will get a diluted audience, and a diluted audience would weaken their appeal to advertisers who want to reach a specialized market of readers" (Janet Laib, "The Trade Press," *Public Opinion Quarterly* 19, no. 1 (1955): 31–44; quote on 38). Also note Julien Elfenbein, *Business Paper Publishing Practice* (New York: Harper and Brothers, 1952).

46. James Greiff, "Saudi Financier Buys Stake in CenTrust," *St. Petersburg Times*, August 13, 1987.

47. David Dahl, "New Accusations Surfacing against CenTrust's Ex-Chief," *St. Petersburg Times*, June 20, 1990.

48. David Dahl, "Gifts to State's Universities Are Falling Short of Pledges," *St. Petersburg Times*, September 23, 1991.

49. David Dahl, "State Comptroller Tells Panel He Was 'Stymied' on CenTrust," *St. Petersburg Times*, January 16, 1993.

50. David Dahl, "Florida Lawmakers Complained in '87 on Behalf of Thrifts," *St. Petersburg Times*, March 29, 1990.

51. "It Looked Bad," *St. Petersburg Times*, August 16, 1991.

Chapter 8. The Future of Business Journalism

1. Biographical material in *Thomas Rollo v. John Glynn et al.*, No. 020079–1982 (N.Y. Sup. Ct., August 11, 1982) (affidavit of Wesley Lindow), 12.

2. Deana Rohlinger and Jennifer Profitt, "How Much Does Ownership Matter? Deliberative Discourse in Local Media Coverage of the Terri Schiavo Case," *Journalism* 18, no. 10 (2017): 1274.

3. Kurt and Gladys Lang, "Noam Chomsky and the Manufacture of Consent for American Foreign Policy," *Political Communication* 21, no. 1 (2004): 96.

4. Paul Muolo, telephone interview with the author, October 19, 2014.

5. Francis X. Dealy, *The Power and the Money: Inside the "Wall Street Journal"* (Secaucus, NJ: Carol, 1993).

6. Kim Zetter, "PC World Editor Quits over Apple Story," *Wired*, May 2, 2007.

7. Harry McCracken, telephone interview with the author, March 7, 2018.

8. Rick Bush, telephone interview with the author, February 16, 2018.

9. Bush interview.

10. Victor Pickard and Josh Stearns, "New Models Emerge for Community Press," *Newspaper Research Journal* 32, no. 1: 50.

11. David H. Weaver, Randal A. Beam, Bonnie J. Brownlee, Paul S. Voakes, and G. Cleveland Wilhoit, *The American Journalist in the 21st Century: U.S. News People at the Dawn of a New Millennium* (Mahwah, NJ: Lawrence Erlbaum, 2007), 84.

12. Pickard and Stearns, "New Models," 20.

13. Investigative News Network, *Member Directory* (Los Angeles: Investigative News Network), https://inn.org/members/.

14. Matthew Nisbet, John Wihbey, Silje Kristiansen, and Aleszu Bajak, "Funding the News: Foundations and Nonprofit Media" (Cambridge, MA: Shorenstein Center on Media, Politics and Public Policy at the Harvard Kennedy School and Northeastern University's School of Journalism, June 2018).

15. Pickard and Stearns, "New Models," 47.

16. Pickard and Stearns, "New Models," 46.

17. *Thomas Rollo v. John Glynn et al.*, No. 20079/82 (N.Y. Sup. Ct., 1982) (exhibit "Proposed New Publication for the Savings and Loan Industry," April 1975).

18. Stephen Kleege, telephone interview with the author, June 15, 2015.

19. "Announcements: Financial Times Annual Results 2017," *Financial Times*, February 13, 2018, https://aboutus.ft.com/en-gb/announcements/financial-times-annual-results -2017/.

20. Richard J. Tofel, *Non-profit Journalism Issues around Impact* (New York: ProPublica, April 2014).

21. Nic Newman, Richard Fletcher, and Antonis Kalogeropoulos, David A. L. Levy, and Rasmus Kleis Nielsen, *Reuters Institute Digital News Report 2018* (Oxford, UK: Reuters Institute for the Study of Journalism, 2018), http://media.digitalnewsreport.org/wp-content/uploads/2018/06/digital-news-report-2018.pdf?x89475.

22. David Olson and Christine Clifford, "An Industry Remembers Stan Strachan," Letters to the Editor, *National Mortgage News*, January 20, 1997.

23. Nic Newman, Richard Fletcher, and Antonis Kalogeropoulos, David A. L. Levy, and Rasmus Kleis Nielsen, *Reuters Institute Digital News Report 2017* (Oxford, UK: Reuters Institute for the Study of Journalism, 2017), https://reutersinstitute.politics.ox.ac.uk/sites/default/files/Digital%20News%20Report%202017%20web_0.pdf.

24. Richard Fletcher and Rasmus Kleis Nielsen, "Paying for Online News: A Comparative Analysis of Six Counties," *Digital Journalism* 5, no. 9 (2017): 1177.

25. Tran Ha, *The 3 Types of News Subscribers: Why They Pay and How to Convert Them* (Arlington, VA: American Press Institute, December 7, 2017), https://www.americanpress institute.org/publications/reports/survey-research/news-subscriber-types/single-page/.

26. Jim Prevor, telephone interview with the author, February 23, 2018.

27. Mike Fabey, telephone interview with the author, January 31, 2018.

28. Maryfran Johnson, telephone interview with the author, February 5, 2018.

29. Alexander Dyck, Adair Morse, and Zingales, Luigi. "Who Blows the Whistle on Corporate Fraud?" *Journal of Finance* 65, no. 6 (December 2010): 2215.

30. Kendra Kozen, "The Enemy Within," *Aquatics International*, January 1, 2010, http://www.aquaticsintl.com/facilities/the-enemy-within_0.

31. Kendra Free, telephone interview with the author, January 31, 2018.

32. Rob Blackwell, telephone interview with the author, January 8, 2018.

33. Whitney Sielaff, telephone interview with the author, February 5, 2018.

34. John Heltman, "Confessions of a Paywall Journalist," *Washington Monthly*, December 2015, 19.

35. Julie Triedman, telephone interview with the author, January 8, 2018.

36. McCracken interview.

37. Justin Lewis, Andrew Williams, Bob Franklin, James Thomas, and Nick Mosdell, *The Quality and Independence of British Journalism: Tracking the Changes over 20 Years* (Cardiff, UK: Cardiff University School of Journalism, 2008); Keith J. Butterick, *Complacency and Collusion: A Critical Introduction to Business and Financial Journalism* (London: Pluto, 2015).

38. Kalyani Chadha and Rob Wells, "Journalistic Responses to Technological Innovation in Newsrooms," *Digital Journalism* 4, no. 8 (November 16, 2016): 1030.

39. Jason Del Rey, "Politico Co-founder's New Media Startup Is Eyeing $10,000 Subscriptions—Eventually," *Recode*, November 30, 2016, https://www.recode.net/2016/11/30/13800100/axios-subscription-10000-politico-founder-new-media-startup.

40. Max Willens, "A Return to Focus: Publishers Are Going High with Subscription Prices," *Digiday*, December 6, 2016, https://digiday.com/media/flight-focus-publishers-going-high-subscription-prices/.

41. Heltman, "Confessions of a Paywall Journalist," 20.

42. Matt Kinsman, email to author, July 10, 2018.

43. Nick Bilton, "The Secret Culprit in the Theranos Mess," *Vanity Fair* (online edition), May 2, 2016, https://www.vanityfair.com/news/2016/05/theranos-silicon-valley-media.

44. Bilton, "Secret Culprit."

45. Fabey interview.

46. Michael Hudson, email message to author, August 15, 2012; Dean Starkman, "The Reporter Who Saw It Coming," *Columbia Journalism Review*, May 3, 2012, 31–33. Hudson's reporting on subprime lending is reflected in his 1996 book, *Merchants of Misery* (Monroe, ME: Common Courage, 1996).

47. Hudson, email message.

48. The *Washington Post* has published a regular column called "The Fact Checker" since 2011. Glenn Kessler, "About the Fact Checker," *Washington Post*, September 11, 2013.

49. Here is an example of how such an approach can question the agenda of major banks: Rob Wells, "New Banking Trend: Loan Mega-pledges to the Underserved," Associated Press, February 13, 1994.

50. Kathleen Quinn, "As S&Ls Sink, a Trade Weekly Is Soaring," *New York Times*, August 27, 1990.

51. "Where's What We Know?," Panama Papers, *New York Times*, April 4, 2016.

52. ProPublica, Documenting Hate (web page), updated March 22, 2019, https://projects.propublica.org/graphics/hatecrimes/.

53. Newman et al., *Reuters Institute Digital News Report 2018*.

54. Gregory Miller, "The Press as a Watchdog for Accounting Fraud," *Journal of Accounting Research* 44, no. 5 (December 1, 2006): 1007; Alexander Dyck and Luigi Zingales, *The Corporate Governance Role of the Media*, NBER Working Paper 9309 (Washington, DC: National Bureau of Economic Research, 2002), 39.

55. Philip Patterson and Lee Wilkins, "An Introduction to Ethical Decision Making," in *Media Ethics*, 6th ed. (New York: McGraw-Hill, 2008), 16.

56. Blackwell interview.

57. Howard Carswell, "Business News Coverage," *Public Opinion Quarterly* 2, no. 4 (1938): 613–21.

58. Diana Henriques, "Business Reporting: Behind the Curve," *Columbia Journalism Review*, December 2000, 19.

59. Paul Duke Jr. and Paulette Thomas, "Thrift Agency Says about 800 S&Ls Won't Meet New Capital Requirements," *Wall Street Journal*, November 7, 1989.

60. "Group Bids for Lincoln," *New York Times*, March 15, 1989.

61. Disclosure: The author has received compensation from the Reynolds Center. I was a 2012 Reynolds Visiting Business Journalism Professor at the University of South Carolina and have been a paid speaker at subsequent Reynolds seminars.

62. Mary Jane Pardue, "Most Business Editors Find Journalism Graduates Still Unprepared," *Journalism and Mass Communication Educator*, October 14, 2013.

63. Gillian Tett, "Silos and Silences Why so Few People Spotted the Problems in Complex Credit and What That Implies for the Future," *Financial Stability Review* 15 (July 2010), 121–29.

64. Donald MacKenzie, "The Credit Crisis as a Problem in the Sociology of Knowledge," *American Journal of Sociology* 116, no. 6 (May 2011): 1778–1841.

65. Bethany McLean, *The Smartest Guys in the Room: The Amazing Rise and Scandalous Fall of Enron* (New York: Portfolio, 2004).

66. Dean Starkman, *The Watchdog That Didn't Bark: The Financial Crisis and the Disappearance of Investigative Journalism* (New York: Columbia Journalism Review Books, 2014).

67. One example of capture in the political journalism realm would involve the lack of reporting on the adultery of Presidents John F. Kennedy and Lyndon Johnson, even though the press knew about it at the time. See Matt Bai, "How Gary Hart's Downfall Forever Changed American Politics," *New York Times Magazine*, September 18, 2014, https://www.nytimes.com/2014/09/21/magazine/how-gary-harts-downfall-forever-changed-american-politics.html.

68. Antonis Kalogeropoulos, Helle Mølgaard Svensson, Arjen van Dalen, Claes de Vreese, and Erik Albæk, "Are Watchdogs Doing Their Business? Media Coverage of Economic News," *Journalism* 16, no. 8 (November 3, 2014): 993–1009, https://doi.org/10.1177%2F1464884914554167.

69. Hudson, email message.

70. Bilton, "Secret Culprit."

71. "2015 George Polk Award Winners," Past George Polk Award Winners, accessed March 28, 2019, http://liu.edu/George-Polk-Awards/Past-Winners#2015.

72. Jane Elizabeth, *7 Characteristics of Effective Accountability Journalists*, @AmPress Report (Arlington, VA: American Press Institute, 2016), https://www.americanpress institute.org/publications/reports/white-papers/characteristics-effective-accountability -journalists/.

73. Randy Martin, *Financialization of Daily Life* (Philadelphia: Temple University Press, 2002), 3.

74. Karl Marx, *A Contribution to the Critique of Political Economy* (Moscow: Progress, 1859).

75. Angus Burgin, *The Great Persuasion: Reinventing Free Markets since the Great Depression* (Cambridge, MA: Harvard University Press, 2012), 156.

76. Johnson interview.

77. The broader definition of business news also tracks the evolution of some news agencies' business models. Michael Palmer noted that one of the first Reuters agreements in 1856 was an exchange of stock-market prices with German and French news agencies; it later evolved into general news. Similarly, one of Bloomberg's first major contracts was for delivery of bond price data to the *Wall Street Journal* and the Associated Press. "Like *Reuters, Bloomberg* moved from financial to general news" (Michael Palmer, "Global Financial News," in *The Globalization of News*, ed. Oliver Boyd-Barrett and Terhi Rantanen [London: Sage, 1998]), 63.

78. "NTN Wins Polk Reporting Award," *National Thrift News*, March 20, 1989.

79. Ben H. Bagdikian, *The New Media Monopoly*, rev. ed. (Boston: Beacon, 2004), 133.

80. Charles Sennott, "How to Report for America," paper presented at the Investigative Reporters and Editors Conference, Orlando, Florida, June 14, 2018.

81. Fabey interview.

Appendix: Methodology

1. LexisNexis Academic was searched for *National Thrift News, American Banker*, Associated Press, and the *New York Times*. Factiva was used for the *Wall Street Journal*, since it is not in LexisNexis. Brief digest or index items referring to longer articles were excluded from the eventual analysis, as were calendar notices about upcoming hearings and items too brief for a full study.

2. The *St. Petersburg Times* is now known as the *Tampa Bay Times*.

3. Kimberly A. Neuendorf, *The Content Analysis Guidebook* (Thousand Oaks, CA: Sage, 2002), 12–13; Bernard Berelson, *Content Analysis in Communication Research* (New York: American Book–Stratford), 171.

4. Berelson, *Content Analysis*; James D. Startt and William David Sloan, *Historical Methods in Mass Communication* (Northport, AL: Vision, 2003); Tracy L. Lucht, "Sylvia Porter: Gender, Ambition, and Personal Finance Journalism, 1935–1975" (Ph.D. diss., University of Maryland, 2007), http://drum.lib.umd.edu/handle/1903/7617.

5. Erica Scharrer, "An 'Improbable Leap': A Content Analysis of Newspaper Coverage of Hillary Clinton's Transition from First Lady to Senate Candidate," *Journalism Studies* 3, no. 3 (2002): 393–406.

6. Kathleen Hall Jamieson, Paul Waldman, and Susan Sherr, "Eliminate the Negative? Categories of Analysis for Political Advertisements," in *Crowded Airwaves: Campaign Advertising in Elections*, ed. James Thurber, 44–64 (Washington, DC: Brookings Institution Press, 2000).

7. Margaret Cissel, "Media Framing: A Comparative Content Analysis on Mainstream and Alternative News Coverage of Occupy Wall Street," *Elon Journal of Undergraduate Research in Communications* 3, no. 1 (2012): 67–77.

8. Division of Supervision and Regulation, Board of Governors of the Federal Reserve System, "Commercial Bank Examination Manual," last updated November 21, 2018, https://www.federalreserve.gov/publications/supervision_cbem.htm.

9. Some of the normative values are accountability, transparency of operations, safe asset management, contributing to the safety, and soundness of the financial system (Wiesław Gumuła, "Banking and Ethics," slide presentation at the Visegrad Summer School, Krakow, Poland; July 15, 2015, http://www.visegradsummerschool.org/edu-materials/banking-and-ethics).

10. Valentina Fetiniuc and Ivan Luchian, "Banking Ethics: Main Conceptions and Problems," *Annals of the University of Petrosani Economics* 14, no. 1 (January 2014): 93.

11. Division of Supervision and Regulation, *Commercial Bank Examination Manual*.

12. Administrator of National Banks, Comptroller of the Currency, *An Examiner's Guide to Problem Bank Identification, Rehabilitation and Resolution: Problem Bank Identification,*

Rehabilitation and Resolution (Washington, DC: U.S. Department of the Treasury, Comptroller of the Currency, January 2001), https://www.occ.gov/publications/publications-by-type/other-publications-reports/an-examiners-guide-problem-bank-identif-rehab-resolution.pdf.

13. Timothy Curry and Lynn Shibut, "The Cost of the Savings and Loan Crisis: Truth and Consequences," *FDIC Banking Review*, January 2000.

14. As with the Keating analysis, I examined the adjectives, adverbs, and other descriptors ascribed to David Paul for manifest content. The "immediate context"—the paragraph or immediately preceding or following paragraphs—of the descriptors was reviewed for supplemental or confirming manifest content.

Index

accountability journalism, 47, 49, 52
Adams, Joseph A., 123
advertising: in business journalism, 10–11, 12; conflicts between editorial content and, 91–93; growth of newspaper, 85–86; in *National Thrift News*, 25–26, 30–31, 98–100; ownership and, 93–95; political-economy theory and, 86–91; professional values in journalism and, 95–98; trade press and, 101–3
Alden Global Capital, 93, 96
Altick, Richard, 89
American Banker, 16, 23, 44, 129, 140, 141, 179; on accounting firms in the Keating scandal, 157; advertising and, 102; on the Congressional investigation of Keating, 151–53; content analysis of, 13–15; corporate culture of, 97; coverage of the Keating Five scandal, 136, 145–46; on criminal probes of Keating, 155–56; on David Paul and CenTrust, 167, 169; on elderly investors in Lincoln Savings and Loan, 153–55; Gerald Loeb awards won by, 43; journalistic ecosystem and, 184; on Keating's ability to intimidate critics, 108; Lee Henkel covered in, 113; libel suit against, 116; negative portrayals of Keating in, 149–51; on regulatory developments in the savings and loan industry, 144; on sale of Lincoln Savings and Loan, 146–47
American Business Press, 101–2
American Continental Corporation, 2, 65–68, 84; Arizona State University archives on, 107; culture of, 70–73; elderly investors in, 153–55; growth of, 60–64; libel suits and, 15–16. *See also* Keating, Charles H., Jr.; Lincoln Savings and Loan
American Economist, 36
American Financial Corporation, 63
American Financial Group, 73
American Lawyer, 55, 97, 104, 105–6, 179
American Press Institute, 187
American Railroad Journal, 35
An, Soontae, 92
Anders, George, 70
Anderson, C. W., 47
Anderson, Jack, 127
Annals of Medicine, 92
antipornography activism of Keating, 73–75
Aquatics International, 54, 97, 105, 178

Aristotle, 50, 77
Arizona Business Gazette, 124
Arizona Republic, 16, 71, 117, 123, 183
Arizona Trend magazine, 15, 82, 126–28, 139
Arthur Andersen, 137, 142
Arthur Young & Co., 142, 156–57, 185
Art of the Deal, 12–13, 77–78
Associated Press, 62, 157; content analysis of, 13–15; coverage of the Keating Five scandal, 136; Lee Henkel covered in, 113
Association of Business Papers, 36
Atal, Maha Rafi, 18, 93
Atchison, Jack, 142, 185
Atlanta Journal-Constitution, 54
AuCoin, James, 40, 51, 53
Audacity of Hope, The, 50
autonomy, journalistic, 89–90
Aviation Week, 6, 14, 48–49, 57, 106, 178, 181; ownership of, 94
Axel Springer, 100
Axios, 100

backwater, business journalism as, 37–39, 187–88
Bagdikian, Ben, 37, 158, 189
Baker, George P., 63
Baker, Gerald, 96
Baldasty, Gerald J., 86, 87
Banks, Henry Louis, 110
Barron, Clarence, 38
Bell, Cheryl, 161
Bennett, Lance, 13, 52, 147, 157, 162
Benson, Rodney, 91
Benston, George J., 83–84
Bentham, Jeremy, 9, 47
Bergen, Lori, 92
Bickwit, Leonard, Jr., 82
Billboard, 57
Bilton, Nick, 181, 187
Binstein, Michael, 62, 76, 126–28, 136
Black, Jay, 91
Black, William, 28, 75
Black Monday, 1987, 41
Blackwell, Rob, 5, 16, 97, 116, 179, 184
Blasco, Andrea, 92
Bloomberg Government, 100
Bloomberg News, 33, 100, 184
Boorstin, Daniel, 12, 34, 77

Boston Globe, 53, 189
Bowden, Charles, 62, 76, 128
boycotts, 99, 103
Branson, David, 127
Breeden, Richard, 83, 145
Broadcasting, 56
Bryant, Jennings, 91
building-and-loan associations, 26–27
Burke, Edmund, 9, 47
Burlingame, Roger, 53
Burns, Robert, 123
Bush, George H. W., 81, 82, 152
Bush, Rick, 174
Business Insider, 100
Business Insider Intelligence, 100
business journalism: advertiser influence in, 10–11, 12; backwater mindset in, 37–39, 187–88; connections to the business estate, 8–9; dilemma of capture in, 186–87; distinctions between trade presses and, 35–36; early warning journalism in, 19; future of, 172–89; improving, 7–9; muckrakers and, 51–52; recommendations for, 18–19; serving the public good, 48–49; trade press genre in, 4–7, 33–37; training for, 184–85; watchdog journalism and, 9–11
business relationship with the press, 11–13
Butterick, Keith, 8
BuzzFeed, 93, 99

Calacanis, Jason, 181
Califano, Joseph, 111
Callahan, Laura, 56
Cannon, Carl, 155
capitalism, 86–88
Capra, Frank, 26
capture problem, 186–87
Carlson, Eugene, 10, 90
Carnegie, Andrew, 51
Carreyrou, John, 187
Carswell, Harold, 7, 187
Carter, Jimmy, 28, 35, 170
CBS, 53
CBS Evening News, 54
CenTrust Savings and Loan, 5, 11, 14, 65, 90, 160–62, 175; negative coverage of, 167–70; as a rogue bank, 163–65; *St. Petersburg Times* on, 160, 162, 164, 166, 167, 170–71;

Strachan and coverage of, 165–66. *See also* Paul, David L.

Cheney, Dick, 82

Chicago Tribune, 53

Chomsky, Noam, 5, 86, 88

Chonko, Lawrence, 95

Cincinnati Enquirer, 62, 63

Cincinnati roots of Charles Keating, Jr., 61–64

Citibank, 126

Citizens for Decency through Law, 73

Citizens for Decent Literature, 73

City Magazine, 128

Civil Rights movement, 22–23, 52

civil society media, 91

Cleveland Plain Dealer, 2

Clinton, Bill, 54

Clinton, Hillary, 17

CNN, 39, 43–44, 54, 56

Coelho, Tony, 81

collaboration among journalistic outlets, 183–84

Columbia Journalism Review, 42, 92, 102

Commercial and Financial Chronicle, 47, 53

communitarianism, 49–50

Competitive Equality Banking Act, 81

complaints about the media, business, 110–11

computational journalism, 49

Computerworld, 46, 56, 97, 179, 188; boycotts against, 99, 103; ownership of, 94–95; separation between editorial and advertising at, 105

conferences, industry, 181

Congressional investigation of Keating, 151–53

Connectiv, 4, 57

content analysis, 13–15

Cope, Debra, 40, 98–99

corporate conflicts with media, 108–10

corporate culture, 70–73, 95, 185–86

Corporate Financing, 43

corporate-government sourcing, 147–48

corporate privacy, 109–10

corporate takeover era, 63–64

Countrywide Credit, 44

Cranston, Alan, 1, 17, 76, 133, 135, 138–40, 154–55

Crawford, Colin, 174

credibility problems of the media, 111–12

C-SPAN, 124–25

culture, corporate, 70–73, 95, 185–86

Curtis, Raleigh T., 38

Dallas Morning News, 4

Daly, Al, 23

Dana, William Buck, 53

Dangerfield, George, 77

Daniels, LeAnne, 53

Danitz, Paul E., 123

Davis, Gerald F., 104

Day, Kathleen, 98–99

DeConcini, Dennis, 1, 65, 82, 133, 135, 138–39, 141, 154–55

DelliBovi, Al, 44

Delorme, Denise E., 99

Democracy's Detectives: The Economics of Investigative Journalism, 49

democratic market society, 85

Den of Thieves, 65

Denver Post, 93, 96

deregulation, 28–30, 30–33, 61

Detroit News, 62, 117, 140

Deukmejian, George, 82

DeWine, Mike, 82

Dillon, Patrick, 155

discrimination, mortgage lending, 54

Dixon, Don, 59

Dobbs, Lou, 56

Documenting Hate, 183

Donahue, 59

Donald Trump v. Timothy L. O'Brien, 115

Dow Jones, 94

Downie, Leonard, 47

Doyle, Gillian, 8, 103–4

Drexel Burnham Lambert, 64, 65, 99, 156, 160

Drier, Peter, 39

Dry Goods Reporter and Commercial Glance, 35

Dutt, Jill, 145

Dyck, Alexander, 48, 54, 103, 158, 178

early warning journalism, 19, 172–73, 182

Economist, The, 47

editorial content and advertising, conflicts between, 91–93

Edmonson, Richard, 38

Elfenbein, Julian, 53–54
Elliot Bell award, 43
Ellison, Lawrence, 5, 46
Emery, John, 101–2
Endres, Kathleen, 4, 11
Engineering News-Record, 46, 53, 57, 97
Enron Corporation, 7, 8, 46, 185, 186, 187
Entman, Robert, 162
Environmental Protection Agency, 109
Epstein, Edward, 89
Etzioni, Amitai, 50

Fabey, Mike, 5, 19, 48–49, 97, 106, 189
Face the Nation, 54
Fannie Mae, 31, 44
Fast Company, 105
Faulkner and Gray, 44
FBI (Federal Bureau of Investigation) probe
   of media leaks at FHLBB, 121–22
Federal Deposit Insurance Corporation, 67
Federal Home Loan Bank Board (FHLBB),
   1, 15, 16, 24, 61; deregulation and, 28, 32;
   Edwin Gray of, 78–81, 113, 115, 143, 144;
   FBI (Federal Bureau of Investigation)
   probe of media leaks at, 121–22; Keating
   Five scandal and (*see* Keating Five); Ke-
   ating's lawsuits against, 109–10; Keating's
   lobbyists and consultants and, 82–83; Ke-
   ating's political contributions and, 81–82;
   Michael Binstein and, 126–28
Federal Home Loan Bank of New York, 44
Federal Reserve Board, 82–83, 139
Federal Savings and Loan Insurance Fund
   (FSLIC), 28
Federation of Trade Press Associations, 48
Fedler, Fred, 99
Feldstein, Mark, 52–53
Fette, Mary Elaine, 62
Financial Deregulation and Monetary Con-
   trol Act of 1980, 35
Financialization of Daily Life, 10
Financial Times, 70, 186
Fire and Fury, 17, 114
First Interstate Bank of Arizona, 84
Flynn, May Belle, 35
Flynt, Larry, 16, 74
Fogarty, Mark, 22, 40, 78, 96, 99, 104, 139; on
   National Thrift News' struggle after the
   S&L crisis, 41–42

Forbes, 37
Forbes, Bertie, 37
Fortune, 36, 47, 110
Fourth Estate, 9, 47, 101
Franklin, Benjamin, 64
Frazer, Tom, 71
Freddie Mac, 99
Free, Kendra, 54, 98, 178
Freedom Marches, 22–23
Freedom of Information Act, 109, 121
Fricker, Mary, 58
Friedman, Milton, 10, 28
future of business journalism, 172–73; fur-
   ther research and, 181–82; journalists
   as owners and, 173–75; market for hard
   news and, 175–79; trade press challenges
   and, 179–81; wary optimism for, 188–89

Galbraith, John Kenneth, 38
Gannett Company, 94
Gao, Paul, 55
Gardner, Michael B., 113
Garn, Jake, 83, 145
Garn-St. Germain Depository Institutions
   Act of 1982, 29, 30
Gartner, Michael, 3
Gawker, 93
Gehlmeyer, Robert, 25
George Polk Award for Financial Report-
   ing, 42–43, 99, 187, 188
Gerald Loeb award, 43
Gerberg, J. Rudolph, 120
Gingrich, Newt, 82
Gleanings in Bee Culture, 36
Glenn, John, 1, 133, 135, 138, 139
Glynn, John, 24–25, 39, 41, 93
Goldstein, Philip T., 118, 120
Gomber, William, 38
Gonzalez, Henry, 14, 147, 151, 157
Gordon, Gregory, 82
"gotcha" journalism, 111–12
Gould, Jay, 51
Graham, Bob, 171
Graham, Katherine, 110
Grande, Judy, 2, 61, 125
Gray, Edwin, 78–81, 113, 115, 143, 144
Great Depression, the, 7–8, 27, 64
Greater Cincinnati Business Courier, 123
Greater Phoenix Business Journal, 73, 122–23

Greatest Ever Bank Robbery, The, 163
Great Society, 28
Great Western Financial Corporation, 44
Greenspan, Alan, 82–83, 84
Grogan, James, 143
Guaranty Savings and Loan Association, 116
Gussow, Don, 70

Hall, Stuart, 162
Hallin, Daniel, 96
Hamilton, James, 49
Harlan, Christi, 99
Harper's America, 51
Hayek, Friedrich, 10
Heltman, John, 101, 179
Henderson, Brad, 23
Henkel, Lee, 113–14, 122, 139, 143
Henley, William Ernest, 126
Henriques, Diana, 9, 184
Herman, Edward, 86, 88
Hesk, Jon, 78
Hewitt, Don, 92
High Rollers, 43
Hill, G. Christian, 58
Hill, John A., 48
Hinkle, Warren, 59
Hollifield, Ann, 102
Hope, Bob, 82
Hovde, Donald, 113
Hoyle, Karl, 143
Hubbard, Timothy, 39, 69–70
Hudson, Michael, 19, 182
Huebsch, Irwin, 40
Hume, Ellen, 3
Hunt, Albert, 3
Hunt, Shelby D., 95
Hunt's Merchant Magazine and Commercial Review, 35, 38
Hustler, 16, 74
Hynds, Ernest, 39

IDG Communications, 94–95
Independent (London), 57
inflation, 30
Inside Job, 18, 58–59, 132, 163, 167, 172, 184
investigative journalism, 52–53
It's a Wonderful Life, 26

Jackson, Brooks, 152

Jacobs, Ramona, 155
Jefferson, Thomas, 64, 120
Jennings, Max, 120, 121
Jesse H. Neal Award, 55, 57
Johnson, Maryfran, 46, 94–95, 97, 179, 188
Johnson, Patricia, 71
Johnston, David Cay, 76, 100–101, 114–15
journalism: accountability, 47, 49, 52; advertising in (*see* advertising); autonomy in, 89–90; business (*see* business journalism); capture problem in, 186–87; communitarianism and, 49–50; computational, 49; early warning, 19, 172–73, 182; as the Fourth Estate, 9, 47, 101; "gotcha," 111–12; journalistic ecosystem and, 183–84; liberal political theory of, 47; muckrakers in, 51–53; paywall, 101, 180; political-economy and, 86–91; professional values in, 48, 95–98; reporter-source relationships and, 103–4; social responsibility theory of, 47; trade press, 4–7, 33–37, 46; watchdog, 9–11, 47, 53–57, 127–28
"journalism of outrage," 52
Journalism That Matters: How Business-to-Business Editors Change the Industries They Cover, 56
Jungle, The, 59

Kalogeropoulos, Antonis, 187
Kandel, Myron, 4, 39, 44
Kant, Immanuel, 9, 47
Kaufman, Henry, 30, 69
Keating, Charles H., Jr., 1–2, 11, 134; anger toward the news media, 107–8, 112–14; as antipornography activist, 73–75; business success of, 60–64; Carl H. Lindner and, 62–63; charitable contributions by, 60, 72–73; Cincinnati roots of, 61–64; complaints about the media by, 122–26; Congressional investigation of, 151–53; contradictions in life of, 60–61; criminal probes of, 155–56; culture of American Continental Corporation and, 70–73; deregulation and, 32; fight with Edwin Gray, 78–81; first SEC case against, 64–65; industry and investors spooked by militancy of, 83–84; lawsuit against FHLBB by, 109–10; Lee Henkel and, 113–14;

Keating, Charles H., Jr. (*continued*): libel
suits by, 15–17, 61, 114–21, 126–28; lobbyists and consultants used by, 82–83;
Michael Binstein and, 126–28; parallels
between Donald Trump and, 17, 75–76,
114–15; Phoenix media and, 116–21; political contributions by, 81–82; prison
sentence of, 156; rhetoric of, 77–78. *See
also* American Continental Corporation;
Lincoln Savings and Loan
Keating, William, 62
Keating Five, 1–4, 16, 112, *130, 133;* corporate-
government sourcing on, 147–48; Keat-
ing's political contributions to, 81–82;
recognition of *National Thrift News'*
coverage of, 42–44; transcript of April 9,
1987, private meeting of, 135–36
Keller, Morton, 52
Keynesian economics, 28
Kielty, Robert, 117, 123, 137, 143
Kleege, Stephen, 1–2, 10, 26, 41, 45, 59, 90,
165; on advertising losses at *National
Thrift News,* 98, 99; on the Keating Five
meeting, 136; reporting of the Keating
Five meeting, 137–40; on reporting of
the taxpayer cost of the savings-and-loan
bailout, 104–5
Korman, Richard, 5, 46, 57, 97
Kurtz, Howard, 3, 127, 128
Kushner, Jared, 75
Kwitny, Jonathan, 59

Lacey, Michael, 118
Laib, Janet, 100
Lang, Gladys, 173
Lang, Kurt, 173
Lanosga, Gary, 53
Leach, Jim, 2
Lee, Rex E., 121
Lerach, William, 155
Lewis, Charles, 94
Lewis, Gerald, 170–71
Lewis, Justin, 8
libel suits, Keating, 15–17, 61, 114–21, 126–28
Lincoln Savings and Loan, 1–3, 12, 30,
60–61, 125; Congressional investigation
of, 151–53; deal with Wall, 144–46; elderly

investors in, 153–55; Keating's acquisition
of, 67–68; leaks about, 112; libel suits and,
15–17; regulatory coverage before crash
of, 143–44; as rejection of ideal of savings
and loans, 45; sale of, 146–47. *See also*
American Continental Corporation; Ke-
ating, Charles H., Jr.; Keating Five
Lindner, Carl H., 62–63, 71, 73; fraud settle-
ment and, 64–65
Lindow, Wesley, 24–26, 34, 39
lobbyists, 82–83, 100–101, 179
Lockheed Martin, 106
Lofgren, Sue, 118
Los Angeles Times, 70, 95–96, 140
Lowy, Martin, 43
Lucht, Tracy L., 37
Luft, Rea, 155

MacKenzie, Donald, 186
Madison, James, 9, 47
Madoff, Bernie, 7
Mafia, the, 22
Making of Donald Trump, The, 114–15
Manning, Michael, 2, 15–16, 67–68
Manufacturing Consent, 88
Martin, Randy, 10, 188
Marx, Karl, 5, 87, 88, 188
Mason, David, 26–27
Maxwell, David O., 44
Mayer, Martin, 153, 163
McCain, John, 1, 71, 81–82, 120, *133,* 135–42,
155
McChesney, Robert, 8, 86
McClure's, 51, 91
McCracken, Harry, 105, 174, 179–80
McCusker, John, 33
McDonald, A. Melvin, 118
McGovern, Pat, 94–95, 174
McGraw, James H., 48
McGraw-Hill, 48, 94, 100
McKenna, William, 34
McLaughlin Report, 59
McLean, Bethany, 46, 186
McNamar, Tim, 29
media, news, 54–55; business complaints
about, 110–11; business relationship with,
11–13; content analysis of, 13–15; corpo-

rate conflicts with, 108–10; credibility problems of, 111–12; improved business reporting by, 7–9; libel suits against, 15–17; negative portrayals of Keating in, 149–51

Media and Business, The, 111

Merrill Lynch, 31, 97, 110

Mesa Tribune, 82, 107, 114–15, 117, 124, *130–31,* 139; Keating's lawsuit against, 120–21

Metzenbaum, Howard, 43

Milken, Michael, 64, 65, 99, 156, 160, 163

Miller, Gregory S., 55, 183–84

Miller, Paul, 103

Mobil Corporation, 110

Modern Medicine, 92

Mollison, Andrew, 82

Montgomery, James F., 44

Moody's, 185

Morgan, J.P., 51, 52

Morris, Julie, 178

mortgage market, 30–33; deregulation of, 28–30, 30–33, 61; lending discrimination in, 54

Mosco, Vincent, 86

Mother Jones, 92

Mott, Frank Luther, 86

Mozillo, Angelo, 44

muckrakers, 51–53

Mueller, Robert, 17

Multi-Housing News, 56

Muolo, Paul, 1, 2, 23, 26, 40, 41, 90; on David Paul, 161, 166; on industry pressure on *National Thrift News,* 99; *Inside Job* and, 58, 59; on ownership of the *National Thrift News,* 93; reporting of the Keating Five meeting, 137–38

Murray, Matt, 9–10, 96

National Association of Homebuilders, 34

National Commission on Financial Institution Reform, Recovery and Enforcement, 7, 27

National Conference of Business Paper Editors, 48

National Jeweler, 46, 56, 98, 102, 179

national media. *See* media, news

National Mortgage News, 44, 65, 82

National News Council, 111

National Press Club, 2, 61, 124–25, *129,* 142–43

National Public Radio, 76

National Review, 115

National Thrift News, 1, 2–4, 18, 19, 130, 172; on accounting firms in the Keating scandal, 156–57; advertising in, 10–11, 25–26, 30–31, 98–100; breaking of the story of the Keating Five scandal, 136–37; conferences and seminars sponsored by, 181; on the Congressional investigation of Keating, 151–53; content analysis of, 13–15; corporate-government sourcing by, 147–48; coverage of the Keating Five scandal, 158–60, 185–86; on criminal probes of Keating, 155–56; on David Paul and CenTrust, 161–62, 167–70; on elderly investors in Lincoln Savings and Loan, 153–55; flipping industry ties, 104–6; founded as business providing hard news, 10; hard news sensibility at, 46–48; *Inside Job* and, 58–59; journalistic ecosystem and, 183–84; launch of, 24–25; on lending discrimination, 54; mortgage market and, 30–33; muckraking by, 52; official sources used by, 185–86; ownership of, 93; political-economy theory and, 88–89; recognition of work of, 42–44; on regulatory developments in the savings and loan industry, 144; on rogue banks, 164; on sale of Lincoln Savings and Loan, 147; scoop on the Keating Five meeting, 137–43; shaped by Strachan, 39–41; struggle after the S&L crisis, 41–42; as trade press, 4–7; watchdog journalism and, 9–11, 127–28

Navy, U.S., 48–49, 61–62

NCB News, 3

Neal, Jesse H., 36

Nelson, Michael, 31

Nemetz, Tobyann, 22, 23–24

Newsday, 53

Newsweek, 42

New York Daily News, 38

New York Financial Writers Association, 43

New York Herald, 85

New York Journal-American, 23

New York Times, 42, 57, 59, 140, 183, 185; on accounting firms in the Keating scandal, 157; on Carl H. Lindner, 64–65; content analysis of, 13–15; coverage of the Keating Five scandal, 136, 145–46, 159; on David Paul and CenTrust, 163, 167, 169; dual-stock ownership structure of, 91; journalistic ecosystem and, 183, 184; Lee Henkel covered in, 113; negative portrayals of Keating in, 149–50; negative slant to economic news coverage in, 110; ownership of, 94; on regulatory developments in the savings and loan industry, 144; on sale of Lincoln Savings and Loan, 147; Stan Strachan at, 23

Nixon, Richard, 15–16, 74

Nolan, Pat, 82

Nolan Act of 1982, 30

Novak, Virginia, 120

Oates, Sarah, 77

Obama, Barack, 49–50

O'Brien, Timothy, 115

O'Connell, William, 34, 83

Ohio Savings Association, 116

Olson, David, 96

Oracle Corporation, 5, 46, 94, 99

Orange County Register, 183

Panama Papers, 19, 182, 183

Pareles, Jon, 57

Parsons, Richard, 44

Parsons, Wayne, 8–9, 31, 33–34, 36, 69

Pashayan, Charles, 81

Patriarca, Michael, 75, 136, 138

Patterson, Philip, 50

Paul, David L., 11, 14, 65, 90, 156, 160–62; Charles Keating and, 163; negative coverage of, 167–70; rare art collecting by, 164–65. *See also* CenTrust Savings and Loan

paywall journalism, 101, 180

PBS Frontline, 71

PC World, 105, 173–74, 179–80

Penny Press era, 53, 85

Pentagon Papers, 70

People v. Larry Flynt, 74

Peterson, Douglas, 100

Pharaon, Ghaith, 168–69

Philips, Chuck, 57

Phoenix Business Journal, 74

Phoenix Gazette, 16, 83, 116–17, 127

Phoenix media and Charles Keating, Jr., 116–21

Phoenix Media Network, 178

Phoenix New Times, 118

Pickard, Victor, 94, 174–75

Pizzo, Stephen, 11, 58, 59, 90, 183; on criminal probes of Keating, 155–56; on David Paul and CenTrust, 161, 165, 170; prior background in real estate of, 184; on rogue banks, 163; on the transcript of April 9, 1987, 135

Poitras, Marc, 53

political-economy theory, 86–88; limits to, 88–91

PoliticoPro, 100

Poor, Henry Varnum, 35, 53

pornography, Keating's activism against, 73–75

Porter, Sylvia, 37, 43

Poynter Institute, 162, 175

Prevor, Jim, 105, 178

privacy, corporate, 109–10

professional values in journalism, 48, 95–98

promotion, discourse of, 12–13

ProPublica, 93, 175, 183

Protess, David, 51, 158

Provident Bank, 63, 64–65

Prudential Capital Markets, 84

Pryce, Gwilym, 77

public ethic, 47

public good, business journalism serving the, 48–49

Pulitzer, Joseph, 89

Pulliam, Eugene C., 17, 117

Pure Food and Drug Act of 1906, 52

Pusey, Allen, 4

quirt, 37, 38

Racketeer Influenced Corrupt Organizations Act (RICO), 155–56

Random House, 173

Ranieri, Lewis, 90, 98, 165–66

Reader's Digest, 92

Reagan, Ronald, 28–30, 61, 65, 144

Regan, Donald, 79, 110, 144–45
Regardie's magazine, 82, 122, 126, 159
Rehm, Barbara A., 97
Renda, Mario, 59, 115–16
reporter-source relationships, 103–4
Report for America, 189
Republic, The, 118
Resolution Trust Corporation, 81
Reuter, Paul Julius, 8
Reuters, 31, 36; as multidimensional news
    outlet, 33
Reynolds Center, 185
rhetorical tradition, 77
Richards, Brian, 123
Riegle, Don, 1, *133,* 135, 138, 139, 142
Riis, Jacob, 51
"robber baron" era, 51
Roberts, Bill, 82, 120
Rockefeller, John D., 37, 46, 51, 91
rogue banks, 163–65
Rollo, Thomas, 24, 25
Roosevelt, Phil, 23
Roush, Chris, 51, 116
Royster, Vermont C., 43
Rozens, Aleksanders, 44
Russian River News, 58, 183

Sack, Robert, 48
Salomon Brothers, 30, 112
San Francisco Examiner, 59
savings and loan industry, collapse of the,
    26–30; National Commission on Finan-
    cial Institution Reform, Recovery and
    Enforcement on, 159; *National Thrift
    News* struggle after, 41–42; rogue banks
    and, 163–65; Strachan's hard news sen-
    sibility and coverage of, 46–48. *See also*
    Lincoln Savings and Loan
Schaffer, Joseph, 123
Scholer, Kaye, 112
Schudson, Michael, 47, 52, 85
Securities and Exchange Commission
    (SEC), 64–65, 117, 119
Seidman, L. William, 145
Seldes, George, 158
Sennott, Charles, 189
Sethi, Prakash, 39
Shame of the Cities, The, 59
Shashaty, Andre, 56

Shearson Lehman Brothers, 31
Shiffer, George, 80–81
Sichelman, Lew, 34–35
Siebert, Fred, 47
Sielaff, Whitney, 46, 56, 98, 101–2, 179
Simons, Howard, 111
Sinclair, Upton, 51, 59
60 Minutes, 53, 92
Smith, George David, 63
Smythe, Dallas, 86, 88
Sobbrio, Francesco, 92
social Darwinism, 51
social responsibility theory, 47
Society for Advancing Business Editing and
    Writing (SABEW), 48
Society of Professional Journalists, 48,
    89–90
Sony, 28
South Carolina Price Current, 33
Sparkman, Robin, 55
Splichal, Slavko, 47
Sporkin, Stanley, 2, 16, 115, 156
stagflation, 28
Standard and Poor's, 84, 185
Standard Oil, 46, 51, 91
Starkman, Dean, 8
Starr, Paul, 7, 89, 91
Stearns, Josh, 94, 174–75
Stedman, Craig, 94–95
Steffens, Lincoln, 51, 59
Stewart, James, 65
St. Louis Post-Dispatch, 57
Stockman, David, 28
Stone, I. F., 158
St. Petersburg Times, 14, 160, 162, 164, 166–
    67, 170–71, 175
Strachan, George, 21
Strachan, Rebecca, 21
Strachan, Ron, 22
Strachan, Stan, 1, 2, 4, 10, 12, 18, 96, *129, 132,
    134;* appearances on CNN, 43–44, 56;
    background on, 21–22; belief in the sav-
    ings and loans industry, 26, 45; in the civil-
    rights era, 22–23; close associations and
    friendships with industry executives and,
    34–35; David L. Paul and, 11; on David
    Paul and CenTrust, 165–66; education and
    early career of, 23; hard news sensibility of,
    46–48; health problems and death of, 44;

Strachan, Stan (*continued*): idealism of, 21, 40–41; independence of, 90–91; journalists as owners as modeled by, 173–74; move to *National Thrift News*, 24–26; *National Thrift News* shaped by, 39–41; offended by abuse of the political system, 45–46; reporting of the Keating Five meeting, 137–43; timeline of life of, 25; transcript of April 9, 1987, private meeting of the Keating Five obtained by, 135–36, 137

Suprynowicz, Vin, 118–19
Sutter, Daniel, 53
Swasy, Alecia, 170
Sweetman, Bill, 57
Symington, J. Fife, 123

Tabor, Gail, 16
Tambini, Damian, 12, 70, 112
Tarbell, Ida, 46, 51, 91
Tavoulareas, William P., 116
Telegraph, 93
Tennant, Don, 95, 99, 103
Tett, Gillian, 46, 186
Thatcher, Margaret, 28
Theranos, 187
Thill, Gary, 97
Thomas, Barbara, 83
Thomas, Bill, 82
Thomas, Paulette, 39
Thomson Corporation, 44
Times-Mirror Company, 94
Time Warner, 44
Timothy White Award, 5, 15, 57, 95, 102
tobacco industry, 92
Tofel, Richard, 93
trade press, 4–7; advertising and, 101–3; as "conscience" of business, 46; distinctions between business journalism and, 35–36; economics of running a, 100–101; future challenges for, 179–81; mentorship in, 96–97; origins of, 33–37; professionalism in, 95–98; watchdog and societal benefits of, 54–57
Trade Secrets Act, 109, 114
training for business journalism, 184–85
Transmission and Distribution World, 103, 174
Tribune Company, 93

Triedman, Julie, 55, 97, 104, 105, 179
Truman, Harry, 24
Trump, Donald, 12–13, 61, 77, 96, 184; *Art of the Deal* by, 12–13, 77–78; parallels between Charles Keating and, 17, 75–76, 114–15; threats of lawsuits against media, 114–15
Trump, Donald, Jr., 75
Trump, Eric, 75
Trump, Fred, 75
Trump, Ivanka, 75
TrumpNation: The Art of Being the Donald, 115
trust in business, decline in, 68–70
truthful hyperbole, 78

United Press International, 82
Upchurch, Jim, 84
U.S. League of Savings Institutions, 32, 34, 153
U.S.S. Freedom, 48–49, 106

VandeHei, Jim, 100, 180
Vanderbilt, Cornelius, 51
Vanity Fair, 181
Variety, 56
Varney, Stuart, 44
Verhoeven, Piet, 105
Vietnam War, 52, 69
Virginia Business Magazine, 116
Vogel, David, 69
Voice of San Diego, 175
Voigt, Mark A., 74
Volcker, Paul, 30, 64, 139
Volkswagen, 28

Waisbord, Silvio, 86
Wall, M. Danny, 83, 128, 143, 152–53, 163; Lincoln's deal with, 144–46
Wall Street (film), 70
Wall Street Journal, 3, 9–10, 36, 40, 58, 140, 183, 185; on accounting firms in the Keating scandal, 156–57; advertising people banned from newsroom of, 91–92; business reporters at, 39; on the Congressional investigation of Keating, 151–53; content analysis of, 13–15; corporate-government sourcing by, 147–48; coverage of

the Keating Five scandal, 136, 140–41, 159; on criminal probes of Keating, 155–56; on David Paul of CenTrust, 160, 164–65; dual-stock ownership structure of, 91; on elderly investors in Lincoln Savings and Loan, 153–55; Elliott Bell award won by, 43; on the FBI probe of FHLBB, 122; General Motors' boycott of, 99; golden age of financial journalism and, 70; journalistic ecosystem and, 183; Keating's description of, 114; Lee Henkel covered in, 113–14; on Michael Milken, 65; as multidimensional news outlet, 33; negative portrayals of Keating in, 149–51; professional standards at, 38; on regulatory developments in the savings and loan industry, 144; on sale of Lincoln Savings and Loan, 146–47; ties between Donald Trump and Gerald Baker of, 96

Ward, Stephen J. A., 47, 50, 77

Warner, Ronald H., 123

Warren, Elizabeth, 184

Washington Monthly, 101

Washington Post, 56, 79, 110, 111, 140; Donald Trump and, 115; dual-stock ownership structure of, 91; journalistic ecosystem and, 184; ownership of, 94; on Strachan's relationship with industry officials, 98

watchdog journalism, 9–11, 47, 53–57, 127–28

Watergate scandal, 70

Watt, James, 56

Weaver, David H., 53

Weblogs, 181

Weld, William, 121

West Valley View, 16, 118–19

White, Byron, 121

Whitson, Arthur Eugene, 119

Wilkins, Lee, 50

Williams, Andrew, 8

Wilson, Arthur Eugene, 119

Wilson, Hillary, 21–22, 23, 90

Wischer, Judy J., 84

Wolff, Michael, 17, 114

Women's Wear Daily, 56

Wood, Hanley, 97

Wood, Van, 95

Woodward, Bob, 116

Wright, Jim, 81

Wriston, Walter, 126

Zingales, Luigi, 48, 54, 103, 158, 178

ROB WELLS is an assistant professor in the School of Journalism and Strategic Media at the University of Arkansas and a former journalist with the *Wall Street Journal, Bloomberg News,* and the Associated Press.

Selling Free Enterprise: The Business Assault on Labor and Liberalism,
    1945–60   *Elizabeth A. Fones-Wolf*
Last Rights: Revisiting *Four Theories of the Press*   *Edited by John C. Nerone*
"We Called Each Other Comrade": Charles H. Kerr & Company, Radical
    Publishers   *Allen Ruff*
WCFL, Chicago's Voice of Labor, 1926–78   *Nathan Godfried*
Taking the Risk Out of Democracy: Corporate Propaganda versus Freedom
    and Liberty   *Alex Carey; edited by Andrew Lohrey*
Media, Market, and Democracy in China: Between the Party Line and the Bottom
    Line   *Yuezhi Zhao*
Print Culture in a Diverse America   *Edited by James P. Danky and Wayne A. Wiegand*
The Newspaper Indian: Native American Identity in the Press, 1820–90   *John M. Coward*
E. W. Scripps and the Business of Newspapers   *Gerald J. Baldasty*
Picturing the Past: Media, History, and Photography   *Edited by Bonnie Brennen
    and Hanno Hardt*
Rich Media, Poor Democracy: Communication Politics in Dubious Times
    Robert W. McChesney
Silencing the Opposition: Antinuclear Movements and the Media in the Cold
    War   *Andrew Rojecki*
Citizen Critics: Literary Public Spheres   *Rosa A. Eberly*
Communities of Journalism: A History of American Newspapers and Their
    Readers   *David Paul Nord*
From Yahweh to Yahoo!: The Religious Roots of the Secular Press   *Doug Underwood*
The Struggle for Control of Global Communication: The Formative Century   *Jill Hills*
Fanatics and Fire-eaters: Newspapers and the Coming of the Civil War   *Lorman A. Ratner
    and Dwight L. Teeter Jr.*
Media Power in Central America   *Rick Rockwell and Noreene Janus*
The Consumer Trap: Big Business Marketing in American Life   *Michael Dawson*
How Free Can the Press Be?   *Randall P. Bezanson*
Cultural Politics and the Mass Media: Alaska Native Voices   *Patrick J. Daley
    and Beverly A. James*
Journalism in the Movies   *Matthew C. Ehrlich*
Democracy, Inc.: The Press and Law in the Corporate Rationalization of the
    Public Sphere   *David S. Allen*
Investigated Reporting: Muckrakers, Regulators, and the Struggle over Television
    Documentary   *Chad Raphael*
Women Making News: Gender and the Women's Periodical Press in Britain
    Michelle Tusan
Advertising on Trial: Consumer Activism and Corporate Public Relations
    in the 1930s   *Inger L. Stole*
Speech Rights in America: The First Amendment, Democracy, and the Media
    Laura Stein
Freedom from Advertising: E. W. Scripps's Chicago Experiment   *Duane C. S. Stoltzfus*
Waves of Opposition: The Struggle for Democratic Radio, 1933–58   *Elizabeth Fones-Wolf*
Prologue to a Farce: Democracy and Communication in America   *Mark Lloyd*

Outside the Box: Corporate Media, Globalization, and the UPS Strike   *Deepa Kumar*
The Scripps Newspapers Go to War, 1914–1918   *Dale Zacher*
Telecommunications and Empire   *Jill Hills*
Everything Was Better in America: Print Culture in the Great Depression   *David Welky*
Normative Theories of the Media   *Clifford G. Christians, Theodore L. Glasser, Denis McQuail, Kaarle Nordenstreng, and Robert A. White*
Radio's Hidden Voice: The Origins of Public Broadcasting in the United States   *Hugh Richard Slotten*
Muting Israeli Democracy: How Media and Cultural Policy Undermine Free Expression   *Amit M. Schejter*
Key Concepts in Critical Cultural Studies   *Edited by Linda Steiner and Clifford Christians*
Refiguring Mass Communication: A History   *Peter Simonson*
On the Condition of Anonymity: Unnamed Sources and the Battle for Journalism   *Matt Carlson*
Radio Utopia: Postwar Audio Documentary in the Public Interest   *Matthew C. Ehrlich*
Chronicling Trauma: Journalists and Writers on Violence and Loss   *Doug Underwood*
Saving the World: A Brief History of Communication for Development and Social Change   *Emile G. McAnany*
The Rise and Fall of Early American Magazine Culture   *Jared Gardner*
Equal Time: Television and the Civil Rights Movement   *Aniko Bodroghkozy*
Advertising at War: Business, Consumers, and Government in the 1940s   *Inger L. Stole*
Media Capital: Architecture and Communications in New York City   *Aurora Wallace*
Chasing Newsroom Diversity: From Jim Crow to Affirmative Action   *Gwyneth Mellinger*
C. Francis Jenkins, Pioneer of Film and Television   *Donald G. Godfrey*
Digital Rebellion: The Birth of the Cyber Left   *Todd Wolfson*
Heroes and Scoundrels: The Image of the Journalist in Popular Culture   *Matthew C. Ehrlich and Joe Saltzman*
The Real Cyber War: The Political Economy of Internet Freedom   *Shawn M. Powers and Michael Jablonski*
The Polish Hearst: *Ameryka-Echo* and the Public Role of the Immigrant Press   *Anna D. Jaroszyńska-Kirchmann*
Acid Hype: American News Media and the Psychedelic Experience   *Stephen Siff*
Making the News Popular: Mobilizing U.S. News Audiences   *Anthony M. Nadler*
Indians Illustrated: The Image of Native Americans in the Pictorial Press   *John M. Coward*
Mister Pulitzer and the Spider: Modern News from Realism to the Digital   *Kevin G. Barnhurst*
Media Localism: The Policies of Place   *Christopher Ali*
Newspaper Wars: Civil Rights and White Resistance in South Carolina, 1935–1965   *Sid Bedingfield*
Across the Waves: How the United States and France Shaped the International Age of Radio   *Derek W. Vaillant*
Race News: Black Reporters and the Fight for Racial Justice in the Twentieth Century   *Fred Carroll*
Becoming the Story: War Correspondents since 9/11   *Lindsay Palmer*
Wired into Nature: The Telegraph and the North American Frontier   *James Schwoch*
The Enforcers: How Little-Known Trade Reporters Exposed the Keating Five and Advanced Business Journalism   *Rob Wells*

The University of Illinois Press
is a founding member of the
Association of University Presses.

———————————————

Composed in 10.75/13 Arno Pro
with Trebuchet MS display
by Lisa Connery
at the University of Illinois Press
Cover designed by Becca Alexander
Cover image: Cartoon with the five senators involved
in the Keating scandal portrayed as finger puppets.
(Stewart Standing, Eclipse Comics; permission
by Todd McFarlane Enterprises, Inc.)
Manufactured by Sheridan Books, Inc.

University of Illinois Press
1325 South Oak Street
Champaign, IL 61820-6903
www.press.uillinois.edu